THE CAPITAL QUESTION
OF CHINA

THE CAPITAL QUESTION
OF CHINA

BY

LIONEL CURTIS

KENNIKAT PRESS
Port Washington, N. Y./London

THE CAPITAL QUESTION OF CHINA

First published in 1932
Reissued in 1970 by Kennikat Press
Library of Congress Catalog Card No: 76-115200
ISBN 0-8046-1093-2

Manufactured by Taylor Publishing Company   Dallas, Texas

PREFACE

SOME years ago groups were formed by the Royal Institute of International Affairs at Chatham House for continuous study of various countries and problems. One was to study the Balkans, another reparations and international debts, a third frontier disputes, a fourth Russia, a fifth the Far East, and so on. The idea underlying this plan was that each group should follow as closely as possible the latest developments in the question or country referred to them, and be ready to provide a paper for discussion by the Institute when called upon to do so. As an honorary secretary of the Institute (a post I no longer hold) I had to keep in touch with these various groups in order to see how far each of them was severally fulfilling the task assigned to it. In course of time, the method began to yield a common result which had not been thought of when it was started. A sense of comparative values began to develop in one's mind. It became apparent that some of these questions were more urgent than others. A day came when I realised that a definite change had taken place in my own outlook. I had come to believe that China, a country in which I had taken no particular interest and had never expected to visit, presented a problem second in importance to no other. A conviction had entered my mind that the next serious threat to the peace of the world would come from the state of the Far East.

I was thus led to concentrate on the study of China, and in doing so realised that my own previous indifference to that country and ignorance of its problems, shared as it is by an overwhelming majority of my fellow-countrymen, is, in itself, a dangerous condition. In dealing with China the Government has no public opinion behind it to determine its attitude, as it has when dealing with India, the League of Nations, the United States or other matters of equal importance.

No human problem can be understood without some knowledge of the past out of which it has grown. I was therefore led to make some study of the history of China and Japan.

This book was begun with three objects in view—firstly, to persuade my readers that China is a question of major importance which could not be further ignored without risk to the whole structure of human society; secondly, to give the historical background within readable compass; and thirdly, to explain the prevailing indifference to the subject and suggest the remedy.

Events, which have moved faster than my pen, have accomplished the first of these objects before the book could be printed. In the last few months no newspaper reader can doubt that the present state of China is a menace to the peace of the world. The second and third objects are, however, rendered more urgent.

It had been my intention to submit proofs of this book to the detailed criticism of a group of my fellow members at Chatham House, whose knowledge of China, past and present, is better than mine. Had I been able to do so, I should issue these pages with less anxiety than I now feel. My reasons for omitting this safeguard is the time it would take. There are moments when *bis dat qui cito dat* is 'the only canticle'. I shall therefore be grateful for any corrections which readers may send me. Effect can be given to them if ever a reprint is possible.

A preface should help potential readers to decide whether a book is worth the time it will take them to read it. From what I have here said, readers can see that the author can make no claim to expert knowledge of China. These pages are merely the result of studies made late in life by one seized with a strong conviction that he, in common with the mass of his countrymen, had too long been ignoring the state of China.

The views taken in the book are contentious. For that reason, amongst others, I felt that before writing it I ought to vacate my post as an officer of the Institute. Chatham House is precluded by its charter from expressing opinions on questions of policy. In view of this cardinal principle, I felt it was better not to hold any official position in the Institute when entering the field of controversy. Its ordinary members, amongst whom are included people of every conceivable point of view, are of course free to form and express any opinion they please.

If I tried to name all those who have helped me by word of mouth with information not to be found in print, this preface would cover pages. I must, however, acknowledge the debt I owe to the Institute of Pacific Relations and to Chatham House and its staff for their help in supplying books and documents. In particular, *The Survey of International Affairs* prepared by Professor Toynbee at Chatham House has accelerated my work by months. In his masterly narrative the tangled story of recent years can be followed in greater detail than is possible in this book. For the earlier years I have largely used the compilations of MacNair, Professor of History and Government in St. John's University, Shanghai (and also at Chicago). These admirable works were printed and published by The Commercial Press, Ltd., of Shanghai, the most valuable agency for distributing knowledge in China. This purely Chinese undertaking has just been destroyed in the fires that consumed Chapei. It is much to be feared that the spare stocks of Professor MacNair's works must have perished in the flames.

I have also to acknowledge with gratitude the kind permission of Mr. H. B. Morse and of his publisher, Messrs. Longmans, to reproduce the plan of the Legation Quarter in Peking, from his monumental book, *The International Relations of the Chinese Empire*. As those who have studied that great work will see, this is only a fraction of the debt which I owe to its author.

L. CURTIS

ALL SOULS COLLEGE, OXFORD
    March 7, 1932

CONTENTS

	PAGE
PREFACE	v

PART I—NARRATIVE

CHAPTER I

INTRODUCTORY 3
    Chinese and Roman Empires compared, 3. Mongol origins, 4. The family unit. Tea and silk, 5. Opium. Villages as material of Empire, 6. Ideographs, paper and printing, 7. Government of scholars, 8. Confucius. Judicial ideas, 9. Unanimous decision, 10. Shi Hwang-ti, Emperor. The Wall and the Huns, 11. Confucian books destroyed. Han dynasty restores state religion, 12. Siniticism. Structure of government, 13. Dynastic ideas, 14. The rule of law. Conflict of Chinese with Western ideas, 15. Defects and qualities of Chinese, 16.

CHAPTER II

THE TARTARS 18
    Rise of Genghis, 18. His conquests. Kublai Khan, 19. Grand Trunk Canal. Journey of the Polos, 20. Peking as described by Marco Polo, 21-4. How Kublai organised his empire, 24. Mings oust Mongols. Capital transferred to Nanking from Peking. Meaning of their names, 25.

CHAPTER III

THE OPENING OF THE SEA ROUTES BY SPAIN AND PORTUGAL 26
    How printing came from China to Europe, 26. Marco Polo's book printed, 27. Its influence on Columbus, who seeks China and Japan by the western route, 28. Cape rounded by Diaz. Division of world between Spain and Portugal. India reached by Vasco da Gama, 29. Expansion of Portu-

x THE CAPITAL QUESTION OF CHINA

guese Empire, 30. Spaniards reach Philippines. Portuguese reach China, 31. Their empires meet, 32. How China acquired the opium habit, 33.

CHAPTER IV

JAPAN IN CONTACT WITH EUROPE 34

Portuguese reach Japan. Its previous history, 34. The Mikados and Shoguns, 35. Hideyoshi unites Japan, 36. Arrival of Jesuit missions, 37. Japan and China assigned by the Pope to Portugal and the Jesuits, the Philippines to Spain and the older orders, 38. Franciscans enter Japan and ignore Jesuit experience. Hideyoshi attempts conquest of China, 39. Korea invaded, 40. China offers Hideyoshi crown. His refusal and renewal of war, 41. His death ends war. Franciscans arouse fears of Spanish aggression, 42. Expulsion of missionaries ordered. Iyeyasu. His relations with the Dutch. Adams as his adviser, 43. Militant character of Papacy explained to Iyeyasu by Adams and a Japanese agent, 44. He founds Tokugawa dynasty of Shoguns on basis of bureaucracy, 45. Persecution of Christians intensified by Tokugawa officials, 46. Revolt of Christians. Japan closed to the world by bureaucracy, 47. Formidable character of Japanese, 48. Far-reaching results of Japan's self-imposed seclusion, 49.

CHAPTER V

CHINA IN CONTACT WITH EUROPE . . . 50

Japan and China contrasted, 50. The Jesuits in China, 51. Conflict with the Friars over God's name, leading to expulsion of Christians, 52.

CHAPTER VI

THE UNEQUAL TREATIES 53

Beginnings of maritime trade between Europe and China. Growing demand for tea, 53. Origin of opium trade. Relations of foreign traders at Canton with Chinese merchants and mandarins, 54. Official corruption. Conflict of legal ideas, 55. Restrictions on Europeans resented. Failure of Macartney mission. Abolition of East India Company monopoly as affecting China trade, 56. Suppression of opium trade leads to war with England, 57. Treaty of Nanking, 58. The most favoured nation policy adopted by America and other Powers. French support of Catholic missions, 59, 60. China opened to all forms of Christianity. Extraterritorial rights, 61. Foreign concessions. Shanghai, 62. Origin of Settlements there, 63-4.

CONTENTS

CHAPTER VII

THE TAIPING REBELLION 65

American influence on Sino-British policy, 65. Its sole motive—trade. Its effect on China, 66. Disruptive effect of Protestant missions, 67. The Tien-Wang seizes Nanking and proclaims himself Emperor, 68. His movement degenerates into banditry, 69.

CHAPTER VIII

ADMISSION OF FOREIGN MINISTERS TO PEKING . . 70

Strained relations between Europeans and Chinese, 70. Aloofness of Chinese officials. The *Arrow* war, 71. Conflict of political conceptions. Ratification of Russian and American treaties, 72. British repulsed at Taku forts. Capture of Parkes. The allies enter Peking. Their treaties signed, 73. Russia secures Amur province by a trick. Emperor forced to receive Foreign Ministers, 74.

CHAPTER IX

END OF THE TAIPING REBELLION AND ITS CONSEQUENCES 75

Taiping rebellion ended by Li Hung-Chang and Gordon, 75. Effect of admitting Chinese refugees into Settlements at Shanghai, 76. The Land Regulations, 77. Their rigid character. Composition of Municipal Council. Its independence, 78. Municipal courts. Difficulty of controlling Chinese majority, 79. Rule of law in the Settlement and difficulties attendant thereon, 80. Creation of Chinese maritime customs service by Hart, 81. Yehonala, her character and regime, 82. Difficulty of handling the modern problem of China from Peking, 83-4.

CHAPTER X

THE PACIFIC OPENED 85

Japan's lost empire. Captain Cook's voyages, 85. British and American activity in the Pacific, 86. Steam creates competition for coaling stations. Admiral Perry sent to Japan, 87. Townshend Harris, his friendship for Japan, 88. Restoration of the Emperor's power, 89. The capital removed to Tokyo, 90. Why Japan succeeded where China failed. Significance of moving capital from Kyoto to Tokyo, 91. War with China avoided in 1874. Extraterritorial rights abolished. War with China, 1894, 92. Japan deprived of Port Arthur by Russia, France and Germany, 93.

CHAPTER XI

SEIZURES OF TERRITORIES BY FOREIGN POWERS 94

Japanese war indemnity secured on Chinese customs. Russia secures railway rights in Manchuria, 94. Germany seizes Kiaochow, and Russia Port Arthur, 95. Lease of Weihaiwei to Great Britain. Further exactions from China, 96. Philippines and Hawaii annexed by the United States, 97.

CHAPTER XII

THE BOXER RISING 98

Reaction on China of emigrants from Canton, 98. Sun Yat Sen, revolutionary. Kang-yi-wei, reformer. The Emperor Kuang Hsü, 99. His abortive reforms. Yehonala resumes authority, 100. The Boxers. Murder of missionaries. Legations attacked, 101. Siege raised by international forces. Flight of the Court. Excesses of foreign troops. Russia seizes Manchuria, 102. Secret agreement between Russia and China, 103.

CHAPTER XIII

THE BOXER SETTLEMENT 104

Dislocation of Chinese bureaucracy. Settlement of indemnities described, 104-5. Remission by the United States, 106-7. Subsequent effect on China of American-trained students. Customs as an agency for collecting indemnities. Consequent weakening of Chinese Government, 108. Dislocation of financial system, 109. Disintegrating force of westernised *intelligentsia*, 110.

CHAPTER XIV

THE LEGATION QUARTER 111

Defect of Peking as capital, 111. Its remoteness from the scene of action in the Yangtze valley, 112. Aloofness of British Legation from Shanghai, 113. No provision for leadership of British community. Hart's letters from Peking, 114. Provisions for establishing the Legation Quarter, 115-18.

CHAPTER XV

THE RUSSO-JAPANESE WAR AND THE CHINESE REVOLUTION 119

Russian position in Manchuria a threat to Japan. Anglo-Japanese alliance, 119. Russo-Japanese war. Treaty of Portsmouth. Russian rights in Manchuria transferred to

CONTENTS

Japan. Effects of Japanese victory on China, 120. Reforms initiated by Yehonala. Her death. Emperor also dies. Yuan Shih-kai as guardian of Pu Yi, his successor. Yuan's retirement. Beginning of revolutionary movement, 121. Yuan recalled. National Assembly at Peking. Another National Assembly at Nanking elects as President Sun Yat Sen, 122. Abdication of Emperor. Sun retires in favour of Yuan, 123. Latent conflict of aims. Yuan's ambition to found a dynasty, 124. Struggle between Yuan and Kuomintang, 125. Foreign loan raised by Yuan enables him to crush southern rebellion. Assumes dictatorial powers. The Great War begins, 126. Japan and Great Britain take Kiaochow. Japan's twenty-one demands on China, 127. Their acceptance with modifications. Re-establishment of monarchy by Yuan, 128. Rebellion in Yunnan. Yuan renounces Imperial title. His death, 129.

CHAPTER XVI

SINO-JAPANESE RELATIONS DURING AND AFTER THE GREAT WAR 130

Character of Yuan's government. Interest of Foreign Powers in maintaining a government of China, 130. Peking government financed by Customs. Japanese objections to China entering war removed by treaties with allied and associated Powers, 131. China declares war, and is represented at Peace Conference, 132. Japanese claims in Shantung restated. Student agitation. China refuses to sign Treaty of Versailles, but joins League of Nations, 133. Japan's failure to secure assent of the United States and of China, 134.

CHAPTER XVII

THE WASHINGTON CONFERENCE 135

Difficulties of Japan. Chinese boycott her trade, 135. The Washington Conference. Japan agrees to evacuate Shantung and reduce the twenty-one points to four, 136. Change in the British outlook wrought by the war, 137. Failure of the United States to support China at Paris, 138. The Washington policy as adopted by the Nine Powers, 139. China's welfare the keynote of this policy. Treaty revision presupposes a Chinese Government competent to negotiate and execute treaties, 140. Shadow governments at Peking maintained by Tuchuns. Vicissitudes of government in the South, 141.

CHAPTER XVIII

SUN YAT SEN AND THE RUSSIAN ALLIANCE . . 142

Division of Customs revenue between North and South. Dr. Sun flies from Canton, 142. His failure to secure British

xiv THE CAPITAL QUESTION OF CHINA

or American help, 143. He accepts Russian aid, and applies for Southern share of Customs, 144. His attempt to seize Customs prevented by the Powers. Borodin and Galens, 145. Teaching of Sun as expressed in his lectures, 146-7. Conflict between Sun's nationalism and Communism. The Kuomintang organised on Soviet lines, 148. Sun's constitution influenced by Russian ideas. His death at Peking, 149.

CHAPTER XIX

THE SHANGHAI INCIDENT 150

Canonisation of Sun. The student movement under Russian influence, 150. Some students shot in Shanghai, 151. The Shameen affair. Boycott of British goods. Institute of Pacific Relations founded, 152.

CHAPTER XX

CHINA WITHOUT A CENTRAL GOVERNMENT . . 153

Tariff Conference meets at Peking, 153. Its collapse through disappearance of Chinese Government. Conflict of Tuchuns and the Nationalist Government, 154. The issues at stake—autocracy at Peking, or republican government on the Yangtze. The capital question as reviewed by Roxby, 155-7.

CHAPTER XXI

ADVANCE OF THE NATIONALIST ARMIES TO THE YANGTZE 158

Inherent conflict between republican aims of Nationalists and their Russianised organisation, 158. Chiang Kai-shek and the Soongs, 159. Their relations with Borodin and Galens. Advance of Nationalists to Wuhan, 160. Borodin secures transfer of government to Hankow, where new British Minister visits it, 161. The British Memorandum of the 18th December 1926, 162. Rendition of British concession at Hankow, 163. Shanghai Settlements protected by foreign troops, 164.

CHAPTER XXII

THE RUPTURE WITH RUSSIA 165

Occupation of Yangtze valley by Nationalists, 165. Counter-intrigues of Borodin. Nationalists occupy Nanking, 166. Attack on foreigners regretted by Chiang Kai-shek, who establishes rival government at Nanking. Raid on Soviet office in Peking, 167. Flight of Borodin and Galens. Chiang Kai-shek resigns, 168. Nanking Government reconstituted under Chiang Kai-shek. Troubles at Canton, 169.

CHAPTER XXIII

THE NANKING GOVERNMENT RECOGNISED BY THE POWERS 170

Second meeting of Institute of Pacific Relations at Honolulu. Its effect on Sino-British relations, 170. Conflict between Japanese and Chinese forces at Tsinan, 171. Japanese warn Chang Tso-lin to withdraw to Manchuria. His death. Peking occupied by Nationalist leaders. Co-operation of Chang Hsüeh-liang as Manchurian ruler deprecated by Japan, 172. British attitude defined by Chamberlain. Kuomintang flag hoisted in Manchuria. Nanking Government recognised by Powers. Peking becomes Peiping, 173. Diplomatic adjustments, 174. Legations remain at Peiping, 175.

APPENDIX TO CHAPTER XXIII

PRESS REFERENCES TO FUTURE SITE OF LEGATIONS 175-83

CHAPTER XXIV

INTERNAL DISSENSIONS 184

Constitution of the Chinese Government, 184. Conference of Generals agrees on disbandment of troops. The Kwangsi rebellion, 185. Further rebellions. Civil war with Feng and Yen ended by intervention of Chang Hsüeh-liang, who occupies Peiping, 186. Tyranny of Kuomintang. Communists troubles, 187. National Convention. Arrest of Hu Han-min. Secessionist Government at Canton. General disorders described, 188. Communist success. Foreign countermeasures on the Yangtze, 189. Tawney on the state of China, 190-2. Floods of 1931. Growth of the opium habit, 193. Organisation of opium smuggling. Its focus in the French Settlement, 194. Its cause traceable to disorders, 195.

CHAPTER XXV

EXTRATERRITORIAL RIGHTS AND THE FEETHAM REPORT 196

Progress in Treaty revision, 196. Cautious attitude of major Powers. Third Pacific Conference, 197. The Feetham inquiry. Dr. Wang demands personal negotiations. Extraterritoriality declared terminable 1st January 1930, 198. Arrangement for maintaining *status quo ante* during negotiations. Arrest of British officer at Hankow, 199. Conference over Provisional Court in Shanghai. Improvement in relations of Chinese and foreigners, 200. Chinese representation on Municipal Council increased. Retrocession of Weihaiwei. Boxer Indemnity settled. Extraterritorial negotiations continued. Volume I. of Feetham Report issued, 201. Its findings, 202. Continuation of negotiations at Nanking. Volume II. of Feetham Report, 203. Its findings. Their effect on British opinion. Questions in Parliament, 204. Reasons for anxiety. Secret interviews with officials. The Thorburn incident, 205. British Chamber of Commerce urges remission of extraterritorial question to conference of Powers. Abolition of extraterritorial rights postponed, 206.

CHAPTER XXVI

The Boxer Indemnity Agreement . . . 207

China Indemnity (Application) Act 1925. Subsequent recommendations of Buxton Committee, 207. New Agreement modifying these recommendations. New Bill submitted to Parliament, 208. Its terms as explained to Parliament, 209. Stipulations in Parliament. Purchasing Committee and Board of Trustees, 210. How the Agreement was interpreted in China. Mr. Macmillan's question in the House, 211.

APPENDIX TO CHAPTER XXVI

Text of Agreement 212-16

CHAPTER XXVII

Japan as Successor to Russia in Manchuria . 217

Russia's need of an ice-free port in Manchuria, 217. How Russia could have colonised Manchuria. Japan as heir to her rights. Contrasted qualities of Chinese and Japanese, 218. Chinese colonisation of Manchuria as result of Japanese policy, 219. Japanese inability to colonise Manchuria as Russia would have done, 220.

CHAPTER XXVIII

Seizure of the Chinese Eastern Railway . . 221

Construction of the C.E.R. Subsequent agreement for its operation between Russia and China, 221. Seizure of railway by Chinese, 222. Russian protests. Admonitions of Powers, 223. Russia invades Manchuria, 224. And enforces her terms, 225-6.

CHAPTER XXIX

Occupation of Manchuria by Japan . 227

Japan impressed by success of Russian policy, 227. Friction incidental to military occupation creates difficulties in

CONTENTS xvii

railway administration. Competitive lines barred by agreements, 228. Which prove ineffective. Growth of disorder and corruption, 229. Boycott alienates Japanese merchants. Korean colonists. Their conflicts with Chinese, 230. Japanese attempt at conciliation thwarted by Japanese chauvinists, 231. Murder of Chang Tso-lin and fall of Tanaka Government, 232. Officers executed by Young Marshal. Consequent aggravation of railway controversies, 233. Weakening of Chinese Government leads to foreign complications. Murder of Nakamura. Military agitation in Japan. The Mukden incident, 234. The Covenant and Kellogg Pact invoked. World-wide implications of Manchurian quarrel, 235. Fourth Pacific Conference at Shanghai, 236. The Lytton Commission, 237.

CHAPTER XXX

REACTIONS OF THE CRISIS ON CHINA . . . 238

Resentment in China. Student agitation, 238. Demand for war with Japan, 239. Chiang Kai-shek and Soong displaced by Canton group. Chinese and Japanese forces in conflict at Shanghai. Further changes in Chinese Government. Manchuria detached, 240.

PART II—COMMENT

CHAPTER XXXI

OUR OWN RECORD CONSIDERED 245

Collective and individual productivity of Chinese contrasted. Danger to world of continued disorders, 245. Anarchy the root of all problems domestic and foreign, 246. British responsibility for disorder. The Washington policy, 247. British policy in conflict with opinion of British in China, 248. Essential condition of Washington policy the strengthening of Chinese Government, 249. Political effect of keeping the Foreign Ministers at Peiping, 250. The plea of economy examined, 251. Political reasons, 252. These reasons examined, 253. Importance to Chinese Government of advice tendered by Foreign Ministers, 254. Dwight Morrow's policy in Mexico contrasted with policy followed in China, 255. His intimate contact with Mexican Ministers, 256. D'Abernon, Houghton, Page, Townshend Harris, 257. Japan's opportunity in China, 258.

CHAPTER XXXII

THE CONSULAR AND DIPLOMATIC SERVICES . . 259

Recruitment and training of British Consuls in China, 259. Their outlook on the situation, 260. Preference for appearances instead of realities the bane of China, 261. Danger of adopting oriental habits of mind, 262. Our missed opportunities in Hongkong. Official disposition to ignore the Feetham Report, 263.

CHAPTER XXXIII

BRITISH POLICY REVIEWED IN THE LIGHT OF THE BOXER INDEMNITY SETTLEMENT 264

Identity of British and Chinese Interests. Difference in legal conceptions, 264. Physical sciences taught, but legal science neglected, 265. Laws framed for ideal rather than real conditions. Looseness of contractual ideas, 266. This vagueness as applied to treaties, 267. What British policy can do to improve matters. The Boxer Indemnity Settlement reviewed, 268. Acceptance of Chinese standards, 269. Safeguards required by Parliament nullified by official action, 270. Official tendency to withold information. Resulting discredit to England in China. Case for a public inquiry, 271. Revision of treaties should depend on observance of treaties, 272.

CHAPTER XXXIV

THE PRIMARY QUESTION AND HOW TO ANSWER IT . . 273

The need for a considered British policy, 273. Official pessimism in China as in India, 274. Why British policy in India is not based on official opinion as in China, 275. The case of Canada; of Egypt; of South Africa, 276. Importance of public opinion as a basis of policy, 277. Suppression of publicity by officials, 278-9. The smoke-screen enveloping China. The remedy stated, 280-1.

CHAPTER XXXV

SOME SECONDARY QUESTIONS 282

Need for inquiry into the relative positions of the Consular and Diplomatic Services, 282. Relations of Hongkong and Peking, 283. The Straits Settlements, South African analogy, 284. The British Minister should be qualified to advise in such matters, 285.

CHAPTER XXXVI

PERSONAL CONCLUSIONS 286

Author's view that British policy can help to restore order in China, 286. Trade as the motive of our policy. A false conception. China's interest the true criterion, 287. Her first interest orderly government, but not enforced by a Foreign Power, 288. Partition of China into separate units examined. Dangerous position of Japan in Manchuria, 289. Destruction of dynastic government in China, 290. Impotence of peasantry, 291. Self-governing institutions the only basis of stable government, 292. Importance to the Chinese Government of intimate contact with Foreign Ministers of political experience, 293. How Nanking might have established effective government in the Yangtze basin, 294. Difficulty of governments in maintaining their own unity, 295. Dispersion of offices at Nanking. The Sun Yat Sen Mausoleum, 296. Failure to grasp the federal principle, 297. The special contribution open to Japan, 298. Her policy conflicts with her diagnosis, because dictated by fear. The remedy for this, 299. Importance of deciding when foreign capital should be lent to China, 300. Need for advice on this point by qualified ministers. England's opportunity in China, 301-2.

POSTSCRIPT

THE LEAGUE OF NATIONS AS AN INSTRUMENT FOR REGENERATING CHINA 303-4

APPENDICES

A. LETTER TO THE "NORTH CHINA DAILY NEWS" FROM TOKYO 305

B. MR. PATRICK YOUNG'S NOTES 309

INDEX 313

LIST OF MAPS

PEKING LEGATION QUARTER, 1900-1902 . . *Face p.* 118
NEIGHBOURHOOD OF SHANGHAI . . .
MANCHURIA AND MONGOLIA . . . } *At end of volume*
CHINA AND JAPAN . . . . .

PART I
NARRATIVE

CHAPTER I

INTRODUCTORY

WHEN Gibbon spoke of Roman emperors as "ascending the throne of the universe" he was using the language of their subjects and contemporaries. There were barbarous races outside the Empire, but these would in time find their place in the government of the civilised world.

The most distant of all these peoples were known as the makers of beautiful fabrics, so precious that they sold in the markets of Rome for their weight in gold. These silks were, in fact, products of a civilisation older than that of Greece, which was organised as an empire while Rome was still a city-republic. Like the later Romans, the Chinese thought of their emperor as ruler of the world. They called China the Middle Kingdom, the centre of the universe. Their own culture was civilisation, the people who lived beyond it barbarians, who ought to pay fealty to the Son of Heaven in the form of tribute. They had formed these ideas before the Christian era, and continued to hold them for nineteen centuries after.

The primaeval forests which once clothed the fertile regions of China were cleared for tillage by Mongol nomads whom hunger had driven to abandon their pastoral life on the steppes. Anthropologists incline to believe that the Mongol race is a higher branch in the tree of human ascent than the races of Europe, or at least as high. Their home in the steppes made the Mongols as different as men could be from peoples bred in the tropical belt. In those treeless and wind-swept regions they were limited to the stage of development possible to men who subsist by hunting and grazing cattle and sheep. They developed to the highest degree a physique capable of resisting hunger and cold, a character indifferent to human suffering and strenuousness in pursuing the purpose in hand. Their manner of life made them highly mobile and skilful in ordering masses of mounted men. Their natural home was the camp. From time to time leaders strong enough to command their loyalty have drilled their hordes into armies which have marched to the farthest coasts of Asia and Europe. On Greek legend they have left their mark in the fable of the Centaurs. Whenever the Mongols overflowed the limits which their upland pastures could support, they had little difficulty in moving to more hospitable regions.

In some remote age a number of these nomads must have percolated into the forests of China, where in changed conditions they still retained some habits of mind contracted through long ages of pastoral life. In nomadic society the family or clan counted for everything, and the organisation of the state in its most rudimentary form was unknown. The village communities which settled along the rivers of China were coincident with families and clans. They had now learned to live by agriculture, and became expert in leading water from the rivers to the land. The family organised as a village was suited to the management of these irrigated systems. The pastoral tradition of the steppes was utterly forgotten, and the grass on the hillsides was used only for fuel.

The sense of devotion to the family was so profound that its living members worshipped their ancestors and expected to be worshipped by their own posterity. Their future welfare depended, therefore, on their having as many children as possible to perform the rites due to them in the world of spirits. To increase and multiply was the dominant motive of their lives: it has made the vast population of China proof against all the destructive forces of war, pestilence, famine and flood. They have learned how to make their soil carry a larger number of human beings than any country of equal area supports. The principal means to this end has been the cultivation of rice under water, which of all methods of agriculture yields, perhaps, the greatest amount of food in proportion to the area tilled. There are in China at least 200,000 miles of canals which contribute their waters to the irrigated fields. Fertility is maintained by a system which carefully returns to the soil the waste products of village life, supplemented by mud obtained in the process of clearing the canals.

Closely packed settlement and a thorough system of manuring the lands which surround the village led to a general pollution of water. In remote ages the Chinese seem to have learned that to boil their water was a safeguard against disease in the bowels. It is this which is thought to have led to the discovery of tea as a means of rendering boiled water agreeable to the taste. China thus learned to produce an article of luxury which, in modern times, the peoples of Europe have so desired that they forced her to trade with them against her will. Silk is another of those discoveries which the rest of the world has insisted on sharing with China. Its people had learned how to unwind from a certain cocoon found in the forest a thread from which could be woven the strongest, lightest and most beautiful fabric known to mankind. The caterpillar which weaves this cocoon had been bred, and mulberry leaves grown for its food, at least 2600 B.C. This valuable fabric was worth carrying across Asia to the markets of Europe, and so revealed to the Roman Empire the existence of China.

The word 'opium' connects the early history of China with that of the civilisation on the shores of the Mediterranean. In the language of Chinese officials the drug is called a-fu-yung. This is clearly the word afyun, the Arabic version of the Greek ὄπιον, and suggests that the drug was first carried to China by Arab traders. But, as we shall see later on, the Chinese did not learn to smoke it until tobacco had been introduced by the Spaniards.

By skill in developing the arts of agriculture, the villages of China grew to be civilised units, which military conquerors could use as materials for a state in its primitive form of autocracy. Like mediaeval Europe, China would seem to have passed through a feudal stage, in which numbers of villages were grouped under one paramount lord, who maintained some kind of order and justice in return for revenues which he drew from the peasants. They would thus be enabled to spend less time on the growing of food and more on the decorative crafts, producing marvels in pottery, jade, metal and silk which the feudal lords could afford to buy. Here, as in Europe, a powerful noble would conquer his neighbours and found a kingdom. A time came when a conqueror more powerful than all the rest would reduce these kingdoms to the provinces of an empire. According to Chinese legend the first such emperor was Fu-hsi, who is said to have reigned four thousand years before the Christian era. This only is certain, that about two centuries before that era there was in China an Empire in certain respects more cultured than that of Rome in the age of the Antonines. Its area and population were probably greater, and its heritage in the crafts, though not in the higher arts, literature, science and philosophy, richer than that which Rome had derived from Greece.

The country, intersected for thousands of miles by navigable rivers and canals, is more uniform in race and language than India or Europe. The languages are said to be eight in number and to have as much in common as French, Spanish, Portuguese and Italian. The meaning of certain syllables is determined by the note upon which they are intoned. The syllable expressed in our letters as chi has perhaps fifty meanings, of which some are distinguished by the tones, while others can only, when spoken, be determined by the context. To record the Chinese language by means of an alphabet was therefore impossible. The Chinese script is a system by which things and ideas are conveyed by separate pictures, which in course of time have become conventional characters called ideographs. The ideograph for scandal, for instance, is said to be based on a picture of three women conversing in a house. The script of China is, in fact, a system for recording unspoken thought. It was common to all China and was used as a means of communication by the speakers of all the languages. The system was perfected hundreds of years before Christ, and the fact that China had one literature in spite of her eight languages goes far to explain how so vast a country and so numerous a people developed a common civilisation.

At an early date the ideographs were scratched on bone. They were afterwards painted on strips of bamboo, and later still on sheets of silk. In A.D. 105 the eunuch Ts'ai Lun, by inventing paper, cheapened the circulation of manuscripts. In the ninth century scribes learned to paste manuscripts face downwards on blocks and remove the wood with engravers' tools in such manner that the ideographs, seen through the back of the paper, remained in relief. By inking the raised ideographs any number of impressions could then be taken on paper.

These momentous inventions did not, however, alter the fact that reading and writing could only be mastered by the few who had leisure to memorise numerous ideographs. As a knowledge of writing is necessary to administrative work, these scholars became the ruling class. Thousands of years ago the ideal of China was a cultured bureaucracy. As the ancient philosopher Laôtze wrote:

> A government conducted by sages would free the hearts of the people from inordinate desires, fill their bellies, keep their ambitions feeble, and strengthen their bones. They would constantly keep the people without knowledge, and free from desires, and where there were those who had knowledge [or enterprise] they would have them so that they would not dare to put it into practice.[1]

The distinction of clerics from laymen, so potent in Europe of the Middle Ages, still dominates China. The early invention of writing in a form which could only be acquired by the few goes far to explain why China, having reached a high state of civilisation before the dawn of our own, has advanced so little beyond it. The people at large looked on the written word with the reverence which human nature invariably attributes to a mystery. An obsession that knowledge is to be found only in scriptures mastered the mind of China.

The ruling class in China were not, as in India, a caste, but scholars, those who could prove their proficiency in knowledge by public examination. Second in honour to them were the merchants, whose calling also demanded some knowledge of letters. As a class they studied to deserve the respect in which they were held. The craftsmen were next in rank; below them the peasants, and then the labourers. Soldiers were reckoned the lowest of all; for, in Chinese theory, decisions by force are absurd; they should rather be reached by agreement and compromise.

In the age when Greece was fighting to save her

---

[1] Laôtze, Taô Teh King, chap. iii.

tiny commonwealths from Persian despotism, Kung-fu-tse was reducing the ideas of his countrymen to a reasoned philosophy. Confucius (for so his name was afterwards latinised by Jesuit missionaries) recognised in the duties imposed by kinship the basis of all social order. He expressed the degrees of duty appropriate to the various relations of son to father, of nephews, brothers and cousins in definite rites. He exhorted his countrymen to "assail their own vices before those of others", and his ethical doctrine has thus elements in common with the teaching of Christ. He also condemned superstitious beliefs as diverting men's minds from the duties they owe to each other. He laid no claim to divine revelation, and described himself as "a transmitter rather than a maker" of wisdom. So his doctrine tended to rivet the eyes of his countrymen on their past. Its unparalleled influence was due to the success with which he reduced to a system the deepest and best ideas of his race. In all that he had to do, the young Chinese was thus taught to think of himself as one of a circle of relatives in connection with whom life was spent. He laboured to deserve their respect and was honest in his business relations with them. The result was a character distinguished for shrewdness and commonsense, for industry and honourable dealing in the ordinary matters of everyday life.

In each village is a hall where the worship of the ancestors of the clan which inhabits it centres. The various family groups select the elders, who see that the rules of the clan are posted in the hall and are also enforced. In larger villages where several clans live together there is usually a temple dedicated to the worship of some local hero or god. The temple officers are elected annually. They maintain order, see to the lighting and roads of the village, to sanitary matters, and generally discharge the functions of a local authority. They also deal with civil and criminal cases; and here again conceptions of justice are based on the idea that the individual is merged in the group. The family or its head is held responsible for the wrong done by one of its members, and the wrong may be atoned for by the punishment of some other member of the group than the actual wrongdoer. In cities the idea has been transferred from families to neighbourhoods, so that all the neighbours, and especially the head-man, can be held responsible for a crime committed by anyone in their area. The legal ideas of Greece and Rome which fastened guilt on the wrongdoer were destined to raise serious difficulties when the civilisations of Europe and China came into contact.

As in Europe, the village communities of China contained the germ from which commonwealths spring. But here as elsewhere, except in Greece and Rome and countries that derive their political ideas from those sources, a custom that everyone must be brought to agree before action can be taken has sterilised the germ.

This attitude towards unanimous consent is to be found running through all Chinese efforts at community activity. Meetings drag out interminably, waiting for some objector to talk himself tired and acquiesce in the wish of the obvious majority. . . . No one may do anything, if someone is sufficiently interested to object; no one will prevent another from doing anything he insists upon doing.[1] Anglo-Saxon people, living in small families, long ago acquired the habit of allowing the majority to rule in public affairs. If fifty-one are for a certain line of action and forty-nine are against, the forty-nine not only yield to the fifty-one, but also more or less cheerfully co-operate with them. In China, as the result of the patriarchal family, if a mere ten are in a position to make an effective resistance, either actively or passively, the preference of the other ninety goes for nothing, and their intentions are balked.[2] Until Chinese villages have repeated the experience of the Saxon *witan-*

[1] John Earl Baker, *Explaining China*, p. 108.
[2] *Ibid.* p. 272.

gemot, and some elements in the population thereby have acquired the habit of rule by the majority, there is little reason to expect that any force other than military will be able to induce the Chinese people to act consistently as a unit on political affairs.[1]

On these remarks, the following comment has been made by one who also is speaking from long personal experience:

> In recent political life the power of the dissenting group is seen not so much in not taking decisions as in 'crabbing' the decisions taken. The minority regards itself at liberty to go on working to reverse the decision often by underhand and underground methods. This leads to a sense of insecurity. No one knows whether the decision will actually hold or be upset; all depends on the incalculable power of the dissentient elements. I call this lack in team loyalty. In almost every group in China I know I find some trace of this.

In the age of Confucius feudalism was gradually yielding to monarchy. So far as we know, the whole of China was first united by the King of Ts'in, who became 'universal Emperor' under the name of Shi Hwang-ti in 246 B.C. The separate kingdoms were thus reduced to the status of provinces.

Of the Emperor Shi Hwang-ti we are told that he planned the Great Wall of China and tried to destroy its entire literature, more especially the books of Confucius—two facts which have more connection than appears on the surface. Though Confucius himself conceived a society wider than the family, the system based on his teaching confirmed the absorption of the Chinese villager in his own family life. A unifying factor was the ever-recurring menace of the Mongol invasion from Central Asia. We know that as early as the eighth century B.C. northern China was constantly worried by human dogs called Hiung-nu, who were destined to ravage Europe a thousand

---

[1] *Explaining China*, p. 274.

years later. It was to exclude these Huns that in 214 B.C. the Emperor Shi Hwang-ti began to build the Great Wall which runs south of Manchuria for 1500 miles from the shores of the ocean to the deserts of Gobi and the mountains of Tibet. The gradual extension of this rampart into Central Asia was probably a factor in diverting the Huns from China to Europe, till, under Attila, they ravaged and almost destroyed the Roman Empire. It is reasonable, therefore, to suppose that in the third century B.C. China had suffered so grievously from internal wars and Tartar inroads that her principalities were at length willing to yield obedience to an overlord.

The Emperor Shi Hwang-ti seems to have realised the difficulty of consolidating China into one political unit so long as the loyalty of its people remained centred in their family groups. With a view to creating a centralised Empire, such as Caesar and Augustus afterwards created for Graeco-Roman civilisation, he tried to extinguish the teaching of Confucius. He was challenging habits of life and thought which, reduced to a reasoned philosophy, had acquired, from the early invention of writing, the sanctity of Scriptures. In 206 B.C. his house was displaced by the Han dynasty. The teaching of Confucius was revived, the unity of the Empire was based on a compromise, and to-day China is reaping its fruits.

Like all monarchs the Chinese emperors were driven to seek in religious beliefs a moral foundation for their authority. The Book of Records and the Book of Odes mention a supreme being under two different names, the one Tien, which means Heaven, the other Shangti, which means 'ruler' or 'father'. The Emperor was henceforth represented as the Son of Heaven, whose peculiar function it was to communicate with the ruler and father of men, from whom he derived his authority. This cult of Heaven and of the Son of Heaven was observed as a state religion to maintain a sense of unity between the Emperor and the scholarly officials through whom he administered the provinces. The illiterate people had little to do with it, and remained content with beliefs which Dr. Hu Shih has aptly termed Siniticism, the native religion of China, just as Hinduism is the native religion of India.

This religion of ancient China contained these elements: (1) The worship of a Supreme God, (2) the worship of the spirits of the dead, (3) the worship of the forces of nature (from among which Tien or Heaven, in all probability, was differentiated and developed into the Supreme God), (4) a belief in the idea of retribution of good and evil, and (5) a very general belief in the efficacy of divination in various forms.[1]

To this Siniticism, Taoism and Buddhism were gradually adapted just as Christianity was adapted to the paganisms of its converts. The people of China are by nature disposed to value the things of this world as good in themselves and as worth enjoying. Such an outlook accounts for the progress they made in civilisation, for a world that is real and enjoyable is also a world that is worth improving. The idea of matter and sense as evil illusions, which tends to asceticism, was imported from India through the medium of Buddhism in the same age that it entered Europe under the guise of the Christian religion. This conception, foreign to so cheerful a people, was also a factor in arresting the progress of their civilisation.

The imperial system in China followed the normal pattern of great autocracies. Over each province the Emperor appointed a viceroy, a governor, a judge and a treasurer. The province was divided into circuits, each under a 'taotai', and the circuits into 'fu' or prefectures under an officer called the 'chi-fu'. The 'fu' was divided into two or more 'hsien' in charge of a

[1] Hu Shih, *Religion and Philosophy in Chinese History*, p. 5.

magistrate called 'chi-hsien'. This 'chi-hsien' was the only representative of the Emperor who came in contact with the people. He was judge of civil and criminal cases, coroner, sheriff, mayor and collector of taxes, and generally responsible for the public welfare. In order to dovetail this imperial officer into the paternal ideas of the people he ruled he was given the title of 'father and mother official'.

By this compromise the people of China were able to retain the structures of their family life and village self-government in the framework of an empire established to resist foreign invasion. The ability of an emperor to rule was accepted as proof of his claim to divine authority, and his incapacity as evidence that the mandate of his house was exhausted. So well was this theory established that Mongol conquerors were able to command the loyalty of Chinese officials, and in a lesser degree that of the people. The numerous dynasties followed the usual cycle. They were founded either by an able Chinese leader or a powerful Mongol invader. They ended with a tyrant who drove his subjects to rebellion, or with a weakling who was used as a tool by women and eunuchs.

The Manchu dynasty, which came to an end when China was proclaimed a republic in 1912, was the last of thirty dynasties. Not once nor twice such dynasties, before they began to decay, established periods of reform throughout their vast domains, such as that which the Roman Empire enjoyed under the Antonines. In these periods agriculture and trade yielded a great superfluity of wealth, and led to the invention of coinage, the greatest of all instruments of commerce. There was leisure for artificers to improve their crafts, and for scholars to develop a heritage of literature and learning.

The civilisation of China embraces at least one-fifth and perhaps one-quarter of human society. Of the rest of mankind a great majority are heirs to a civilisation which has its roots in tiny commonwealths on the shores of the Mediterranean Sea. On opposite sides of the globe these two great sections of human society have developed in separate compartments, and are now facing the problem of living together in a world that is one.

The idea which has vitalised Western society was first conceived in the city-republics of ancient Greece. Their citizens were conceived as subject only to the collective authority of the local community of which they were members, expressed in the form of ascertainable laws derived from the reasoned experience of the people themselves. For more than two thousand years Western civilisation has been slowly translating this dynamic idea into institutions. Ways have been found of moulding the law in accordance with general experience, of controlling the public purse and of making rulers accountable for their acts and obedient to law. That freedom of public discussion, in which alone the rule of law can survive, has been largely established. The principal means to these ends were elected assemblies and also courts in which laws, not executive orders, were supreme.

The rule of law, by reducing the element of uncertainty in human affairs, promotes enterprise. It was no coincidence that the Anglo-Saxon people, who had carried the principle farthest, excelled in commerce. China was brought into touch with a civilisation, the essence of which was strange to her people, largely by British and American traders. The result can be seen in the present tangle of China's relations with the rest of the world.

The people of India are in many respects less fitted for self-governing institutions than those of China. The idea that law is above the ruler has, however, been established in India and her people are now assuming the burden of governing themselves with some hope of success. In the minds of the people of

China the imperial regime did nothing to implant this idea. Its absence goes far to explain why twenty years after the fall of the last dynasty so little has been done to establish the verities of responsible government. It further helps to explain why the Western Powers and China find it so hard to adjust their mutual relations.

To the Western mind a contract or treaty is, in theory at any rate, an agreement stated in definite terms which are meant to be executed by both the parties under all conditions. To the Chinese mind this is not so even in theory. A contract or treaty is not felt to be binding if the conditions to which it applied can be shown to have changed. Agreements conceived in this way have therefore little effect in reducing that element of uncertainty which hampers action in practical life.

Enough has already been said to suggest that the Chinese are deficient in the power of corporate action in any field wider than that of their family life. Their aptitude for forming secret societies is no real exception to this rule. This deficiency can be seen in the military sphere, in any commercial or industrial business which outgrows the family circle, and above all in the field of government. It is this which subjects a stalwart and cheerful people to afflictions on a scale unparalleled in human experience. They have learned to expect from government nothing but punishment and taxation, and from nature every kind of catastrophe. In the presence of disorder, pestilence, famine and flood they contrive to work for themselves and their families long after a people not born to calamity would have sunk in despair.

This unequalled capacity of the individual to look after his own affairs explains why this people, humbled to the dust by more highly organised nations, steadily continue their effective conquest of neighbouring regions. There are competent observers who hold that Batavia, the Malay Peninsula, Burma and Siam, as well as Manchuria, will all in a few generations be part of China.

History which deals with men in the mass cannot do otherwise than present the Chinese in their least favourable aspect. It leaves the impression of a race inferior to Western nations. To visit the country and make friends with its scholars and merchants, craftsmen and peasants, servants and labourers, is once for all to discard that impression. An indefinable sense of their worth is forced on the mind. This isolated people resembles a vast body of ore ready to yield metals that are useful, precious and beautiful, when metallurgists have learned how to treat its refractory qualities.

CHAPTER II

THE TARTARS

At the dawn of the Middle Ages China was ruled by a native dynasty known as the Sungs, who established their court first at Nanking and then at Hangchow. Their hold on the country north of the Yangtze was weak. In the twelfth century a Tartar power known as the Kin dynasty had established itself at Chungtu, on the present site of Peking, and controlled China from the Yangtze river to the Great Wall.

The word Tartar is a misspelling for Tatar, but none the less worth preserving because it reminds us that our ancestors thought of these Mongol hordes as fiends let loose to destroy mankind. It dates from a pun made by St. Louis of France, who sought to comfort his mother by saying, "If the Tatars come here we will send them to Tartarus (Hell) whence they came".

In the days when King John was ruler of England there appeared on the shores of Lake Baikal a leader, greater than Attila himself, whose name was Temuchin. In 1206 he assembled his hordes on the Onon, an upper tributary of the Amur river, and there assumed the title of Genghis Khan (Chinese Chengsze = inflexible warrior). By collusion with Tartars south of the Great Wall, he was able to pass that barrier, seize Chungtu and overrun China to the Yangtze river. In 1219 he turned west to try conclusions with Islam, which now centred in Persia and Turkestan under the rule of Mohammed Shah. Through the gap north of the Pamirs Genghis moved enormous siege trains with Chinese artificers to work them. Mohammed Shah, defeated on the Jaxartes, was hunted till he perished on an island in the Caspian. Samarkand, Bokhara, Merv and Herat were laid in ruins, and their inhabitants butchered. In 1222 he chased the Shah's heir Jelal ed-Din across the Indus. The westward advance of his hordes was only stayed when they reached Silesia.

From the Indus Genghis himself returned to China, but died before he could finish its conquest. That task was completed in 1278 by his grandson, Kublai Khan, who thereafter ruled from the shores of the Pacific well into Russia and

from the Frozen Sea to the straits of Malacca. With the exception of Hindustan, Arabia, and the westernmost parts of Asia, all the Mongol princes as far as the Dnieper declared themselves his vassals, and brought regularly their tribute.[1]

The foresight of Genghis enabled his grandson to keep his hold on these vast conquests. For, unlike Attila, he had always intended to rule where he conquered, and had organised chains of communication with inns and post-horses along the routes which his armies had followed through Central Asia. Chungtu, the capital of the Kin dynasty, was selected by Kublai Khan as the terminus of these routes. Some fifty miles south of the Great Wall, it was close to the waters of the Pei-ho river, which runs through Tientsin to the Gulf of Chihli at Taku. By constructing canals, or connecting old ones, he created a waterway down the river to Tientsin and thence by further canals south to the Yellow River and the Yangtze river at Chinkiang. From that point the canal was

[1] Gowen and Hall, *An Outline History of China*, p. 150.

continued south through Soochow to Hangchow, a former capital of China in the province of Chekiang.

Such was the famous Grand Trunk Canal, still in existence to-day, through which Kublai Khan could pass his troops into and up the Yangtze river, and also into the network of canals south of its estuary. Through this artery he could also draw to his capital from the whole Yangtze valley and south of it unlimited stores of grain which those regions produced to feed the army which guarded his court. From that point he could keep in touch with his western dominions through the routes which Genghis had organised. He could also dominate China to the south, with the Wall and the Mongol hordes at his back. This seat of his power was known to his subjects as Khan-baligh—the city of the great king—and to Europe as Canbaluc.

The first Europeans to reach this city were two brothers, Nicolo and Maffeo Polo. Starting from Venice in 1260 they went to the Crimea and thence to Bokhara. They there fell in with certain envoys and journeyed with them to the court of Kublai. As the enemies of Islam the Tartars were friendly to Christians. Their great ruler was anxious to learn all that the Polos could tell him of Europe, and especially of the Emperor, of the Pope and of Rome. Finally he despatched them to ask the Pope to send him a hundred missionaries to expound the Christian religion. They reached Acre in 1269 to find that Clement IV. was dead. After waiting two years for the election of his successor they started to return, Nicolo taking with him his son Marco, who was then a youth of seventeen. At Acre they obtained a letter from the Papal Legate, M. Tebaldo de' Vesconti di Piacenza, explaining what had happened. From Armenia the Legate recalled them to say that he had been raised to the Papal Chair. As Gregory X. he commissioned two Friars to accompany them with letters and presents to the Grand Khan. The Friars accompanied the Polos as far as Armenia; but, their courage failing them, they returned from Armenia to the coast, with the far-reaching result that Kublai resorted to the Buddhists of Tibet for the civilising influence he desired.

The three Polos, however, decided to proceed with the letters and presents, and in 1275 reached the Grand Khan in his summer palace not far from the present site of Peking. They were welcomed by the monarch, who seems to have taken a fancy to Marco, a youth of rare intelligence, who had learned to speak the Tartar language. In the service of Kublai he visited many parts of China and India, and in the course of his journeys acquired from others some knowledge of Japan. After seventeen years the Grand Khan allowed the three Venetians to return to their home, which they reached in 1295 after his death. In the course of this journey Marco acquired some knowledge of Africa. In 1298 he was taken prisoner in a sea fight by the Genoese, and beguiled his captivity by dictating to a fellow prisoner an account of his travels. He thus describes the fortress from which the Tartar Emperor governed the greater part of the Eurasian continent:

> The grand khan usually resides during three months of the year, namely, December, January, and February, in the great city of Kanbalu, situated towards the north-eastern extremity of the province of Cathay; and here, on the southern side of the new city, is the site of his vast palace, the form and dimensions of which are as follows. In the first place is a square enclosed with a wall and deep ditch; each side of the square being eight miles in length, and having at an equal distance from each extremity an entrance-gate, for the concourse of people resorting thither from all quarters. Within this enclosure there is, on the four sides, an open space one mile in breadth, where the troops are stationed; and this is bounded by a second wall, enclosing a square of six miles, having three gates on the

south side, and three on the north, the middle portal of each being larger than the other two, and always kept shut, excepting on the occasions of the emperor's entrance or departure. Those on each side always remain open for the use of common passengers. In the middle of each division of these walls is a handsome and spacious building, and consequently within the enclosure there are eight such buildings, in which are deposited the royal military stores; one building being appropriated to the reception of each class of stores. Thus, for instance, the bridles, saddles, stirrups, and other furniture serving for the equipment of cavalry, occupy one store-house; the bows, strings, quivers, arrows, and other articles belonging to archery, occupy another; cuirasses, corselets, and other armour formed of leather, a third store-house; and so of the rest. Within this walled enclosure there is still another, of great thickness, and its height is full twenty-five feet. The battlements or crenated parapets are all white. This also forms a square four miles in extent, each side being one mile, and it has six gates, disposed like those of the former enclosure. It contains in like manner eight large buildings, similarly arranged, which are appropriated to the wardrobe of the emperor. The spaces between the one wall and the other are ornamented with many handsome trees, and contain meadows in which are kept various kinds of beasts, such as stags, the animals that yield the musk, roe-bucks, fallow-deer, and others of the same class. Every interval between the walls, not occupied by buildings, is stocked in this manner. The pastures have abundant herbage. The roads across them being raised three feet above their level, and paved, no mud collects upon them, nor rain-water settles, but on the contrary runs off, and contributes to improve the vegetation. Within these walls, which constitute the boundary of four miles, stands the palace of the grand khan, the most extensive that has ever yet been known. It reaches from the northern to the southern wall, leaving only a vacant space (or court), where persons of rank and the military guards pass and repass. It has no upper floor, but the roof is very lofty. The paved foundation or platform on which it stands is raised ten spans above the level of the ground, and a wall of marble, two paces wide, is built on all sides, to the level of this pavement, within the line of which the palace is erected; so that the wall, extending beyond the ground plan of the building, and encompassing the whole, serves as a terrace, where those who walk on it are visible from without. Along the exterior edge of the wall is a handsome balustrade, with pillars, which the people are allowed to approach. The sides of the great halls and the apartments are ornamented with dragons in carved work and gilt, figures of warriors, of birds, and of beasts, with representations of battles. The inside of the roof is contrived in such a manner that nothing besides gilding and painting presents itself to the eye. On each of the four sides of the palace there is a grand flight of marble steps, by which you ascend from the level of the ground to the wall of marble which surrounds the building, and which constitute the approach to the palace itself. The grand hall is extremely long and wide, and admits of dinners being there served to great multitudes of people. The palace contains a number of separate chambers, all highly beautiful, and so admirably disposed that it seems impossible to suggest any improvement to the system of their arrangement. The exterior of the roof is adorned with a variety of colours, red, green, azure, and violet, and the sort of covering is so strong as to last for many years. The glazing of the windows is so well wrought and so delicate as to have the transparency of crystal. In the rear of the body of the palace there are large buildings containing several apartments, where is deposited the private property of the monarch, or his treasure in gold and silver bullion, precious stones, and pearls, and also his vessels of gold and silver plate. Here are likewise the apartments of his wives and concubines; and in this retired situation he despatches business with convenience, being free from every kind of interruption. On the other side of the grand palace, and opposite to that in which the emperor resides, is another palace, in every respect similar, appropriated to the residence of Chingis, his eldest son, at whose court are observed all the ceremonials belonging to that of his father, as the prince who is to succeed to the government of the empire. Not far from the palace, on the northern side, and about a bow-shot distance from the surrounding wall, is an artificial mount of earth, the height of which is full a hundred paces, and the circuit at the base about a mile. It is clothed with the most beautiful evergreen trees; for whenever his majesty receives information of a handsome tree growing in any place, he causes it to be dug up, with all its roots and the earth about them, and however large and heavy it may be, he has it transported by means of elephants to this mount, and adds it to the verdant collection. From this perpetual verdure it has acquired the appellation of the Green Mount. On its summit is erected an ornamental pavilion, which is likewise entirely green. The view of this altogether,—the mount itself, the trees, and the building,—form a delightful and at the same time a wonderful scene. In the northern quarter also, and equally within the precincts of the city, there is a large and deep excavation judiciously formed, the earth from which supplied the material for raising the mount. It is furnished with water by a small rivulet, and has the appearance of a fish-pond, but its use is for watering the cattle. The stream passing from thence along an aqueduct, at the foot of the Green Mount, proceeds to fill another great and very deep excavation formed between the private palace of the emperor and that of his son Chingis; and the earth from hence equally served to increase the elevation of the mount. In this latter basin there is great store and variety of fish, from which the table of his majesty is supplied with any quantity that may be wanted. The stream discharges itself at the opposite extremity of the piece of water, and precautions are taken to prevent the escape of the fish by placing gratings of copper or iron at the places of its entrance and exit. It is stocked also with swans and other aquatic birds. From the one palace to the other there is a communication by means of a bridge thrown across the water. Such is the description of this great palace.[1]

From the writings of Marco Polo it is clear that Kublai had inherited from Genghis Khan the power of mastering the multitudinous detail in which effect must be given to large and simple ideas. His Chinese Empire was held in subjection by Tartar garrisons quartered in its numerous cities. In the civil administration responsible posts were given to Christians, but Chinese scholars were also employed, just as three centuries later the Mogul conquerors used the Brahmins and Kyasthas in Hindustan. The Emperor's attention was largely confined to the appointment of these officers. Their primary duty was

[1] Marco Polo, Book II. chap. vi.

to see that the revenues, which partly consisted of grain, were properly collected in the various provinces and sent to the capital. The Chinese invention of printing enabled him to tax his subjects by the issue of paper money, and, to back this currency, he accumulated stores of the precious metals. So thorough was his system that goldsmiths and silversmiths had to obtain material for their crafts from the treasury of the Court.

The hardihood and mobility of his Tartar horsemen, supported by his vast revenues, enabled Kublai to make his military power felt for thousands of miles south and west of China. But his conquests, like those of the Czars at a later date, were brought to a standstill when they reached the sea. In 1274, and again in 1281, his attempts to invade Japan led to disaster.

The virility of the Tartars, which had its roots in the pastoral life of the steppes, was sapped by the luxury of the Chinese towns. In 1368 the last of Kublai's line was expelled by Chu Yuan-Chang, a native of Anhwei, who founded the Ming dynasty. He abandoned the northern fortress from which a foreign dynasty had dominated China, and fixed his court on the Yangtze river at a place which was called Nanking, or the Southern Capital. The native dynasty presently found their attention absorbed by the task of watching the ever-recurring threats from the north. In 1411 Yungloh, the third of his line, had returned to the fortress of Kublai to superintend the defence of the Wall. The name of Peking, or the Northern Court, dates from this time.

CHAPTER III

THE OPENING OF THE SEA ROUTES BY SPAIN AND PORTUGAL

The Franciscans had used the routes opened by Genghis Khan.

The first missionary sent by the Pope to China, John of Monte-Corvino, arrived in Cambaluc about 1294, just after Marco Polo left for Europe. He remained at Cambaluc as head of the mission till his death in 1328. In 1305 he wrote home that he had already baptized six thousand converts, that he had built a church in Cambaluc, that he had learned the Tartar language and had translated into this language the New Testament and the Psalter. The next year he wrote that he had built another church in Cambaluc on land presented by a resident Italian merchant, and that he had prepared six pictures, representing scenes from the Old and New Testaments, for the instruction of the ignorant, with explanation in Latin, Tarsic and Persian characters.

In 1307 Pope Clement V. raised John of Monte-Corvino to the rank of archbishop, and sent three Franciscans, with rank of bishop, to assist him. They worked for five years in Peking, living on a subsidy from the Khan, then moved to Fukien, where a strong mission was established and a church built with funds given by a local Armenian woman. There were missionaries of the Roman Church at the same time at Yang-chou and in Turkestan.

These missionaries, spending their lives in China, learning the language and mingling with the people, must have come in contact with printed literature at every turn. John of Corvino in the first dozen years of his work, even before reinforcements had arrived, had already translated the

New Testament and Psalter, and prepared pictures and texts for the ignorant, and that at just the time when in China it was the natural thing to have every important literary work printed. There is no question that the Chinese who were associated in the work of translation would have suggested that the translations and the pictures should be brought before the public in what to them was the usual and natural way. Whether the missionaries agreed and thus became the first European patrons of the art of printing, we have no means of knowing. That religious image prints, prepared, like the pictures of John of Monte-Corvino, "for the ignorant", began to appear in Europe some time within the half century after these early missionaries laid down their work, may not be altogether a coincidence.[1]

In the course of a thousand years the art of making paper, which Ts'ai Lun had invented in A.D. 105, had travelled by slow stages to Europe. It had reached Samarkand in 751, Bagdad in 793, Egypt by 900 and Morocco by 1100. Spaniards were making it in 1150, Frenchmen in 1189, Italians in 1276 and Germans 1391. In the fourteenth century the art of printing, first pictures and then words, from wooden blocks, as in China, was practised in Europe. In course of time the alphabetical scripts of Europe suggested the idea of cutting each letter on a separate block and casting copies in metal. Each letter could thus be multiplied to any number required, by a purely mechanical process. This invention of movable types cast in metal was first made in the latter half of the fifteenth century either by a Dutchman, Coster, at Haarlem, or else by a German, Gutenberg, at Maintz.

The invention brought to a close the epoch known as the Middle Ages and opened the chapter of Modern History.

The writings of Marco Polo had attracted but little attention till one of the early printers selected

[1] Carter, *The Invention of Printing in China*, p. 122.

his book for the exercise of his art. It thus came to the notice of Christopher Columbus, and a copy is still extant with his notes on the margin. How it worked on his vivid imagination we can best realise by reading for ourselves the account of Japan which he found in those pages. And in doing so let us bear in mind that when speaking of miles Marco Polo is thinking, by force of habit, of Chinese 'li'. The strait which divides Japan from Korea is 110 miles wide at its narrowest point. Its actual distance from China is less than 500 miles.

Says Marco Polo:

Zipangu is an island in the eastern ocean, situated at the distance of about fifteen hundred miles from the mainland, or coast of Manji. It is of considerable size; its inhabitants have fair complexions, are well made, and are civilized in their manners. Their religion is the worship of idols. They are independent of every foreign power, and governed only by their own kings. They have gold in the greatest abundance, its sources being inexhaustible, but as the king does not allow of its being exported, few merchants visit the country, nor is it frequented by much shipping from other parts. To this circumstance we are to attribute the extraordinary richness of the sovereign's palace, according to what we are told by those who have access to the place. The entire roof is covered with a plating of gold, in the same manner as we cover houses, or more properly churches, with lead. The ceilings of the halls are of the same precious metal. . . . So vast, indeed, are the riches of the palace, that it is impossible to convey an idea of them. In this island there are pearls also, in large quantities, of a red (pink) colour, round in shape, and of great size, equal in value to, or even exceeding that of the white pearls.[1]

The Genoese sailor, having heard of the daring suggestion that the earth might be shaped like a ball, conceived the idea that China and Japan might be reached by crossing the sea in a westward direction. After failing to interest the Portuguese King, he

---

[1] Marco Polo, Book III. chap. ii.

III THE OPENING OF THE SEA ROUTES

applied to Ferdinand and Isabella of Spain, who undertook to provide him with ships. On sighting the West Indies in 1492 the passage we have quoted from Marco Polo must have recurred to his mind. When he reached the mainland of South America in 1498 he thought it was China, and in 1506 died in that error.

In 1486 a Portuguese captain, Bartholomeu Diaz, had rounded the Cape of Good Hope. So, in 1493, when Columbus returned from his first voyage, Pope Alexander VI. issued a bull, assigning to the kings of Spain and Portugal all lands "such as have not actually been heretofore possessed by any other Christian king or prince". By the Treaty of Tordesillas in 1494 the two monarchs agreed to fix the line dividing their empires in the middle of the Atlantic from north to south.

To the draftsmen of papal bulls and treaties the idea of the earth as a ball instead of a plate had still to be proved; so nothing was said as to what was to happen if the two empires should meet on the other side of the world.

The project of finding a western route to Asia and its seeming success had obscured for the moment the achievement of Bartholomeu Diaz. But when, in 1494, the Portuguese realised that the papal bull debarred them from using this western route, their interest in the route explored by Diaz revived. The leader entrusted by their King, Manoel, with the task of following it up was Vasco da Gama. In January 1497 he sailed from Lisbon with four tiny vessels, rounded the Cape in December, and dropped anchor in Calicut harbour on the 20th May 1498.

This port on the west coast of India was an emporium at which goods passing from China and the Indies to Europe were collected. The sea-borne trade from Calicut to the Persian Gulf and the Red Sea was controlled by the Arabs, to whom the appearance of Europeans in ships at an Indian port came like a bolt from the blue. Under pressure from the merchants of Mecca the Hindu ruler of Calicut imprisoned da Gama and his officers. They were presently released; but the insult was never forgotten and twice revenged, by Cabral at the head of a second expedition in 1500 and by Vasco da Gama himself, who returned at the head of a powerful squadron in 1502. He then met the combined Arab fleets off the coast of Malabar and almost destroyed them.

The task of developing these achievements fell to the great Albuquerque, who proceeded to survey the maritime problem of the eastern trade. At this period the island of Ormuz in the mouth of the Persian Gulf was the focus of sea-borne trade west of India. From Mesopotamia to Malabar articles of commerce were shipped to that point. To the east of India the trade was collected at Malacca on the straits between the Malay Peninsula and Sumatra, the maritime road which connects the Bay of Bengal and the China Seas. Goods destined for Europe were shipped from Malacca and Ormuz to Egypt by the Arabs, who controlled the whole of these seas.

In a series of desperate engagements Albuquerque seized and occupied the island of Socotra at the mouth of the Red Sea, Ormuz at the mouth of the Persian Gulf, and then Goa on the coast of India, which he made the capital of the Portuguese Empire in the East. From this base he was able to capture Malacca, which was then tributory to the Emperor of China. The Arabs were swept from the seas. Till the close of the sixteenth century the whole trade from the East to Europe was controlled by the Portuguese. The spices and silks for her markets were carried by sea to Lisbon, and thence distributed to the ports of Europe by Dutch traders. So much was accomplished when Albuquerque died at Goa in 1515.

When Albuquerque stormed Malacca in 1511 the

III THE OPENING OF THE SEA ROUTES

eastern limit of the Portuguese Empire was carried to that point. The King of Portugal had styled himself "Emperor of India"; but his great servants in the East had realised better than their master the relative weakness of the kingdom behind them. Almeida had strongly opposed Albuquerque's schemes for occupying ports like Ormuz and Malacca. But even the forceful Albuquerque realised that so small a power as Portugal must rest content with the empire of the sea.

About 1517, the year in which Luther challenged the Pope's authority at Wittenberg, Portuguese ships reached Canton. In the next few years there were several violent collisions between Portuguese and Chinese forces. An envoy, Thomé Pires, sent to visit the Court of Peking in 1521, was arrested and probably died in prison. Requests for permission to trade were rebuffed. It was not till 1557 that the Portuguese, by bribing the local officials, were able to open a trading station on Macao, a peninsula at the mouth of the Canton River.

The Portuguese had thus reached by sea the fabled Empire of Cathay which Marco Polo had explored by land. The spherical theory was becoming so evident as to bring the empires of Spain and Portugal into conflict on the other side of the world. Magalhães, a Portuguese mariner, incensed by failure to secure an increase of pay, deserted the service of Manoel, and offered to prove by a westward voyage that the Spice Islands belonged to the empire of Charles V. in terms of the bull issued in 1494. The offer was accepted, and in 1520 he passed the straits which bear his name (Magellan) and reached the Philippine Islands, where he perished in 1521. But one of his ships, the *Victoria*, returned to Spain by the Cape of Good Hope in 1522, thus proving beyond dispute that the human race lived on a ball suspended in space.

The settlement of a line down the Pacific to divide the two empires was at once demanded by Spain. After long negotiations this line was fixed in 1529 by the Treaty of Saragossa at 17° east of the Moluccas. In the light of the facts then known it was not realised by either party that this line would assign the Philippines to the Portuguese. When, in later years, the Spaniards annexed the islands they simply ignored the letter of the treaty; for the Portuguese were too weak to assert their technical claim.

In America, Spain, with vastly greater resources, was confronted by races to whom horses as well as guns were unknown, races far weaker than those of Asia. By 1521 the empire of Mexico had fallen to Cortes, and by 1532 Pizarro was master of Peru. The Americas had, in fact, become provinces of the Emperor Charles V. And with these conquests went hand in hand the forcible conversion of the natives to the Christian religion. For with Catholics and Protestants alike the maxim that subjects must follow the religion of their ruler was accepted as a matter of course. In 1543 the same policy was applied to the Philippines. The islands were conquered and a Spanish governor appointed to rule them from Manila, which the Spaniards founded as capital of the province. The task of converting the natives to the Christian religion was entrusted to the orders of St. Augustine, St. Dominic and St. Francis.

Thus in the middle of the sixteenth century the western and eastern outposts of the Spanish and Portuguese Empires were confronting each other with little more than 500 miles of open sea between them. To the people of those regions it was also made clear that forcible conquest and conversion to the Christian religion were part of the same process. Behind the conventional terms in which popes had issued their mandates to kings was a stern reality.

The conquest of the Philippine Islands by Spain

presently led to a large immigration of Chinese, who there acquired the habit of smoking tobacco which the Spaniards brought from America. Their surgeons had learnt to treat malaria by mixing opium and arsenic with the tobacco smoked by their patients. The Chinese copied this treatment and presently found that opium could be smoked by itself. It was thus, through tobacco, that a useful drug began to demoralise this enormous section of the human race.

CHAPTER IV

JAPAN IN CONTACT WITH EUROPE

IT was only in 1542 that an acquaintance with the islands of Japan themselves was obtained. In this year Martin Alphonso de Sousa being Governor of India, and Francis Xavier arriving there, Antonio Da Motto, Francisco Zeimotto, and Antonio Peixotto went in a junco from Siam to China, when a great tempest, called Tufao (from the Chinese Tai-fum, or the Japanese Tai-fu, great wind), drove their junco for twenty-four hours on the open sea, and brought them among the islands of Japan: they landed on one of those islands, called Tanegashima, in the Sea of Satsuma. The Portuguese taught the inhabitants of the island how to make arquebuses (espingardas), an art which quickly spread through the whole of Japan.[1]

In order to understand the effect on Japan of this introduction of firearms, we must glance for a moment at her previous history. In theory the government was, as in China, an absolute theocracy. In Japan, however, the dynasty never changed. In the time of Charles the Great, A.D. 793, Kwammu Tenno, the fiftieth Mikado of his line, was ruling Japan from Kyoto. From the close of the eleventh century the structure of society was becoming feudal in character and subject, therefore, to grave disorders when weak monarchs sat on the throne. At the close of the twelfth century order was restored by a powerful

[1] *History of the Church of Japan*, composed by the Religieux of the Company of Jesus who have been resident in that country from the year 1575 to the present year 1634, an unpublished manuscript in the library of Ajunda in Lisbon, quoted by Murdoch and Yamagata (p. 33) in their *History of Japan*.

soldier, Yoritomo, upon whom the Mikado conferred the title of Sei-i-tai-Shogun (Barbarian-subduing-great-general). His position was closely comparable to that acquired by Charles Martel as mayor of the Palace under the degenerate Merovingian monarchy. But so ancient and sacred was the Japanese dynasty that the Shoguns never dared to end it, as Pippin ended the House of the Merovingians. It lived through centuries of poverty and neglect till its glorious restoration to power in the nineteenth century, surviving by means of adoption the causes which are usually fatal to dynasties.

The Shogun dynasties were themselves subject to those causes. Yoritomo's sons were side-tracked, just as their father had side-tracked the Mikado. Till 1334 Japan was ruled by the Hōjō, as Shikken or regents, under fainéant Shoguns. In 1281 the Hōjō, Tokimune, was able to defeat the expedition of 100,000 men which was sent by Kublai Khan to conquer the islands. In Japanese history this victory figures as the Spanish Armada in our own. A great storm played a similar part in it.

The Hōjōs were displaced by the Ashikaga dynasty. Yoshimitsu, the third of this line (1368–1393), is still execrated in Japan, because he obtained from the Emperor of China the title of king, by the payment of tribute. The islands relapsed once more into feudal chaos; but the Ashikaga Shoguns were like the Mikados reigning, though not ruling, in the era when ships from Europe were feeling their way into the Pacific through the Straits of Malacca and round Cape Horn. Their power existed only in name. As in Germany, feudal lords, called Daimyo, were each paramount in their own fiefs. The Buddhist monks, living in fortified monasteries, were also powerful near Kyoto. They were, like the Templars, truculent soldiers as well as priests. Such was the state of Japan when the first visitors from Europe arrived at its shores.

In the previous decade there had come into the world three children destined to reduce to order the feudal chaos into which they were born, Nobunaga in 1533, Hideyoshi in 1536, and Iyeyasu in 1537. As in Europe, the introduction of gunpowder enabled competent soldiers to compel the obedience of feudal chiefs to a centralised government.

Nobunaga was the head of a small fief in Honshiu, the largest island of Japan. From the Portuguese he learned to make firearms and powder, and also the principles of fortification as then practised in Europe. When murdered in 1582 by a trusted follower he had made himself dictator of four provinces with absolute control of the Shogun and Mikado.

Hideyoshi was the son of a woodcutter, and is classed by historians with men like Caesar, Genghis and Bonaparte. In no age or country was it harder for a peasant to surmount the obstacles of humble birth. As a boy Hideyoshi is said to have discerned the future greatness of Nobunaga and got himself engaged as the personal horse-boy of the rising dictator. His genius was recognised by his master, who raised him to the rank of soldier. Hideyoshi quickly rose to be chief of his staff and also his trusted political adviser. He was leading an expedition when he heard of his master's murder. Quickly returning, he suppressed the rising. By October 1586 he

had far outstripped his predecessor Nobunaga in grandeur of State, in power, in honour, and in riches. . . . Into his hands come nearly all the gold and silver of Japan, together with the other rich and precious things; and he is so feared and obeyed that with no less ease than a father of a family disposes of the persons of his household he rules the principal kings and lords of Japan; changing them at every moment, and stripping them of their original fiefs, he sends them into different parts, so as to allow none of them to strike root deep.[1]

[1] Murdoch and Yamagata, *History of Japan*, p. 209.

These are the words of Father Froez, a Jesuit missionary in Japan at the time. His remarkable order had started its work in Japan in 1549, only ten years after its foundation by Loyola, a Spaniard. The revolt of Luther had quickly provoked a revivalist movement in the Catholic Church, and in 1539 Loyola conceived the idea of founding an order based on military rather than on collegiate principles. Another Spaniard, Francis Xavier, was chosen by Loyola to act as its secretary. In 1540 he was sent by Loyola to King John III. of Portugal, who had applied to Rome for missionaries to convert his Indian Empire. In 1542 Xavier landed at Goa. In 1545 he visited Malacca, and wrote thence urging King John to establish the Inquisition at Goa to repress Judaism, advice which was taken after his death. It was there also that he met in 1547 a Japanese exile, Yajiro, and resolved to attempt the conversion of Japan. In 1549 he reached Kagoshima with his Japanese friend, and thence made his way to Kyoto.

Failing to learn the language of Japan, and discouraged by the few converts he made, Xavier now conceived the idea that if China could be brought to adopt Christianity Japan would presently follow suit. In 1552 he managed to reach St. John's Island, off the mouth of the Canton River, but died of fever before he could reach the mainland.

The strenuous lead given by Xavier was eagerly followed by his order. The feudal lords of Kiushiu, the western island of Japan, were eager for trade, and as Portuguese traders were more willing to come if permitted to have their own confessors, and were glad to carry Jesuit priests, the Daimyo allowed the missionaries to land. In 1567 they founded a station at Nagasaki, which quickly grew from a fishing village to a flourishing port. They were viewed with jealousy by the Buddhist monks; but Nobunaga, a descendant of Shinto priests, was bent on curbing this militant group. He had also learned to value the supplies of powder and firearms brought by the traders, so the Jesuit missionaries enjoyed his protection. By 1581 they had built 200 churches and claimed 150,000 converts, mostly in Kiushiu. In 1582 Valegnani, as Visitor General in Japan, arranged for four young nobles to visit Lisbon, Madrid and Rome.

Hideyoshi was as anxious as Nobunaga to encourage the Portuguese trade, but distrusted the influence which their priests were gaining with the Daimyo. His suspicions were also roused by the growing power of Spain in the Philippines. In 1580 the throne of Portugal had passed to Philip II. of Spain; so the story which follows throws an interesting light on the natural history of dual-monarchies.

Though Loyola and Xavier were both Spaniards, their order was identified with the Portuguese interests in the Far East. Spain had entrusted the conversion of the Philippines to older foundations, Franciscans, Dominicans and Augustinians, in whose eyes the Jesuits were impertinent upstarts. So strong was the mutual jealousy that the Pope in 1585 had tried to separate their spheres in accordance with the facts of geography, now better known than they were when the line was drawn in 1529 by the Treaty of Saragossa. By papal decree China and Japan were assigned to the Portuguese and their Jesuit priests. The Philippine Islands, which the Spaniards had occupied, were reserved to the older orders. They were always seeking a chance to evade their exclusion from the wider and more interesting field.

By 1591 Hideyoshi was master of all Japan. Distrusting the loyalty of the Christian Daimyo, he was anxious to employ them on conquests beyond the sea. So he called on the Governor at Manila, Don Gomez de Marinas, to acknowledge Japan as his suzerain power. Don Gomez realised that here in the furthest outpost of their empire the Spaniards were facing a military power of a different order from any they had met in the Philippines or Americas. He decided to temporise, and in 1593 agreed to send an embassy to Japan. The Franciscans seized the opportunity of getting the Governor to include Father Baptiste and three others of their order in the embassage.

On reaching Japan Baptiste secured permission for the four Franciscans to remain, by swearing to Hideyoshi that the Philippines would accept his demands. They then started to preach and even to build churches. Unlike the Jesuits they had not studied the politics of the country, and were blind to the dangers which threatened the whole missionary movement. They ignored the advice of the Jesuits, criticised and obstructed their work, and even seized one of their churches at Nagasaki.

The disasters to which their zeal was leading were postponed for a few years by events in a different field. Hideyoshi's mind was entering that stage when despots begin to regard their power as divine. He dreamed of an apotheosis as war-god of Japan, and erected a temple for his worship as such. As a step towards world dominion he was planning the conquest of China. So the Philippines, which offered an easy prey, were for ever lost to Japan, and the temporising policy of Don Gomez was justified in its wisdom. The mirage which drew Napoleon to Moscow perhaps in the end affected the map of the world less than the dream that lured Hideyoshi to attempt the conquest of China.

As Belgium is to the British Isles, so is Korea to those of Japan. In attacking China, Hideyoshi had either to secure the Koreans as his allies or else to conquer them. Their King refused his approaches.

Two letters [he wrote] have already passed between us, and the matter has been sufficiently discussed. What talk is this of our joining you against China? From the earliest times we have followed law and right. From within and from without, all lands are subject to China.... When we have been unfortunate she has helped us. The relations which subsist between us are those of parent and child. This you well know. Can we desert both Emperor and parent and join with you? You doubtless will be angry at this, and it is because you have not been admitted to the Court of China. Why is it that you are not willing to admit the suzerainty of the Emperor instead of harbouring such hostile intents against him?[1]

Hideyoshi prepared for war and hostilities opened in 1592.

At one time there were 200,000 Japanese serving oversea, the greatest force that ever was sent on such service down to the date when Great Britain was called upon to preserve her supremacy in South Africa.[2]

Equipped with firearms they were more than a match for Koreans armed with bows and arrows, and were soon in Seoul. But, like Napoleon, Hideyoshi had ignored the factor of sea power. The Koreans had an admiral of genius called Yi Sun-sin who destroyed the Japanese fleets and controlled the sea. The invaders were reduced to the verge of starvation, and might have been utterly destroyed if the Chinese had come to the aid of Korea in time.

By 1593 the position of the Japanese forces was so desperate that negotiations were opened with the Chinese Court. They were long drawn. The Chinese, underrating the reverence in which the Mikado was held, not unnaturally thought they could tempt the ambition of the peasant dictator. So the Emperor offered to invest Hideyoshi as King of Japan. In 1596 the Japanese envoys returned bearing a letter in the following terms:

The influence of the holy and divine one (Confucius) is widespread; he is honoured and loved wherever the heavens

[1] *Ibid.* p. 311.   [2] *Ibid.* p. 359.

overhang and the earth upbears. The Imperial command is universal; even as far as the bounds of ocean where the sun rises, there are none who do not obey it. In ancient times our Imperial ancestors bestowed their favours on many lands; the Tortoise knots and the Dragon writing were sent to the limits of far Fusang (Japan), the pure alabaster and the great seal character were granted to the mountains of the submissive country. Thereafter came billowy times when communication was interrupted, but an auspicious opportunity has now arrived, when it has pleased us again to address you.

You, Toyotomi Taira Hideyoshi, having established an Island Kingdom, and knowing the reverence due to the Central Land, sent to the West an envoy, and with gladness and affection offered your allegiance. On the North you knocked at the barrier of ten thousand li, and earnestly requested to be admitted within our dominions. Your mind is already confirmed in reverent submissiveness. How can we grudge our favour to so great meekness?

We do therefore specially invest you with the dignity of King of Japan, and to that intent issue this commission. Treasure it up carefully. Over the sea we send you a crown and robe, so that you may follow our ancient custom as respects dress. Faithfully defend the frontier of the Empire; let it be your study to act worthily of your position as our minister; practise moderation and self-restraint; cherish gratitude for the Imperial favour so bountifully bestowed upon you; change not your fidelity; be humbly guided by our admonitions; continue always to follow our instructions. Respect this![1]

This gracious proposal was addressed to a ruler of sterner mould than Yoshimitsu had been. Hideyoshi was roused to fury when he learned its contents, and hastened to pour troops into Korea. He had learned the lesson of sea power and had brought his navy to a high state of efficiency. It swept the Korean fleet from the seas; for a sordid intrigue at Court had removed Admiral Yi, and placed a drunken coward in command.

The Koreans were now supported by Chinese

[1] *Ibid.* p. 352.

armies. For two years bloody campaigns were fought through the great peninsula. After one victory the Japanese sent the ears and noses of 38,700 foes, packed in barrels, to be buried in a mound which is still shown to visitors in Kyoto. Their command of the Straits, however, was again threatened by the reappearance of Admiral Yi in command of a squadron.

The struggle was ended with the life of the despot, whose ambition had forced an unwilling people to attempt the conquest of China. In September 1598 Hideyoshi and Philip II. of Spain died within three days of each other. Immediate steps were taken to withdraw the Japanese forces. So ended an enterprise which won for Japan nothing but the mound at Kyoto and a hatred which still smoulders unquenched in the Belgium of Eastern Asia.

With a war like this on his hands it is not surprising that Hideyoshi was long content to ignore the Franciscan envoys who were busy supplanting their Jesuit rivals in the missionary field. In 1596 their activities were forced on his notice. A Spanish ship, the *San Felipe*, commanded by one Landecho, was wrecked on the coast of Tosa. Her valuable cargo was seized by the local prince. Landecho called on the central government to order its return; and to strengthen his case produced a map of the world, on which he displayed the vast extent of the Spanish Empire. When asked to explain how so many nations had been brought to obey the King of Spain, Landecho replied:

> Our Kings begin by sending into the countries they wish to conquer religieux who induce the people to embrace our religion, and when they have made considerable progress, troops are sent who combine with the new Christians, and then our Kings have not much trouble in accomplishing the rest.[1]

[1] *Ibid.* p. 288.

His words were reported to Hideyoshi, who denounced the Franciscans for using their position as envoys to conduct propaganda. He ordered a general expulsion of the missionaries. Some twenty-six were condemned to have their noses and ears cut off and then to be hung on crosses and stabbed through the heart with a lance. Amongst the condemned, three Jesuits suffered at Nagasaki for the folly of their rivals. A number of the order, however, were enabled to evade the decree of expulsion by the loyalty of their Japanese converts.

The death of Hideyoshi was followed by a lull in the persecution. His successor, Iyeyasu, though a pious Buddhist, was at first too cautious to antagonise his Christian subjects. But the conflicts aroused by the Protestant revolt in Europe were beginning to trouble Pacific waters. In 1594 Philip II., by closing the port of Lisbon to the Dutch, had driven them to challenge the monopoly of trade which Portugal maintained in the Far East. The Portuguese were no match for the Hollanders. In 1600 a Dutch vessel, the *Liefde*, reached Japan. The Jesuits denounced her as a pirate, and Iyeyasu sent for her English pilot, Will Adams. His ability impressed the new dictator, who insisted on retaining Adams in his service as master shipbuilder. For the rest of his life Adams lived in Japan, teaching the Japanese how to build and navigate ships in the Western fashion, and also the science of making charts. Through his influence the Dutch in 1609 were able to establish a thriving factory at Hirado, in the western island of Kiushiu. In 1613 an English factory was also founded at Hirado on his advice. But it never prospered, because Saris, who commanded the fleet sent by the English East India Company, was too small a man to listen to Adams or use his influence at the Japanese Court. Iyeyasu was anxious, as Hideyoshi had been, to encourage the traders, and in 1602 offered to protect them, so long as no priests were brought in their ships. Protestant nations were as yet untouched by the missionary zeal which inspired the Catholics; so Iyeyasu favoured the Dutch and declined ingenuous offers made by the Spaniards to destroy their factories at Hirado. When a Spanish sailor and priest obtained leave to survey the coast, he does not seem to have grasped their object, till the speed with which they completed their work aroused his suspicions and led him to discuss the matter with Adams. The English pilot explained that in Europe such conduct on the part of a foreign power would be treated as a hostile act.

The Roman priesthood [he added] had been expelled from many parts of Germany, from Sweden, Norway, Denmark, Holland, and England, and that although his own country preserved the pure form of the Christian faith from which Spain and Portugal had deviated, yet neither English nor Dutch considered that that fact afforded them any reason to war with, or to annex, states which were not Christian solely for the reason that they were non-Christian.[1]

It is not to be wondered that Iyeyasu on hearing these words should have said: "If the sovereigns of Europe do not tolerate these priests, I do no wrong if I refuse to tolerate them."

The information given by Adams was presently confirmed from a number of different sources. Araki, a Japanese Jesuit, who had gone to study at Rome under Cardinal Bellarmine, visited Madrid, and heard

the statesmen and monks there calmly discussing the subjugation of Japan to the King of Spain and to the Pope of Rome. On returning to Japan he preferred the claims of patriotism to those of religion, and plainly told the Tokugawa authorities of what was really toward in the councils of Spain.[2]

[1] Morse and MacNair, *Far Eastern International Relations*, p. 43.
[2] Murdoch and Yamagata, *History of Japan*, p. 690.

IV JAPAN IN CONTACT WITH EUROPE

It is more than possible that Araki was really from the outset an agent in the secret service of Iyeyasu. From Japanese sources we know that

> Iyeyasu sent Nishi Soshin to Western countries with a commission to investigate Christianity . . . while abroad for three years he became a Christian and studied Christianity, and then, returning, gave Iyeyasu a minute report on what he had studied. Iyeyasu now clearly saw the harmful nature of Christianity, and resolved to prohibit it altogether.[1]

In Japan governing circles were thus fully apprised of affairs in Europe. They knew of the wars between Protestants and Catholics which were presently to lay Germany in ruins. The knowledge they acquired of the Inquisition was destined to be used by this imitative people with their native thoroughness.

While eager to promote commerce with Europe, Iyeyasu was equally determined to suppress its religion. Native Christians were put to death, and the foreign priests were ordered to leave Japan, but their lives were spared.

Hideyoshi had completed the task of uniting Japan begun by his master, Nobunaga. Iyeyasu was resolved to render it permanent by founding a dynasty, and in this he succeeded. Of noble birth, he was able to induce the Mikado to invest him with the title of Shogun, and so to transmit that office to his family, the Tokugawas. From his death in 1616 to the restoration of the Mikado to power in 1867 the rulers of Japan were sprung from his loins. A great realist, he seems to have recognised that heredity cannot be trusted to produce rulers of ability. He deliberately copied from China the 'government of sages' established in obedience to the teaching of Laôtze. The successes and failures of the Tokugawa regime were alike due to the system of bureaucracy created by its founder.

[1] *Ibid.* p. 495.

From a government of officials it is possible to secure the highest efficiency in maintaining a system already established, and even in carrying that system to its logical conclusion. But on questions of policy, involving a change in the system, respect for technique and its own position renders it blinder than ordinary men. It belongs to the order of mechanism rather than of mind, and no more than an engine can call in question the merits of the gauge to which it is built.

The bureaucracy created by Iyeyasu was unable to appreciate his idea of encouraging trade with Europe, but thoroughly competent to enforce and improve his tentative measures for extinguishing the Catholic religion. The priests, Europeans as well as native, were subjected to a persecution more searching than the Inquisition had ever established in Spain. While native Christians were massacred wholesale, the efforts of the persecutors were directed to securing the apostacy of Spanish and Portuguese priests. When mere crucifixion was found, for obvious reasons, to inflame the zeal of their followers, they were plunged into boiling and sulphurous pools, or hung by the feet head downwards in pits. One conspicuous success rewarded the persecutors, and did much to discredit the Church in a country where indifference to pain is a point of honour. But, apart from this one exception, the priests of the rival orders endured to the death these exquisite torments with a heroism unsurpassed by Jewish or Protestant victims of the Holy Inquisition, which had never devised such lingering anguish.

At the root of this hideous cruelty were fears that, like curses, fulfil themselves. In 1637 the Christian peasants of Kiushiu, unable to endure further, rose and occupied the fortress of Shimabara.

Whatever the movement may have been in its inception —whether economic or religious—it at all events soon became a Christian one. The rebel generalissimo—a *samurai* youth of 17, Masuda Shirō by name—was a Christian who preached and celebrated Mass twice a week; all round the parapet were a multitude of small flags with red crosses, and many small and some large wooden crosses, while the insurgent war-cries were 'Jesus', 'Maria', and 'St. Iago'—the latter the battle-cry of Spain.[1]

As their own guns proved too light for the work, the Tokugawa Government accepted an offer of assistance from the Dutch, who threw 426 shot into the castle and drove the besieged "to build places like cellars into which they crowded". Meanwhile hunger was doing its work and the fort was stormed by *samurai* troops. In the action there perished 37,000 peasants, while the Government troops lost at least 13,000 in killed and wounded.

In the fear engendered by this movement, the bureaucracy resolved on a step which, in its consequences, was far-reaching as any in modern history. They resolved to close Japan to intercourse with countries beyond the sea. In order that the Government itself might retain some knowledge of events in the outer world, the pliant Dutch were allowed to send one ship a year. Their colony was moved from Hirado to an island of a few acres in the harbour of Nagasaki, where they lived as prisoners, and submitted to great indignities. When the annual ship arrived from Holland the superintendent of the factory was obliged to make a report to the Shogun on foreign events in the course of the year.

Japan was thus closed to the world by a nervous bureaucracy. Of vastly greater importance were the steps taken to close the world to their own countrymen. An ordinance was issued forbidding any Japanese vessel to go abroad, or any Japanese subject to leave the country on pain of death. No ship might be built larger than would carry some 2500 bushels of rice. The build and rig were prescribed in exact regulations.

[1] *Ibid.* p. 652.

The intended effect of all this was to render the vessels at once so cumbrous and so crazy that facing the fortunes of an oversea voyage in them would be at once profitless and foolhardy.[1]

The Japanese are described by the English who first met them as "a desperate warlike people and ready to adventure for good pay". A maritime people, like the English, they had greater need for room to expand beyond the seas. In 1604 Michelborne and Davys (who had given his name to the straits which divide Greenland from America) attacked a Japanese junk near Singapore. The Japanese swordsmen fought them in silence, and slaughtered a number of the English, including Davys himself. In his letters Michelborne speaks of

the Japons as not being suffered to land in any port of India with weapons, being a people so desperate and daring that they are feared in all places where they come.[2]

The garrison of Molucca which beat off the Dutch attack in 1606 was largely Japanese. The Dutch themselves employed them to garrison the Moluccas. When in 1623 they seized the English colony at Amboyna it included Japanese soldiers. In all the regions they opened to the world adventurers from Europe found no one to match their own daring and resource but the Japanese. As they learned to use guns their diminutive stature became an advantage.

In 1638 the people of Japan were fully acquainted with world geography. In 1613 the Franciscan, Father Sotelo, had conducted an embassy from Japan, through the Spanish provinces of South America and Mexico, where, in the church of St. Francis, sixty-eight of them were baptized and confirmed. On arriving in Spain they were entertained in Seville and Madrid as the guests of the King. There was little in the arts of building and navigating

---

[1] *Ibid.* p. 695.   [2] *Ibid.* p. 580.

IV JAPAN IN CONTACT WITH EUROPE

ships as then practised by Europeans which this highly intelligent and imitative people had not already mastered. Their population, many times greater than that of the British Isles at that period, was seeking an outlet. By 1608 as many as 15,000 were settled in the Philippines. With or without their natural allies, the Dutch or the English, the Japanese with a navy of their own could have taken these islands from Spain whenever they chose to do so; and rulers of the calibre of Hideyoshi or Iyeyasu would certainly have done it. A glance at the map is sufficient to show that, once established in the Philippines, the Japanese must have quickly felt their way to Borneo, the Moluccas and New Guinea. In the course of two centuries they must have discovered and annexed Australia and New Zealand. Their navies must have mastered the Pacific more thoroughly than those of England mastered the Atlantic. They would scarcely have brooked exclusion by Spain from the whole American seaboard. They might well have supplanted the Spaniards in America, and to-day the civilisations of Europe and Japan would be facing each other in regions south of the great lakes. As it is, the civilisation of Western Europe dominates the ocean which washes the shores of Japan; while she, following the path traced by her peasant dictator, has seized Korea and is driven to seek in China the means of supporting her teeming millions.

CHAPTER V

CHINA IN CONTACT WITH EUROPE

THE people of Japan, like those of England, were possessed in a marked degree by devotion to their island home and to those who lived in it. They developed a sense of nationalism and a patriotism never surpassed in intensity; and this in a later age has enabled them to adapt their institutions to those of Western Europe with incredible speed and facility. Their insular feudalism also developed the Samurai, a class with a moral code which has features resembling those of 'the English gentleman'. The islands, too, were easily controlled by a central government. Their effective seclusion for over two centuries is proof of the fact.

With China it was otherwise. Its people considered themselves as a civilisation, or rather as the only civilisation. But the country was much too large for its people to conceive, as did those of Japan, the idea of a nationality. Provincial mandarins, eager for pickings, could easily lull the contemptuous instinct of the court at Peking to exclude the foreign 'barbarians', by representing the dues collected on trade as tribute dutifully brought by subject peoples. Traders of Europe who were ready to be fleeced and submit to humiliations were allowed to load their ships at Canton, with expensive commodities like silk, tea, porcelain and rhubarb.

With rare exceptions, the only Europeans who

got into the country were missionaries. The Friars had been welcomed by Timur the grandson of Kublai, and had made numerous converts. But when in 1368 the Tartars were expelled by the Mings, the Christians were suppressed as clients of the fallen dynasty. In 1580 the Jesuit Ricci succeeded, where Xavier had failed, in entering China through Macao. In 1601 he gained admission to Peking, and interested the Emperor, Wan Li, in his astronomical instruments. The Emperor's wife, mother and son were converted and baptized under the names of Helena, Maria and Constantine.

The Ming dynasty had by now exhausted its mandate. In 1644 the last of that house died by his own hand, and a Tartar conqueror sat once more on the throne of Peking. Again Christianity suffered by its close connection with a fallen dynasty.

So far from regarding the Chinese as heathens Ricci preferred to dwell on points which Buddhists and Catholics had in common—the use of the cross, mitre and dalmatica, the resemblance of their fasts, litanies and relics, their candles, bells and holy water, and also their prayers for the dead, the celibacy of their clergy and their doctrines of atonement. As for the state religion he identified Heaven worshipped under the name of Tien with the God of the Christians. The local deities he identified with saints, and endeavoured to harmonise the worship of ancestors with prayers for the dead.

Schaal and Verbiest, two able successors of Ricci, by their knowledge of science secured the protection of the Emperor and obtained an imperial edict declaring that ancestor-worship was a political rite and that Tien-chu (Lord of Heaven) was the name of the one true God.

Meanwhile the Dominicans and Franciscans had made their way into China from the Philippines, and in 1645 persuaded Innocent X. to issue a bull declaring Chinese rites as idolatrous. It was further declared that Shangti, not Tien-chu, was the Chinese word to be used to express the idea of God.

In 1656 the Jesuits induced Alexander VII. to reverse the decision of Innocent X. But in 1704 Clement XI. restored the ruling in favour of the Friars, and issued a bull condemning the worship of ancestors as idolatry. He further denied that either Tien-chu or Shangti was the name of the true God. A legate was sent from Rome to serve the bull on the Manchu Emperor Kang Hsi who now reigned at Peking. The Son of Heaven, who alone of men had access to God, thus learned that the Pope had presumed to issue a decree contrary to his own. The unlimited claim to authority of the Vicar of Christ in Rome was thus in direct conflict with the no less unlimited claim of the Son of Heaven in Peking. The issue which had brought the Church into conflict with the Roman Empire was revived. And in this case the Pope, by denouncing ancestral worship, was threatening the basis of Chinese civilisation. So Kang Hsi expelled the Dominicans and Franciscans. A second legate was then sent from Rome to excommunicate the Jesuits and their followers. Kang Hsi handled the crisis with moderation; but in 1724 his successor, Yung Cheng, forbade the teaching of Christianity and confiscated the property of the churches. Some Jesuits were able to live at Peking under the protection of emperors who valued their knowledge of Western science and sheltered them from the jealousy of Chinese scholars. It was through the Jesuits that France acquired the position she still holds in the West as a centre of sinological studies.

CHAPTER VI

THE UNEQUAL TREATIES

THE Portuguese were able to frustrate the attempts made by the Dutch to open trade with Canton; so in 1624 the Dutch created an establishment of their own at Formosa. In 1637 Captain John Weddell of the English East India Company, ignoring the Portuguese at Macao, forced the Bogue, silenced the Chinese forts, and, proceeding to Canton, disposed of his cargo and loaded with sugar and ginger. In 1685 the English Company secured the right to a factory at Canton, but took no great interest in the trade for the next thirty years.

Slight as the sea-borne traffic was it was fast creating in Europe a demand for Chinese products other than silk. In 1660 Pepys wrote in his diary, "I did send for a cup of tee, a China drink, of which I never had drunk before". The East India Company began to purchase small quantities from Chinese junks at Madras to use as presents to friends at Court. By the reign of Queen Anne tea had become fashionable in London society, and in 1715 the Company opened a regular trade at Canton. The taste for tea then spread so rapidly throughout the English-speaking world that by the end of the century 2 lbs. per head of the population were consumed in Great Britain.

There was no corresponding demand in China for the products of Europe, and the traders were put to it to find some commodity other than silver to give in exchange for their cargoes of silk, porcelain and tea. This problem of exchange found its solution in opium smuggled from India in contravention of Chinese law. In 1770 the Company assumed a monopoly of opium in Bengal and in that year 200 chests were sent to China.

In the eighteenth century the Court of Peking would have closed the country to trade with Europe, as did Japan, but for the fact that the duties paid by the traders were represented as tribute from nations which recognised the Emperor of China as Lord of the Universe. The trade was therefore confined to Canton, the nearest port reached by the ships from Europe. There was no intention of allowing the barbarians to enter the country. A location was provided on the fore-shore where the traders of each European nation were allowed to build their factories and lodgings. On specified days they were suffered to walk under superintendence in public gardens on an island opposite. Their intercourse was limited to a guild of Chinese merchants called the Co-hong, which was organised for the purpose. These merchants were usually men whose capacity for business and standards of honour earned the respect of the foreigners. With officials it was otherwise; for mandarins were expected to live by exacting fees from those who required their assistance. For their attitude towards the industrious people they misgoverned a parallel may be quoted from the pages of Dickens.

"For myself, my children," said Mr. Turvydrop, "I am falling into the sear and yellow leaf, and it is impossible to say how long the last feeble traces of gentlemanly deportment may linger in this weaving and spinning age. But, so long, I will do my duty to society, and will show myself, as usual, about town. My wants are few and simple. My little apartment here, my few essentials for the toilet, my frugal morning meal, and my little dinner will suffice. I charge your dutiful affection with the supply of these requirements, and I charge myself with all the rest."

This vast and isolated empire, like that of the Romans, had developed no public opinion competent to restrain official exactions. Corruption could be checked only by the hand of a strong emperor, and it grew apace as a dynasty weakened. At the close of the eighteenth century the Manchu dynasty was already in decline. The system whereby the balance of exchange was adjusted by smuggling opium from India gave the fullest scope to the recognised practice of squeeze. The largest profits on the traffic were made by officials whose duty it was to prevent it.

The Hong system was workable so long as British trade (which exceeded that of all other nations together) was monopolised by the East India Company, and therefore subject to the control of their superintendent. But contact, however restricted, between societies so widely different was bound to issue in conflict. According to European ideas a man is responsible for his own conduct. In China justice is communal, the family, neighbourhood or guild is responsible for wrong done by its members, and justice can be satisfied by the punishment of any member of the group involved, irrespective of his individual guilt. One case from a number on record will illustrate the point. In 1784 a salute fired from a ship called the *Lady Hughes* caused the death of a Chinese. The supercargo was arrested, and in order to save him the Company surrendered a gunner, who was strangled.

The tragedy preparing for China had its roots, as tragedy usually has, in a great obsession. For ages she had lived as a civilised world to herself and had gained no knowledge of the world without. The visits which Europeans had paid to her shores had not been returned. Their trade, lawful and illicit, was a source of enormous profit to the mandarins and merchants of Canton, and the Court at Peking was prevailed on to tolerate their presence under close restrictions on the theory that they came to pay in the form of customs the tribute due from barbarian kingdoms to the Son of Heaven. So late as 1860 when the British and French took Peking they found the chair in which the American Minister had just been received inscribed "for the tribute-bearer Ward".

Their treatment as inferiors was a constant offence to the Europeans, and especially to the British, whose navy in the eighteenth century was accustomed to dominate the seas. They resented the laws which forbade their leaving the factory to walk in the streets of Canton, less as an injury to their health and comfort than to their dignity. This resentment was rendered more dangerous by the knowledge that English warships could in a few hours silence the forts of the Chinese and sink their junks.

One obvious way out of the difficulty was for England, following the precedents set by the Portuguese at Macao, to establish a station under her own control on some uninhabited island. In 1793 Lord Macartney was sent on a special embassy to China to negotiate a settlement on these lines, and ask for an exchange of diplomatic representatives. The mission failed because Macartney refused to pay the Emperor the homage held to be due to him from a subject nation, and returned bearing a letter in which George III. was addressed as a vassal of China.

The East India Company was able to avoid any positive rupture so long as its officers remained in exclusive control at Canton. But when its monopoly was abolished in 1833 and the China trade opened to all British merchants who wished to send ships to Canton, the British Government appointed Lord Napier as superintendent of British trade. An officer commissioned by Government could not, like a superintendent appointed by a company, agree to address his letters only to merchants. The Viceroy declined to receive Lord Napier's letters except in the form of petitions forwarded through the Hong. He thus brought to a head the latent issue of inequality, no empty question of status, but an issue which affected every European trading in Chinese waters.

The crisis was delayed by the death of Lord Napier, to be rendered acute in a few years by a movement at Peking to enforce the laws prohibiting opium. The 200 chests sent from India in 1770 had by 1830 grown to 4000 per annum. In the course of the next decade the imports had increased to more than seven times that quantity. Originally started to correct the balance of exchange the illicit import was now draining China of silver. In 1838 the Emperor appointed the leader of the anti-opium movement, Lin Tse-hsü, as commissioner for enforcing the laws. Lin demanded and obtained through Captain Elliot, the successor of Lord Napier, a surrender by the merchants of opium to the value of over £1,000,000. He then went on to demand the surrender of certain Europeans for alleged crimes on Chinese soil and, when this was refused, closed the port of Canton to trade. British warships arrived to support Captain Elliot, and in November 1839 hostilities began. Chinese forts and junks were easily silenced and sunk by the British men-of-war. Facts so unpleasant were slow to percolate through ranks of courtiers to the incredulous ears of the Son of Heaven, and the issue was delayed by the immense time which it took in the days of sailing ships to send forces to China. By 1842 the British had captured a number of cities on the Yangtze, had cut the route by which the tribute of grain was sent by the Grand Canal to Peking and were threatening Nanking. The stoppage of supplies vital to the very subsistence of the Court at Peking at length brought home to the Emperor that this was something more than a local affair with barbarians in Southern China.

The Treaty of Nanking which ended this war was signed on H.M.S. *Cornwallis*. The equality of the two nations was admitted in terms. The British obtained what Macartney had asked for, an island off the coast of China, where they could live under their own laws and flag, and conduct their business unhampered by the manifold exactions of Chinese officials. The bare rock of Hongkong rapidly became the greatest emporium of the East. It also provided a residence for the representative of the British Government in China.

The Hong monopoly at Canton was abolished, and Canton, Amoy, Foochow, Ningpo and Shanghai were opened to foreign trade.

On the question of opium the treaty was silent. In despatches Palmerston admitted that the traffic was illegal, and the British negotiators urged the Chinese to legalise and regulate it. But the genuine believers in prohibition at Peking received sinister support from officials at Canton. The mandarins stood to gain more from illicit than from legalised traffic. So to-day prohibition in America is favoured not only by smugglers but also by officials they corrupt.

The British Government, while agreeing to regard the importation of opium into China as contrary to law, did nothing to restrict its export from India. In the cultivation of opium the British East India Company had now discovered a lucrative source of revenue. The dangerous example was followed by Indian Princes. When the Company was abolished the British Government inherited a system under which the opium revenues had become an all-important item in the budgets of the Indian Empire. In official circles a conviction grew up that opium was necessary to the health of the Chinese.

Anxious, though unable, to avoid further conquests in India, the British Government consciously adopted the policy of demanding nothing from

VI THE UNEQUAL TREATIES

China but what was thought necessary for the purpose of trade. They resolved to claim no exclusive rights, and in the Treaty of the Bogue, signed in 1843, secured the right that any privilege accorded to other nations should *ipso facto* be accorded to England. Henceforward the most favoured nation clause became a common form in treaties which foreign nations made with China.

At this period the trade conducted by American merchants with China rivalled that of the British. The Chinese merchants in Boston were a factor in American politics. So Mr. Caleb Cushing was sent by Daniel Webster, the Secretary of State, as Commissioner and Envoy Extraordinary and Minister Plenipotentiary to negotiate a treaty with China. His instructions were to recognise as valid the laws of the Empire, but also to "assert and maintain, on all occasions, the equality and independence of your own country". On the 3rd July 1844, he obtained the signature of the Treaty of Wanghia, in terms of which the U.S.A. secured the same privileges as the British had exacted in the Treaty of Nanking, but agreed to treat opium as contraband. On the 24th October 1844, the French followed suit in the Treaty of Whampoa. The Powers of Europe, and even some South American Republics, obtained similar privileges by insisting on the principle which England had first enunciated in the most favoured nation clause.

In Asia the French Government has always supported Catholic orders, even when endeavouring to suppress them in France; for in foreign affairs traditional policies often survive domestic revolutions. So in 1844 France was more interested in pushing the Catholic religion in China than in fostering trade, and Louis Philippe instructed his envoy, de Lagrené, to secure facilities for the Catholic missions.

The ideas which inspired de Lagrené in 1844 can be gathered from an article in the *Revue des deux*

Mondes, thought to have been written by a member of his staff.

Let us in our policy and our commerce imitate the conduct, at once prudent and courageous, of the Catholic missions, which have for more than two centuries exerted such noble efforts in the cause of religion. Protected and proscribed, honoured and persecuted by turns, raised to-day to the dignities of the imperial court, to be thrown into prison or conducted to execution to-morrow, the missionaries persevered in their glorious task, without being for a moment dazzled by the prospects of a precarious favour, or cast down by the inflictions of the most fearful hostility. All the Catholic nations of Europe, French, Spaniards, Italians, Portuguese—all their congregations, Lazarists, Dominicans, Franciscans, Jesuits, have been leagued in this remote crusade to take Asia in the rear, and reduce to the spiritual dominion of Rome the most ancient, the most civilised, but at the same time the most corrupt of Asiatic communities. China is at this day parcelled out into bishoprics or vicariats apostolic, wherein the new apostles have divided among themselves the rude labours of conversion. The progress is slow, but this has not damped their hopes. The faith advances only by insensible degrees, but it never recedes. God only knows how many years or how many centuries, how much devotion, and how much martyrdom may be required to complete the work.

France has at all times distinguished herself in the first rank of Christian nations, and in China she has not been wanting in the duties imposed by her traditions, or suggested by the exigencies of the public good. This may serve at least as some compensation for the inferior place which we have held in the order of material interests; and if we are obliged to acknowledge the extent to which England and the United States have eclipsed us by the still unceasing growth of their commerce and navitation, we may, in our turns, pride ourselves on the brilliant services rendered by the Catholic missions of France to the cause of religion and civilisation.[1]

De Lagrené secured for France the privileges accorded to America in the Treaty of Wanghia,

[1] MacNair's *Modern Chinese History,* p. 202.

and also a rescript establishing the liberty of the Catholic worship. The church properties confiscated in 1724 were restored by a further rescript issued in 1846.

The Protestant missions were not satisfied with the rescripts granted to de Lagrené, from the terms of which it might be inferred that the veneration of images was a necessary feature of Christianity. A further declaration was therefore obtained at their instance, in which it was made clear that Chinese subjects were to be allowed to adopt and practise Christianity in all its forms.

Under British initiative the states of Europe and America thus secured for their nationals the right to live, trade and teach in China without coming under the operation of her laws. Their consuls, to whose jurisdiction alone they were subject, acquired a position of exceptional importance. The British consuls were organised as a corps, separate from the rest of the consular service. Cadets were expected to master the language and also the technique of the intricate system established by the Treaty of Nanking. In Sir Harry Parkes, Sir Robert Hart and Sir John Jordan this service produced men who have left their mark on the Far East.

A law so different in principle from that of Europe must constantly have driven Europeans obliged to live under it into armed resistance. The case of the strangled gunner above quoted is enough to illustrate that point. The only arrangement possible at the time was to place foreigners under the jurisdiction of their own laws administered by their own consuls. But none the less the system led to dangerous abuses and was one of the factors which undermined the authority of government in China. It offered a motive to unscrupulous Chinese to acquire the status of foreign subjects. Some consuls, especially of certain Latin communities, were not incorruptible, and naturalisation was sold broadcast to Chinese who had motives for living beyond the reach of their own laws. It can scarcely be supposed that such consuls would be strict in enforcing the law of their own country against the natives of China to whom they had sold their nationalisation.

Consuls were appointed to the five Treaty Ports, the number of which was afterwards increased. In most of these ports the consuls obtained from the Chinese Government areas known as 'concessions', as homes for their nationals and sites for their godowns. These concessions were leased to the Foreign Power, whose local consul then issued titles to his own nationals, established a court to administer their law, and made provision for municipal government. At Canton a French concession as well as an English concession was established. At Hankow five, and at Tientsin eight foreign concessions have existed side by side.

Shanghai was the sole exception, a port at the mouth of the Yangtze which was destined to prove more important than all the others. For the Yangtze drains 750,000 square miles, one-half of China proper. More than one-tenth of humanity—some 180,000,000 industrious folk—convey their produce down this artery. A thousand miles from its mouth steamships collect the merchandise brought to its waters in junks and barges down tributaries, creeks and canals. If the Mississippi and St. Lawrence met to discharge their waters through the estuary of the Hudson River, the position of New York would, in point of natural advantages, be comparable with that of Shanghai. It may yet become the greatest city that the world has seen.

The old Chinese city of Shanghai stands on the left bank of the Whangpoo, which flows for sixteen miles through mud flats to the estuary of the Yangtze, and is tidal for a long distance above Shanghai. A channel deep enough for any ships which existed in 1842 is swept by the constant rush of the tide. It is now deepened by dredging, so that all but ships of the largest tonnage can lie in the stream, which at Shanghai is 500 feet wider than the Thames opposite London.

Here Captain (afterwards Sir George) Balfour took up his residence as British Consul in 1843. He failed, however, to persuade the Taotai, the Chinese official in charge, to grant a concession. As a compromise, 138 acres were reserved on the left bank of the river below the Chinese city, where British subjects might purchase land from the peasants, which was not thereafter to be sold or let to the Chinese. Titles subject to a just rent were issued by the Taotai, through the Consul, and were registered at the consulate.

In 1845 Land Regulations were jointly enacted by the Consul and the Taotai. "Three upright merchants" were appointed by the British Consul to administer the municipal affairs of the Settlement.

In 1849 the French Consul secured land near the city wall, above the area reserved for the British, as a residence for his nationals.

On the other side of the British area, American missions and shipping interests began to acquire land. In 1854 the American Consul took up his residence on the river front just below the Soochow Creek. This so-called American Settlement was ultimately incorporated with the British area as the International Settlement. The present map of Shanghai is due to these facts. Its peculiar institutions are the outcome of American insistence on treaty rights.

In 1848 Mr. Griswold, the American Consul, took up his residence in the British Settlement, hoisted the stars and stripes, and in the face of British and Chinese protests kept it flying on the ground that

England had disclaimed all right to exclusive privileges.

On the 6th April 1849, Luh, the Chinese military intendant, issued a proclamation to the effect that foreigners other than French might buy land in the French Settlement, but must register it with the French Consul. Griswold refused to accept this interpretation of the treaties, and so established the practice that foreigners might purchase land in all the Settlements and register their titles with their own consuls. Other consuls followed the American example. The area reserved for the British was thus transformed into a settlement in which all nations with extraterritorial rights stood, in law, on a footing of legal equality.

CHAPTER VII

THE TAIPING REBELLION

THE peculiar development of Shanghai was the result of American influence, and, as we shall see in subsequent chapters, the whole course of events throughout the Pacific was profoundly affected by the schism which established the United States as a separate sovereignty.

The British Commonwealth was definitely weakened by the loss of the American Colonies. Wise in the knowledge of that weakness, its government was sincere in its efforts to develop its commerce without expanding its empire. In India and elsewhere, events, powerfully aided by British traders and officers, were too strong for it, and the flag followed where trade went. But in China, the young Republic, jealous of its status as a foreign Power, influenced the course followed by the parent commonwealth with decisive effect. Accepting the British initiative, the U.S.A. secured for its citizens the same privileges. At critical junctures, however, it drew attention to the declarations of Ministers in London and refused to accept from British officers in China practical arrangements which seemed to conflict with the principle of equality. Mr. Griswold's action in hoisting his flag in the British Settlement and American insistence on the right of Americans to register properties with their own consuls are cases in point. There were other causes at work, but the watchful attitude of the

United States, adopted by virtue of its separate sovereignty, sufficed of itself to secure that in China the British Government would not be diverted by British merchants or officers from the path of commerce which it honestly wished to tread.

England has thus pursued in China a policy which developed no other motives than trade. The privileges sought and obtained for missionaries, in common with other nations, were merely the logical results of that policy, for facilities once secured for merchants could not be denied to philanthropists.

We have now to trace the results of this policy on China. The ink was scarcely dry on the Treaty of Nanking before they began to appear.

According to a contemporary observer:

> The peace was hastened, not more by the really formidable character of the British expedition than by the universal anarchy and confusion that reigned internally; by the entire failure of every scheme grounded in ignorance, and defeated by its own folly; and, in fine, by the apprehension of a general revolution against the government, which was losing its hold on the minds of the people.[1]

A Chinese official who had witnessed the fall of Canton wrote:

> Henceforth we shall be an object of contempt to other nations, and the native villains will gain strength and oppose the government.

The mandarins, powerless to cope with foreign governments, encouraged the populace and also the secret societies in their hatred of foreigners. To the Chinese their Manchu rulers were foreigners also, but this fact was ignored. War had filled the country with firearms, and officials made no attempt to keep them out of the hands of the rabble. The seas also were infested with pirates.

[1] Sir John Davis, *China during the War and since the Peace*, London, 1852, vol. i. pp. 6 and 7.

THE TAIPING REBELLION

Had foreigners never come near China, the Manchu dynasty would have burnt to the socket as twenty-nine others had done before. Its guttering flame, so nearly blown out by the British guns, was afterwards sheltered, for the reason that revolutions are bad for trade. Merchants and diplomats assumed that whenever its time came, as sooner or later come it must, another and stronger dynasty would be found to replace it. A history much longer than that of Europe could be trusted to repeat itself. Assumptions so natural in the nineteenth century were falsified, however, by factors which are now easier to discern.

Durable governments rest on ideas in the minds of those who obey them. The Chinese had thought of their emperors as divine and regarded their power to rule, so long as it lasted, as proving their supernatural authority. Some thirty dynasties had risen, flourished and declined, by virtue of these beliefs in the minds of a people secluded from those influences which Greece let loose on the world when she opened her tiny jar. By the Treaty of Nanking, and others which followed it, China was rapidly exposed to ideas certain to prove fatal to those upon which her dynasties had rested their power for thousands of years. To Europeans of the nineteenth century it was plain enough that the Manchu dynasty must eventually fall. It was not then plain, as it now is, that the ancient foundations upon which all the dynasties had rested were about to dissolve once for all. The essential solvent was not the traders, nor yet their governments nor their guns, but the Protestant missionaries and the schools they founded.

In 1847 a native of Kwangtung called Hung Suitsuen (better known as the Tien-Wang or Heavenly King) received instruction from the Rev. Issachar J. Roberts, an American missionary. When refused baptism by his mentor, he formed an "association for the worship of God" (Shangti), the supreme being with whom the Emperor alone was supposed to have intercourse. His most loyal follower, the Chung Wang, on the eve of his execution in 1864, wrote of him:

> His doctrine was that a man serving Shangti would be free from all calamity or misfortune, whilst snakes and tigers would devour all disbelievers. Those who did serve other gods were guilty of sin.

He proclaimed his doctrine as a new revelation of Christianity. The Trinity included the Father, Christ the Heavenly elder brother, and the Tien-Wang himself as the Heavenly younger brother.

> Our Heavenly Prince [he announced] has received the Divine Commission to exterminate the Manchoos ... and to possess the Empire as its true sovereign.

From these proclamations it is clear that China was now drifting from her ancient anchorage in Confucianism, Taoism and the religion of Buddha.

In 1850 the Tien-Wang allied himself with the Triads, a powerful secret society opposed to the Manchus, and chose as the title of his dynasty Taiping or Great Peace. By 1853 the Taiping leader was dominating China south of the Yangtze. On the 19th March 1853 he stormed Nanking, and put to the sword the Manchu garrison, their women and children, 20,000 in all. In the ancient capital of the Ming dynasty he proclaimed himself Emperor.

From Nanking his armies attempted the conquest of Northern China, but were checked before they could reach Tientsin. Forces organised south of the Yangtze learn to depend for their movements on canals, and are apt to find themselves hampered in regions where no such facilities exist. Whatever the reason may have been, the Taiping forces were stopped and destroyed before they could threaten

Peking. The outbreak of war with the Foreign Powers in 1856 enabled the Tien-Wang to retain control of the Yangtze valley till 1864. He failed to establish the semblance of a government and the movement developed into organised pillage.

CHAPTER VIII

ADMISSION OF FOREIGN MINISTERS TO PEKING

THE mandarins, as we have seen, had drifted into the policy of conniving at mob violence. When the mob burned factories in Canton, the Governor readily paid compensation; but Europeans had no protection and therefore no liberty to move in the streets of the city. The British were on excellent terms with the Chinese merchants with whom they came into personal contact. Coolies were ready to earn wages even from military forces conducting operations against their country, and served its enemies with loyalty and zeal. But the Treaty of Nanking had left unchanged habits of mind centuries old in the great mass of the Chinese not in direct business relations with foreigners, whom they still regarded as inferiors, barbarians and even as devils. To understand their feelings we have only to imagine what our own ancestors would have felt if in the Middle Ages Chinese merchants, backed by powerful fleets, had been able to assert in London, Bristol and Liverpool the privileges which Europeans had secured for themselves in the Treaty Ports.

In the records of Macartney's embassy there is no indication that Englishmen of that period regarded the Chinese as inferiors. But as they became conscious of the overwhelming power which steam and mechanical improvement was placing in their hands a change was taking place. They were not in the

CH. VIII ADMISSION OF FOREIGN MINISTERS 71

temper to tolerate their continued exclusion from the streets of Canton contrary to treaty rights. A situation in which Chinese and British each regarded the other as racial inferiors was highly explosive.

Its dangers were gravely enhanced by the fact that the British representative at Hongkong had no access to the government of China at Peking. The following letter from Sir John Bowring (24th April 1854) to Commissioner Yeh shows that he was even denied personal access to responsible officers of the Chinese Government at the Treaty Ports:

> To give effect to the provisions of the Treaty, personal and unrestrained intercourse between the officers of both Governments was indispensable, at all events, for the transaction of important business, even if not necessary for exchange of the common courtesies of life. At those ports where the practice does happily exist, it is oftener exacted than willingly accorded. At Foochow and Canton either the error is committed of deputing inferior officers to meet the consul, or he is refused an interview altogether, and, as regards Canton in particular, at this very hour no personal intercourse has taken place with the higher authorities.

In 1856, while China was still in the throes of the Taiping rebellion, a dispute as to whether a vessel called the *Arrow* was subject to Chinese or British law provided the inevitable spark. In October Sir Michael Seymour seized the defences of Canton and demanded that foreigners should be allowed to reside in the city in accordance with treaty rights. In November the Barrier forts opened fire on American ships, which replied and captured them without difficulty. But America declined to join in the war. The murder of a missionary, Père Chapdelaine, brought France into active alliance with England, and in 1857 Russia joined the allies. In December of that year Canton was taken and occupied by the British.

England was seriously hampered by the outbreak of the Indian Mutiny in 1857, and the Chinese were also better prepared than they had been in 1839. On the other hand, British warships were now under steam power, and the forts as well as the war-junks of China lay at the mercy of vessels which could move regardless of wind and tide.

In the previous war the Emperor had acted as though the treatment of foreigners was a provincial and not an imperial question. Two utterly different ideas of the state, of its nature and functions, were in conflict, the one European, the other Chinese. The West, though it did not know it, was forcing on China its own political concept. The British Government was resolved to compel the Imperial Court itself to handle the foreign relations of China. The first and necessary step was to compel the Emperor to receive the envoys of Foreign Powers in his palace at Peking. The French agreed, but the Russians and Americans declined to support this policy.

By June 1858 the British and French had compelled the Chinese to accept treaties at Peking which the Emperor signed on the 4th July. Under these treaties the equality of foreigners with Chinese was admitted in terms. They were not in future to be styled 'barbarians' in official correspondence. Christianity was to be tolerated, and the whole of the Yangtze valley opened to trade. The Russians and Americans followed the accepted policy of requiring similar privileges under the most favoured nation clause. The Russian Minister went from St. Petersburg overland via Kiakhta to Peking and there ratified the treaty. The American Minister, Ward, agreed to go by Pehtang, was given no interview at Peking, was there exposed to discourtesies, and finally agreed to exchange ratifications at Pehtang.

The British and French decided to proceed by the ordinary route via Tientsin, and to go with their fleets up the river to that port, ignoring the fact that the right to select their route had not been specified in the treaty. On the 24th June 1859 they met with a serious repulse at the Taku forts, at the mouth of the river. A year later Lord Elgin and Baron Gros returned with an overwhelming force. Sir Harry Parkes, who was sent by Elgin to negotiate with Peking, was captured and some of his party were murdered. Sir Reginald Johnston has recently discovered from archives obtained in Peking that the Chinese Government believed that Parkes was the British Commander-in-Chief, and also that, when deprived of his leadership, the British attack would collapse. This tragic delusion was doubtless due to the forceful character of Parkes, who, owing to his mastery of the Chinese language as well as his personal qualities, was the intermediary through whose lips and pen everything which passed between Elgin and the Court at Peking was conveyed.

In October 1860 the British and French forces entered Peking and rescued Parkes. The Emperor's summer palace, five miles from the city, was burned in reprisal for what seemed like a wanton act of treachery. Had Elgin realised the curious delusion in the Chinese mind as to the status of Parkes, he surely might not have thought that this act of vandalism was necessary.

An indemnity of 8,000,000 taels was exacted in the treaty imposed on the Chinese. The Emperor was further compelled to agree to legalise the opium trade, to cede Kowloon, a beach on the mainland opposite Hongkong, and to sanction the recruiting of Chinese coolies for labour abroad.

The English and French Governments had no intention of allowing their troops to remain at Peking longer than was necessary to obtain a settlement of the points at issue. The Court assumed that they meant, if they could, to keep it permanently, as the Manchus themselves had done. General Ignatieff, the Russian plenipotentiary, made skilful use of this misapprehension. In return for a promise to induce Lord Elgin and Baron Gros to withdraw from Peking, he obtained from Prince Wang the Amur province north of Manchuria, which was afterwards extended to include Vladivostok opposite the coast of Japan. The train of events which led to the collision of the Russian and Japanese Empires was thus laid. It was not till a year later that Prince Wang discovered his own error in supposing that the British or French Governments meant to keep their soldiers in China, and so realised that he had given away something for nothing.

The struggle had largely grown from a discord between the political ideas of Western Europe and China due to her long seclusion from contact with foreign states. The Court at Peking had been mainly concerned with appointing or replacing the officials who governed the provinces. Their success or failure in collecting and forwarding to the capital the revenues upon which it subsisted were the main criterion by which they were judged. It was for the local governors to collect the tribute which barbarians paid in the form of customs, and also to restrain their disorderly conduct. Such disorders were treated as a matter of police. When foreigners with their guns and steamships proved too strong for provincial governors, the Emperor and his courtiers were too far removed from actualities to realise the necessity of confirming the terms of peace they made. Till 1860 the Imperial Court had no Minister or office equipped to deal with foreign affairs.

By the treaties forced on China in 1860, the Imperial Court was obliged to receive the Ministers of the Powers. In 1861 England, France and Russia established legations at Peking, and the U.S.A. in the following year. In order to deal with those Ministers the Court had to create the Tsung-li Yamen or board charged with the conduct of foreign affairs.

CHAPTER IX

END OF THE TAIPING REBELLION AND ITS CONSEQUENCES

WHEN the peace was signed at Peking, the Yangtze valley and the country south of it was still dominated from Nanking by the Tien-Wang and his followers. So long as the Foreign Powers were at war with China they observed a policy of strict neutrality as between Nanking and Peking. But when they had made peace with the Manchu dynasty they allowed it to engage foreign officers in their service, and also import munitions of war, a privilege still denied to the rebels. This change of policy enabled a young Chinese official to prolong the tenure of the Manchu dynasty into the twentieth century. In 1853 Li Hung-Chang had raised a militia battalion which did such good service against the rebels that in 1862 he was made Governor of Kiangsu. He adopted the policy of using foreign methods and leaders in fighting the rebels. In 1860 an American sailor, Ward, had begun to organise troops (largely composed of deserters from the British forces) which came to be known as the "ever-victorious army". Ward was killed in 1862 and Li Hung-Chang then secured the services of Gordon, the British officer who ended his days in Khartoum. In 1864 Nanking was stormed, the Tien-Wang died by his own hand, and the rebellion was finally crushed. When it ended the rebels had reduced the villages of the Yangtze to ruins, and massacred their inhabitants to the number of 20,000,000.

Though the native city of Shanghai had been in the hands of the rebels, the sanctity of the Foreign Settlements was secured by the fact that British, French and American warships could lie at the wharves and land troops when necessary. By the regulations Chinese, other than servants of the foreigners, were excluded. But these regulations were not enforced against refugees escaping from the native city and the general anarchy of the Yangtze valley. To the number of 500,000 they flocked to the Settlements as cities of refuge, the only place of security in central China. The foreign holders of land, who had not the heart to expel them at first, presently found in their continued presence a lasting and lucrative source of profit. Immense prices were paid by Chinese for leases of land granted by foreigners. When peace was restored in 1864 about 90,000 Chinese preferred to remain in the Settlements reserved for foreign residents under the treaties. This of course involved heavy expenditure on police and sanitary measures, and Chinese and foreigners were taxed alike to meet the cost. But municipal control remained entirely with the small minority of foreign landholders. The physical protection of foreign warships thus brought into being the greatest of Chinese cities ably and honestly ruled by a mere handful of foreign merchants.

The flight of Chinese from the rebels into the International Settlement created a problem which could scarcely be handled by "three upright merchants" appointed by the British consul. In allowing the consuls of other nations to exercise in the Settlement a jurisdiction equal to his own, the British consul had lost the right to arrange for its government with the Taotai in a conference of two. So in 1854 a meeting of the land-renters, summoned to meet the

British, American and French consuls, framed regulations under which the land-renters were to elect representatives who should organise a police force, provide municipal services and impose the necessary taxation.

The validity of these regulations was open to question by nationals other than British, American and French. Many other defects were revealed by experience, and in 1866 a revised constitution (in the shape of new Land Regulations) was produced in Shanghai. In this draft the English and French areas were included as one municipal whole. A proposal that delegates should be elected by native guilds, for consultation on matters affecting Chinese residents, was discussed, but was dropped for reasons which cannot now be explained. The draft regulations were forwarded by the consuls to the foreign Ministers, but years were to pass before they all agreed. When in 1869 the Land Regulations had been finally approved by the Ministers, the provisions for Chinese representation had disappeared, and the French had decided to keep their Settlement apart in the hands of their own consul.

Under these Regulations, foreign residents owning or renting property of a certain value within the Settlement were entitled to elect a Municipal Council of nine. This Council was entrusted with the task of administering the affairs of the Settlement. Its accounts and its budget had to be submitted for approval to a meeting of the foreign electors. This meeting of electors had exclusive power to impose certain specified taxes, and also to approve by-laws for the better enforcement of the Land Regulations. But by-laws passed by the meeting of electors, to become valid, must be sanctioned by the Ministers of Powers in treaty with China.

Any constitution is bound to reveal defects when put into actual working, especially when the community for which it is framed is rapidly growing and changing. The Council of nine, with a heavy and continuous burden resting upon them, developed a higher sense of responsibility than the voters in their annual meeting. The Council could realise the importance of giving the Chinese majority some voice in public affairs, and also a proportionate share of the benefits to the cost of which they had to contribute. But the Council's proposals for reform were too often negatived by the public meeting, or frustrated by the absence of a quorum. When reforms had received the approval of the public meeting they had then to run the gauntlet of the Ministers at Peking. The result has been that, apart from a few amendments approved in 1899, the municipal constitution remained rigid and unaltered, as it was drafted in 1866, till changes were forced by the cataclysm of 1925.

From the outbreak of the Taiping rebellion till 1928 the task of maintaining order in the greatest of Chinese cities lay with a handful of foreign merchants. In the area reserved for the British in 1843, the British Government stood on exactly the same footing, in international law, as Sweden, Brazil or any other of the Treaty Powers. But in actual fact control for the most part lay with the British, who owned most of the property. From 1890 to 1914 the Council normally consisted of seven British members, one American and one German, who after 1914 was replaced by a Russian. A Japanese member was first elected in 1916. From 1927 to 1930 there were five British, two American and two Japanese members. Thus, before Chinese members were included in 1928, the British always had a majority. Through the consuls the British Minister at Peking had direct control of the British concessions in other Treaty Ports. In the International Settlement at Shanghai he lacked such control. There was no guarantee that measures taken by the British majority and their officers to govern a large and turbulent Chinese community there would harmonise with the aims of policy as seen from the wider standpoint of Peking. Yet Shanghai, not Peking, was the real focus of China's relations with the rest of the world. In the distant legations the problems that confronted the Municipal Council were imperfectly grasped.

Apart from the yield of its normal trade, wealth from all over China seeks the relative security of the Settlements; and where riches collect criminals gather as wasps to honey. Shanghai is also the principal centre of illicit traffic in opium, which breeds criminal organisations as ruthless and rich as those which exist to frustrate prohibition in America. In no city are the police faced by more baffling problems.

In the minds of the foreign residents, and especially in British and American minds, the authority behind the Municipal Council was law, enforceable through courts. A foreigner was entitled to be sued or tried in his own consular court. In the International Settlement there were fourteen such courts. The Municipal Council itself could be sued in a court consisting of the consuls sitting together. But what was to happen when the bulk of the population in the International Settlement was Chinese? In 1863 Sir Frederick Bruce, the British Minister in Peking, contended that the authority of the Municipal Council in Shanghai should "not extend beyond simple municipal matters, roads, police and taxes for municipal objects". He added "that the Chinese not actually in foreign employ shall be wholly under control of Chinese officers as much as in the Chinese city". But as Morse, the American historian, wrote:

> The merchants resident in Shanghai were more clearly conscious than the envoy, on his pinnacle in Peking, of the practical difficulties attendant on a strict interpretation of the letter of the treaties, and the admission of dual and

rival jurisdictions, on a footing of independence, within the same area.[1]

In his recent report on Shanghai Mr. Justice Feetham made the following comment:

The contrast between the authority of the Council of the Settlement and Chinese official authority, as represented by its local officer, the Taotai, was the contrast between an authority exercising limited powers in accordance with a defined constitution, and subject to the control of independent Courts of law, and an authority exercising powers of an arbitrary character, not subject to any defined legal limit, which controlled its own Courts and was not controlled by them.

It is impossible for arbitrary and unlimited powers and legal and limited powers to exist side by side, and to be exercised simultaneously by two independent authorities in the same area and in respect to the same persons. The first will inevitably swallow up or destroy the second. The Council of the Settlement, if they were to exercise any effective control over the Chinese residents, and to collect revenue from them, were compelled to insist on restricting the power of the Chinese authorities in respect of the Settlement portion of the Chinese population, and they seem to have recognised at a very early date that this was a question of life or death—that not only the welfare of Chinese residents, and therefore, also, to a large extent the prosperity of the Settlement, were involved, but that the very existence of their whole system of government was at stake.[2]

The result of this controversy was a compromise in favour of the Municipal Council. Chinese courts were established in the Settlement to try civil and criminal cases in which Chinese were defendants. On various occasions these courts have appeared to give decisions, not on the merits of the case, or in accordance with law, but in deference to political or administrative pressure from outside. But despite these difficulties, which have still to be faced, the rule of law in the Settlement was established in principle.

[1] H. B. Morse, *The International Relations of the Chinese Empire*, vol. ii. p. 128.   [2] *Feetham Report*, vol. i. p. 98.

END OF THE TAIPING REBELLION

Such a situation could never have lasted as it has for some eighty years, were it not for a certain good humour and tolerance in the Chinese nature, and the high standard of honesty maintained by the foreign oligarchy in the International Settlement. Shanghai has been happy in the personal integrity of its councillors, and is justly proud of their record in the matter. It is now on the whole the most promising instance of international co-operation which the world has yet produced.

When in 1853 rebels had captured the native city of Shanghai, the Imperial officials arranged for the British, American and French consuls to control the collection of customs on foreign imports in the Foreign Settlement. In 1863 Robert Hart, a young Ulsterman in the British consular service, was appointed by the Chinese Government to control the collection of foreign customs, which continued under his hand till he left China in 1908. No administrator has ever faced a task of greater delicacy with more consummate tact. Throughout he maintained the position of the Chinese maritime customs as a branch of the Imperial Government. He appointed under him inspectors recruited from the services of the Foreign Powers trading with China on salaries and pensions commensurate with the importance of their duties. Their Chinese subordinates were also paid on similar principles. He thus sought to create for China a working model of the kind of mechanism used by Western governments for administration, and in it Chinese officials were trained to standards different from those which the mandarins observed in their offices.

It was this service, together with the areas reserved for the residence of foreigners in the Treaty Ports, which served to bridge the gulf between two societies almost as different from each other as if they had developed on separate planets. The bridge might hold so long as one or other of the two was not in violent commotion. It was even strong enough to steady for a time the tottering fabric of China. The survival of the Manchu dynasty into the twentieth century was due to the achievements of Hart no less than to those of Li Hung-Chang.

To these two leading figures must be added one of the most remarkable women in history. Yehonala was born in 1835 as member of one of the oldest Manchu clans. In 1852 she was chosen as concubine for the Emperor Hsien Feng under the title 'Feminine Virtue', and in 1856 bore him his only son. In 1860, when the allies were approaching Peking, she advised the Emperor to remain there and face them. The Emperor, however, listened to the advice of a certain official, Su Shun, who saw that he could dominate his master if once he could get him away from the influence of his brothers. So the Emperor fled to Jehol, where he fell so ill that he never returned to Peking. On his sick-bed he was told that Yehonala was in love with Junglu, a young officer of the guards, and was thus persuaded to sign a decree placing the regency during his son's minority in the hands of Su Shun, Prince Yi and Prince Tuan Yua. The two princes, however, shrank from assenting to Su Shun's advice that Yehonala should at once be murdered. Their scruples were to prove fatal to their plans. Yehonala had secured the seal by which alone validity could be given to Imperial decrees. When the Emperor died, Yehonala set out with her son for Peking. An attempt to murder her *en route* was frustrated by her presence of mind. By virtue of the seal she held she was able to give to a decree vesting the regency in herself that authority which the decree issued by the three conspirators lacked. It was they who lost their lives and the Dowager-Empress reigned in their stead. Her son died in 1875, and except for a few months in 1898, when his suc-

IX END OF THE TAIPING REBELLION

cessor tried to assert himself, she remained the real ruler of China till her death in 1908.

Yehonala belongs to a type familiar in the history of dynasties. Her nearest counterpart is the Empress Irene, who ruled Constantinople in the time of Charlemagne. Like the rest of her kind, she cared more for her own power than for that of her country, which was humbled beyond measure throughout the period of her masterful rule. One after another of the neighbouring kingdoms which had paid tribute and rendered fealty to the Court of Peking passed to the rule of Foreign Powers. In 1885 France acquired the suzerainty of Annam. In 1886 Upper Burma was annexed by the British. In 1894 China's claim to control Korea was challenged by Japan. The dispute led to hostilities, which were quickly settled by Japan's mastery of the sea. One fact alone is sufficient to explain this result. The millions which should have been spent on the navy of China had been wasted by Yehonala on the building of palaces.

From these and far deeper indignities might China have been spared at the hands of a foreign dynasty if the Taiping rebellion had been led by a statesman instead of a bandit, as was that which expelled the descendants of Kublai. Up to the nineteenth century China had thought of herself as the world, and during it she was called upon to realise a world even greater than herself, and to find her place in it. A native government established on the Yangtze would have come into intimate contact with those forces of Western civilisation on which China had now to adjust her life. With its feet planted, one south and the other north of the great river, into which the streams of her life drain, and are now brought into ever-closening contact with the world without, it might have established and developed her political union. This, the supreme need of its people, could never be met from Peking. In origin a fortress whereby conquerors could dominate China, it was at best a Byzantium from which a native dynasty could strive to repel the forces threatening her independence. In the long run Peking could no more preserve the unity of China than Constantinople could maintain the unity of Graeco-Roman civilisation.

To the British and American Commonwealths the treaties which removed their Ministers to Peking, while opening the valley of the Yangtze to their commerce, were fraught with evil. They created a system under which the principal agents controlling their policy were far removed from the region in which British and American merchants and missionaries were developing intimate but difficult relations with Chinese in the heart of their country. It led to the growth on Chinese soil at the mouth of the Yangtze of the International Settlement as a city-republic which neither China nor yet the Foreign Powers could control. In course of time it also led to diplomats realising for themselves in Peking an International Settlement within fortified walls, thus creating a vested interest which has helped to obscure from themselves the common interests of their own peoples and those of China.

The world's two greatest civilisations were meeting each other in the Yangtze valley; but the problems to which their impact gave rise were thus destined to be handled by the statesmen of China and of the Foreign Powers at a point six hundred miles from that central artery.

CHAPTER X

THE PACIFIC OPENED

IN a previous chapter we have seen how the Japanese learned from Adams to make charts and to build and navigate ships on Western lines. Equipped with such knowledge, this seafaring race must have explored the Pacific for themselves if their own rulers had not forbidden them to apply it. Till near the close of the eighteenth century they could easily have planted the flag of Japan on every island great and small, and have occupied the coast of America north of the Spanish colonies. Their people and culture would thus have spread to the space which was naturally theirs. How greatly they needed such space is proved by the frequent recurrence of famines in Japan.

The outlet lost by refusal of knowledge fell to a people free to search for it. In 1768 Captain Cook was commissioned by the Royal Society to observe the transit of Venus about to occur on the 3rd June 1769, from the Southern Pacific. He rounded Cape Horn, reached Tahiti in time for his task, and named the group to which it belongs "the Society Islands" to commemorate the event. After charting the coasts of New Zealand and Eastern Australia, he returned home by Java and the Cape of Good Hope on the 12th June 1770.

In 1772 he sailed to New Zealand by the Cape, visited the Marquesas, the Friendly Islands, the

New Hebrides, New Caledonia, Norfolk Island and the Isle of Pines. He then made for the Horn, surveyed Tierra del Fuego, and returned to England in 1775. In that same year was fought the battle of Lexington. The loss of facilities for sending convicts to American plantations led the British Government to think of the regions opened by Cook as a site for depositing human refuse.

In 1776 Cook embarked on his last voyage. Its object was to settle the question whether ships could pass north of America from the Pacific to the Atlantic. He first made his way to Tasmania by the Cape route, and thence to Tonga and the Society Islands, discovering on his way the larger islands of the Cook Archipelago. On his voyage north he rediscovered Hawaii (which the Spaniards had found and afterwards lost), and named the group after Sandwich, First Lord of the Admiralty. He next struck the shores of America where the State of Oregon now is, and charted the coast up to Behring Straits till a wall of ice blocked his path. On his way home he revisited the Sandwich Islands, and there perished in a fracas with the natives on the 14th February 1779.

In 1782 Great Britain acknowledged the separate sovereignty of the United States. In 1788 those States adopted the constitution which enabled them to realise their destiny as one Commonwealth. In that same year Great Britain established a convict settlement at Botany Bay.

A major cause of the rupture with England had been the commercial system under which the enterprise of American merchants had been confined to trade with the mother country. The Chinese trade, monopolised by the British East India Company, was now opened to the enterprise of American vessels, and the mercantile community of Boston took so active a part in it that at one period the American tonnage in Chinese ports surpassed the British. The ships, like English vessels, came east by way of the Cape of Good Hope, which is just the same distance by sea from Boston as from London or Liverpool. The appointment of American consuls, and their influence on British policy in China, has already been noticed. These consuls were also supported by American ships of war.

A naval as well as a mercantile rivalry was thus established with England in Far Eastern waters. New England merchants were just as eager as those of the old country for the opening of markets in these regions.

In the years which followed the Treaty of Nanking, ships driven by steam power began to appear in Chinese waters. The need of stations where ships could count on supplies of coal was quickly realised. England had acquired such a station at Hongkong. American captains were eager to follow suit, and actually hoisted the Stars and Stripes in Formosa and the Bonin Islands. But their Government at Washington shrank from demanding the approval of Congress for these annexations, as required by the constitution. The British Empire as it now is would never have come into being if annexations had needed an Act of Parliament to confirm them. So large are the unforeseeable effects of a written constitution!

American admirals and merchants, none the less, saw in Japan a field in which to emulate the achievements of England and France in opening an Eastern Empire to the trade of the West. An occasion was offered by ill-use of American sailors wrecked in Japan. In July 1853 Commodore Perry, with four steamships, dropped anchor in the bay of Yedo, and demanded from the Government of the Shogun protection for shipwrecked Americans, the opening of ports to trade and the right to purchase supplies, especially coal. Having made these demands he departed, promising to return next year for the answer —with more ships. This he did, and in 1854 his demands were conceded in the Treaty of Kanagawa under which the Shogun agreed to admit an American consul to residence in Japan.

To this post was appointed Townshend Harris, a cultivated and travelled citizen of New York who had served as a consul in China. In persuading the Shogun to receive him and to open Japan to American trade, he was able to point to what was happening in China and to what therefore Japan might expect at the hands of European Powers, unless she made haste to concede the pacific demands of his own Government. He was thus able to secure his honourable reception by the Shogun at Yedo in 1857, and the signature of a treaty in 1858 on the deck of the *Powhatan* in Yedo bay, upon which the subsequent relations of Japan to the Western Powers were largely founded. The American Government thus reaped the advantages of a forceful policy without incurring the odium which it brought on those who employed it.

It was even more happy in sending to Japan a master of that American courtesy which is, in essentials, second to no other in the world. Townshend Harris was studious to preserve the self-respect of the strangely isolated people with whom he was dealing. And he also realised that, by studying the deeper interests of that people, he would best secure those of his own. Stricken with a dangerous illness in the course of his difficult negotiation, prayers were offered for his recovery, which was also attributed to the nurse O-Kichi, appointed by Government to attend him. The people of Japan, who have never forgotten their debt to Harris, have recently raised a temple to O-Kichi on the site of the house where "William Adams, known as Miura Anjin, the first Englishman to settle in Japan, who resided in a mansion built on this spot, instructed Iyeyasu, the first Tokugawa Shogun, in gunnery, geography, mathematics, etc., and constructed for him several ships on the European model". So runs the inscription on the temple dedicated to the lady who restored the American diplomat to health. The career of Harris, like that of Page, D'Abernon, Houghton or Dwight Morrow, is worth studying to remind us how much a nation in the throes of a perilous crisis may owe to the experience and sympathy of a foreign envoy.

For more than a century leaders of thought in Japan had been seeking to burst from within the seclusion imposed on the Island Empire by the government of the Shoguns. The Tokugawa regime was viewed with increasing jealousy by the rival clans of Satsuma, Tosa, Chosiu and Hizen, who hoped to restore to the ancient Imperial dynasty at Kyoto the authority usurped by the Shoguns at Yedo. The intellectuals were thus in sympathy with the feudal chiefs, but their joint aims were embarrassed by the fact that the Emperor Komei was under the influence of reactionary courtiers in Kyoto, who, like those at Peking, still hoped to exclude all foreigners from the country. These difficulties were suddenly removed when the Shogun, Iemochi, and the Emperor Komei died within a few months of each other. In February 1867 the young Emperor Meiji came to the throne at the age of fourteen. In the following November the new Shogun, Yoshinobu, was advised by the heads of the leading clans to resign his authority into his hands. This advice he accepted at Kyoto on the ground that "the laws cannot be maintained in the face of the daily extension of our foreign relations, unless the government be conducted by one head".

When, however, in January 1868, the Tokugawas were deprived of control of the young Emperor's bodyguard by the other clans, the ex-Shogun and his followers escaped from Kyoto to Yedo. After several defeats he surrendered in May 1868 and was then allowed to retire into private life. The rebellion was finally suppressed in July 1869.

In April 1868 the young Emperor took the charter oath before an assembly of Daimyo, and undertook that his Government should be guided by public opinion, for which purpose a deliberative assembly should be established. "Knowledge", said the Emperor, "should be sought for all over the world, and thus shall be strengthened the foundations of the imperial polity." In these words the seclusion imposed on Japan by the Tokugawa regime for over two centuries was officially ended. Through the British representative, Sir Harry Parkes, the foreign Ministers were invited to a personal audience. The policy was thus consciously adopted of learning from the great Powers of the world all that would help Japan to be ranked as one of them.

In 1869 the young Emperor was removed from the reactionary surroundings of Kyoto. His Court was established in the vast fortress which Iyeyasu had created for his dynasty at Yedo. In order to indicate that it was now the seat of the Emperor himself its name was changed to Tokyo.

In the course of the next decade the Emperor's Government had succeeded in dissolving the feudal system, in pensioning off the retainers of the Daimyo, in founding a system of universal education, and creating a mercantile marine. The army was organised under German experts on the basis of conscription, and the navy created under British advisers.

From this chapter, and also from Chapter IV., can be gathered the reasons why Japan reacted to Western influence in a manner so strangely different to that of China. The limited size of the country had combined with its isolation to create loyalties. As in the

Middle Ages England resisted absorption by Europe, so Japan had resisted absorption by China. From this had developed an intense devotion of the people to their country, which found its expression in reverence paid to a native dynasty. As in England, the feudal system had arrested the growth of national unity. But it also created the intense loyalty which the feudal retainers paid to their chiefs, who continued to exercise real authority over them, even in the period when a single clan had usurped to itself the central power. There were thus plenty of chiefs experienced in public responsibility, as well as devoted to the national ideal, when the advent of foreigners gave the finishing stroke to the waning power of the Tokugawas. The significant fact is that these chiefs, instead of destroying their country in a struggle for personal power, were able to unite in the project of restoring the ancient dynasty at Kyoto to genuine authority. In them the young Emperor found advisers experienced and able enough to realise the importance to Japan of learning the secrets of Western knowledge, and also of bringing her social structure into line with modern conditions. Their success is explained by the great authority which they themselves exercised over their own retainers. The rapid dissolution of the feudal system was in fact made possible by loyalties which that system had helped to create.

In nothing was the wisdom of the Emperor's advisers more signally shown than in moving his Court to a capital close to the greatest port of Japan, where its people were now coming into ever-closening contact with traders from all the world. At Tokyo the rulers of Japan and the envoys of Foreign Powers were in contact with the human problems they were called upon to handle, as they could not have been in the cultured and historic seclusion of Kyoto.

In 1871 a mission was despatched to the United States and Europe to

study the institutions of civilised nations, adopt those most suited to Japan, and gradually reform our government and manners, so as to attain the status equal to that of civilised nations.

It was led by Iwakura, Minister of Justice, and included Okubo, Minister of Finance, Ito, Vice-Minister of Public Works, and Yamaguchi, second Vice-Minister of Foreign Affairs. Returning in 1873 the commissioners found that disputes over Korea, the Liuchiu Islands and Formosa had brought Japan to the verge of war with Korea and China. Their travels had made them realise how little Japan was as yet prepared for such an adventure, and their whole influence was exercised to prevent it. Okubo argued that, if Japan and Korea went to war, both would become the prey of Russia. His view prevailed with the young Emperor, and in October 1874 he was sent to Peking with secret instructions to effect a settlement. This, with the aid of the British Minister, Mr. Wade, he accomplished.

It is not to our purpose in these pages to trace the steps by which Japan in the course of the next twenty years secured the abolition of the extraterritorial treaties imposed on her by the Foreign Powers. In July 1894 the fundamental treaty providing for the termination of these rights was signed with Great Britain.

A week later Japan was at war with China. Before the end of the year she had wiped the Chinese fleet from the sea, had taken Port Arthur, invaded Korea, and was threatening Peking. In March 1895 Li Hung-Chang was suing for peace at Shimonoseki. On the 17th April a treaty was signed there in terms of which China agreed to recognise the independence of Korea, to cede to Japan the Liaotung Peninsula,

Formosa and the Pescadores Islands, and to pay an indemnity of £40,000,000. In July 1896 a further treaty was signed granting to Japan extraterritorial rights together with all and more than the privileges enjoyed by the Western Powers.

In the Treaty of Shimonoseki, Port Arthur and the Liaotung Peninsula were ceded to Japan. A joint note was, however, addressed to Japan by Russia, France and Germany intimating that these Powers would decline to recognise the cession. In view of this pressure from the Western Powers, Japan agreed to withdraw this claim in return for an increase in the war indemnity. And so the train was laid for the subsequent seizure of Port Arthur by Russia and the war with Japan on Chinese soil, which sealed the fate of the dynasty in Russia as well as in China.

CHAPTER XI

SEIZURES OF TERRITORIES BY FOREIGN POWERS

CHINA was now faced by the task of raising in Europe the millions necessary to pay the indemnity to Japan. In order to do this she was forced to pledge the revenues accruing from the foreign customs, from the salt gabelle and even from likin[1] in the Yangtze basin. In case of default the Inspector-General of Customs was to take charge of all these services in the interest of the lenders. The Chinese Customs Service, organised under European officers, was thus transformed into an instrument of foreign control.

From this period began the general scramble by Western Powers for railway and mining concessions.

In 1895 Li Hung-Chang was sent to Europe ostensibly to represent China at the coronation of the Czar Nicolas. An emissary was sent by Count Witte, the Russian Minister of Finance, to meet Li Hung-Chang in Egypt, who induced him to come straight to St. Petersburg via Odessa, before visiting the countries of Western Europe. He there agreed to concede to Russia the right to connect the Trans-Siberian Railway with Vladivostok across Manchuria. The agreement was embodied in a treaty under which Russia and China undertook to defend each other if either were attacked by Japan.

The humiliation inflicted on the people of China by the Japanese victory revived their dislike of the

[1] Transit dues on goods levied locally.

presence of foreigners in their country. The missionaries scattered throughout the provinces were the easiest target for this resentment. Strong measures were taken by the American as well as by the British and French Governments to protect their nationals. In November 1897 two German missionaries were murdered in Shantung. The German Government seized the excuse to occupy the port of Tsingtao in Kiaochow Bay, and to exact railway and mining concessions in Shantung.

Encouraged by the German initiative, the military leaders in Russia advised the Czar to seize Port Arthur and the Liaotung Peninsula. This project was opposed by Witte as contrary to the spirit of the friendly alliance embodied in the secret treaty of 1896. Overriding his scruples, Nicolas supported his military advisers and authorised the seizure. In December 1897 a Russian squadron occupied Port Arthur. The consent of the Chinese Government was obtained by the machinations of Count Witte himself. The following is his own account of the matter:

> The Chinese Government was reluctant to comply with our demands. The Empress Regent, together with the young Chinese Emperor, had gone to her summer residence, in the vicinity of Peking. Under the influence of English and Japanese diplomats, she obstinately refused to make any concessions. Seeing that under the circumstances, should we fail to reach an agreement with China, bloodshed was likely to take place, I wired to the agent of my Ministry in Peking to see Li Hung-Chang and Chang Ing Huan, another high official, and to advise them in my name to come to terms with us. I instructed the agent to offer these two statesmen valuable presents amounting to 500,000 and 250,000 rubles respectively. This was the first time I resorted to bribing in my negotiations with Chinamen.
>
> Largely under the influence of the fact that a number of our warships, cleared for action, lay off Port Arthur, the two statesmen went to the Empress intent on persuading

her to yield. Finally, the Empress consented to sign the agreement. This came as a pleasant surprise to His Majesty. The agreement was signed on March 15, 1898, by Li Hung-Chang and Chang Ing Huan, on the one hand, and our Chargé d'affaires, on the other. The act was a violation of our traditional relations with the Chinese Empire. . . . It was a fatal step, which eventually brought about the unhappy Japanese War and the subsequent revolution. On the other hand, the Chinese Empire is tottering, and out of the civil war now raging a republic is bound to arise. The fall of the Chinese Empire will produce an upheaval . . . for many years to come.[1]

Great Britain was openly opposed to the action taken by Germany and Russia as contrary to the principle of the open door. In order to maintain the balance of power in the Gulf of Pechihli, a Chinese minister suggested that England should apply for a lease of Weihaiwei. After some hesitation this application was made and promptly accepted by the Chinese Government. The lease to Great Britain of Weihaiwei was signed on the 1st July 1898.

At this period various Powers used the condition of China's weakness to exact concessions at Treaty Ports, Russia at Newchwang, Germany at Tientsin, Japan at Amoy and Foochow, and all these Powers as well as Belgium and France at Hankow. At Shanghai the Chinese Government agreed under pressure from France and England to extend the Settlements. In May 1899 the International Settlement was increased from 1500 acres to 5584. In January 1900, 358 acres were added to the French Settlement.

The German Government had long been hoping to secure for herself the reversion of the moribund Spanish Empire in the Far East. But these hopes were frustrated by a sudden turn of events in the western hemisphere. The condition of Cuba had led to the outbreak of war with Spain on the 21st April

[1] MacNair, *Modern Chinese History*, p. 564.

1898. On the 1st May Admiral Dewey destroyed or captured the Spanish squadron in Manila Bay. German warships were instantly sent to Manila under Admiral von Diedrich, whose attempt to impede the American operations was met by Dewey with a threat of war supported by the British admiral, Chichester. Manila was then taken and occupied by American forces on the 13th August 1898. The decision to annex the entire archipelago, embodied in the Treaty of Paris signed by Spain on the 10th December 1898, was prompted by the previous seizure of ports in China by Western Powers. As part of the same movement the islands of Hawaii were annexed to the United States on the 8th July 1898.

CHAPTER XII

THE BOXER RISING

THE events recorded in the last two chapters had vast reactions in China, but to understand them we must for a little retrace our steps.

In the course of the nineteenth century the foreign communities of the Treaty Ports in the valley of the Yangtze, as well as along the coast and the missions throughout the interior, had permeated China with Western ideas. They had acted like yeast in masses of dough, and the earliest effects were apparent in the south. The Cantonese, whose junks by the thousand did trade with Hongkong, had learned to contrast the methods and results of Western government with those of the Manchu dynasty. Kwangtung was the province from which vast numbers of emigrants went to Singapore and also to Western America and Australia. The emigrants there learned what the practice of popular government means. It is claimed that the Kuomintang, the party which now dominates China, was founded in Australia. The movement for revolution was mainly financed by funds supplied by the Chinese communities in Singapore and the Dutch East Indies.

These facts go far to explain why the movement for reform in China has its deepest roots in the soil of Kwangtung. The two foremost apostles of the movement were natives of that province.

Sun Yat Sen was born of a Christian father in

1867 and educated under Christian influences, chiefly British. At Hongkong he was trained as a medical doctor, was qualified in 1892, and started practice at Macao, where he came in contact with leaders of revolution who had sought the protection of the Portuguese Settlement. In 1894 he organised a raid on Canton from Hongkong which missed fire; so he fled for his life to Hawaii and thence through America to London. In October 1896 he was kidnapped and imprisoned in the Chinese Legation in Langham Place, but managed to throw out a note into the street to his former medical instructor, Sir James Cantlie, appealing for protection as a British subject. He was instantly released on the orders of Lord Salisbury.

For seventeen years, from 1895 to 1912, death by violence constantly threatened him. No fear of torture and death, however, deflected Sun from his purpose. With opinions moulded by his missionary education and the democratic ideas he had absorbed, he was convinced that, if the Manchus were expelled, their place must be taken by a republic.[1]

There was, however, another and more conservative movement which hoped to achieve reform through the agency of the Emperor himself. The leading exponent of this view was another Cantonese, Kang-yi-wei, who was older than Sun Yat Sen and trained entirely under Chinese influence. His books on reform in Japan and Russia attracted widespread attention.

Yehonala was now in retirement. In Chapter IX. we have seen how in 1860 she secured the throne for her only son. When he died in 1875 she then raised to the throne her nephew, a grandson of the Emperor Tao Kuang who had reigned in the critical period from 1820 to 1850. This boy was made Emperor under the name of Kuang Hsü, which means "con-

[1] Morse and MacNair, *Far Eastern International Relations*, p. 642.

tinuation of splendour". In 1889 she had formally resigned the office of regent, though, as we have seen, this did not prevent Yehonala from spending the money which should have been used for the fleet on building a sumptuous palace for herself. As events afterwards proved, the young Emperor was clay in the hands of this masterful woman whenever she chose to exert her power.

On her sixtieth birthday she was formally presented by more than 10,000 women of China with a copy of the New Testament. The Emperor Kuang Hsü read it, and his interest in projects of reform was aroused. He turned to the works of Kang-yi-wei, which were now attracting widespread attention. The author was commanded to see him and authorised to translate his ideas into practice. So under the direction of Kang-yi-wei a comprehensive programme of reforms was prepared. In the summer of 1898 the Emperor proceeded to enact them. The flux of enlightened decrees, which continued from June to September, alarmed Yehonala, and when Li Hung-Chang was dismissed from office on the 4th September she decided to put the Emperor under restraint. Kuang Hsü got wind of her plans, and resolved to arrest Yehonala and execute Junglu, her old lover and principal supporter. The task was entrusted to Yuan Shih-kai, who disclosed his instructions to Junglu and transferred his loyalty to the cause of Yehonala. On the 22nd September the Emperor was placed under restraint. His life was probably saved by the active intervention of the foreign legations, added to the difficulty of finding another successor to the throne. Kang-yi-wei fled for his life. Decrees were issued cancelling those of the Emperor.

North of the Yangtze the secret societies, inspired by hatred of foreigners, were now getting beyond control. From bands which called themselves "Fists of Righteous Harmony" the movement came to be known as the Boxer Rising. On its banners were inscribed "Cherish the Dynasty and exterminate Foreigners", a motto which explains the subsequent attitude to the movement of the Manchus and Yehonala herself. The persecution of native Christians was accompanied by threats to foreign missionaries. On the last day of 1899 Mr. Brooks, an English missionary, was murdered near Tsinan. The vigorous action taken by all the foreign Ministers in the course of the year 1899 led to the appointment of Yuan Shih-kai to take the place of an anti-foreign governor in Shantung. But foreign intervention could only add fuel to the flames. Decrees were issued by Yehonala deprecating robbery and pillage, but encouraging law-abiding and loyal people to drill for their own defence. As in the movement which led to the Taiping rebellion, the Manchus were hoping to evade the stream of popular resentment by directing it towards the foreigners.

In 1900 the storm burst, and missionaries by the hundred were massacred in various parts of China. Yuan Shih-kai was strong enough to maintain comparative order in the province of Shantung. But this served to concentrate the movement in Chihli. In Peking and Tientsin the Boxers were openly drilling their forces.

The Manchu nobles were in favour of encouraging the Boxers to attack the legations. Junglu, supported by Chinese ministers, opposed them strenuously, but on the 4th June was overborne. Such foreigners as were able, and some Chinese Christians, took refuge in the legations. On the 20th June Yehonala threw in her lot with the Manchu nobles, declared war on the foreigners and ordered the legations to leave Peking within twenty-four hours. The German envoy, Baron von Ketteler, against the advice of all his colleagues, decided to carry his protest to the Tsung-li Yamen, and was killed on the way there.

For eight weeks the foreign legations were fighting for their lives, and would have been overwhelmed but for the strange fact that Junglu commanded the besieging forces, and at critical junctions restrained their action.

Of the garrison, 76 had been killed and 179 wounded when on the 14th August 1900, the allied forces entered Peking and raised the siege. To this composite army Japan had furnished 8000 men, Russia 4800, England 3000, the U.S.A. 2100, France 800, Austria 58 and Italy 53. The Germans had none in China to send; but an expeditionary force of 7000 men under Marshal von Waldersee was hastily despatched from Europe, and reached Peking on the 17th October. In view of the German envoy's murder, the allies agreed to allow von Waldersee to assume the position of commander-in-chief.

When the siege was raised Yehonala had escaped in disguise, taking the Emperor with her, to Sianfu, in the distant province of Shensi. To teach him his place, she ordered his favourite concubine to be drowned in a well before leaving Peking.

By ordering a general massacre of foreigners and attacking the foreign legations, the Manchu dynasty had done everything possible to discredit China in the eyes of the world. This explains, while it cannot excuse, the vengeance taken by the allies on the local inhabitants when Peking and the neighbouring regions lay at their mercy. Of this painful episode it suffices to say that contemporary records show that the Japanese were better restrained than the Europeans.

The Russian Government lost no time in seizing Southern Manchuria from Port Arthur as far north as Tiehling and west to the border of Chihli.

Their methods were brutal but effective. At Blagovyeshchensk five thousand Chinese—men, women, and children—were driven into the river and drowned, the feeble resistance of the Chinese was everywhere easily overcome, the whole of Manchuria was occupied and treated as though it was conquered territory, and at Newchwang the Russian flag was hoisted and a Russian administration established.[1]

On the 11th November 1901 a secret agreement between China and Russia was signed which gave the Russians a control of Manchuria that almost amounted to annexation. Under this agreement China allowed Russia to connect Port Arthur with the Trans-Siberian railway by a line to Harbin.

These separate arrangements with Russia are explained by the fact that the Empress had entrusted to Li Hung-Chang the task of making a settlement with the Powers who had occupied Peking. It was rightly believed that a secret understanding existed between China and Russia to support each other. The fact, which we now know from the memoirs of Witte, that Li Hung-Chang had two years before accepted a bribe of 500,000 roubles goes far to explain the one-sided nature of this secret agreement.

[1] Sir Harold Parlett, *Diplomatic Events in Manchuria*, p. 12.

CHAPTER XIII

THE BOXER SETTLEMENT

THE final settlement with the allies was signed on behalf of China by Li Hung-Chang and Prince Ching on the 7th September 1901. On the 7th November 1901 Li Hung-Chang died.

We shall here deal only with those points in the settlement which had lasting and decisive effects on the main current of after-events.

It was felt by the Powers that the corps of officials was largely responsible for aiding and abetting the Boxer Rising. As a mark of their displeasure, the Chinese Government was compelled to prohibit the examinations by which the official corps was recruited in all cities where foreigners had been ill-treated. This provision had the effect of dislocating the ancient system under which officials were selected and trained for the public service.

The indemnities exacted from China were fixed by Article VI. The following account is given of the matter by the British China Indemnity Delegation, of which Lord Willingdon was chairman, in their report dated the 18th June 1926:

> The total amount of the Indemnity imposed on China by the Final Protocol, signed by the Chinese plenipotentiaries and by the accredited representatives of eleven foreign Powers on the 7th September, 1901, amounted to 450 million taels. This amount, which was intended to cover the actual military expenses incurred by the Powers in

China in 1900, and the claims of their subjects who had suffered loss or damage from 'Boxer' outrages, was to be paid in instalments, with interest at the rate of 4 per cent per annum, the instalments to be spread over a period of forty years. The total sum which China had to pay in respect of interest and amortisation of principal, under the scheme agreed upon by the Powers and accepted by the Chinese Government, amounted to 982,238,150 taels, a sum which (taking the Haikwan tael at 3s.) is equivalent to £147,335,722.

The following table . . . shows the percentages due to each of the participating countries:

Russia	29 per cent
Germany	20 ,,
France	15 ,,
Great Britain	11 ,,
United States	7 ,,
Japan	7 ,,
Other Powers	11 ,,
Total	100 ,,

From the foregoing table it will be seen that the British share of the so-called Boxer Indemnity (principal and interest) amounted to £16,573,810, which is about $11\frac{1}{4}$ per cent of the total sum payable by China to all the Powers combined.

In connection with these figures, it is important to note that the amount fixed upon as due from China to Great Britain was arrived at after every claim submitted by British subjects for losses sustained had been subjected to a very rigid scrutiny and most careful revision by the British Government. Not only had the claims, as originally passed, been cut down so drastically as to cause some legitimate grumbling on the part of those who had suffered loss, but the amounts were still further reduced in order to meet a difficulty which had arisen from the fact that the total claims finally presented by the various Powers concerned were in excess of the total amount of the Indemnity which China had agreed to pay. This Indemnity had been fixed by the Final Protocol at 450 million taels; but when the Powers presented their several claims, it was found that the satisfaction of these claims would necessitate the payment of a further sum of 10,296,293 taels. As

China could not be called upon to make good this discrepancy, it was necessary for the Powers to come to a mutual agreement with regard to the reduction of their claims, so that in the aggregate they should not exceed the amount of the Indemnity already provided for in the Protocol. There was a good deal of discussion among the Powers' representatives as to how this reduction should be effected. The proposal favoured by the majority, that the reduction should be *pro ratâ* for all the Powers, was at first opposed by the British Minister on the ground that a *pro ratâ* reduction would cut down the British percentage from $13\frac{1}{2}$ per cent to $11\frac{1}{4}$ per cent of the total amount of the Indemnity, although Great Britain (unlike some other Powers) had already reduced and cut down her claims and was demanding nothing from the Indemnity but a reimbursement of actual expenses and payments which she would have to make to those of her subjects whose claims had been scrutinised and adjusted. However, in order to facilitate and hasten the final settlement of these troublesome and protracted negotiations, the British Government gave way on this point, and the British share of the Indemnity was, therefore, fixed at the lower percentage already named.[1]

It would thus appear that the £16,573,810 received by Great Britain was actually less than the amount required to compensate British subjects for losses sustained by them. That British subjects had more to lose and lost more than those of any other Foreign Power is not in question. It is clear, therefore, that Russia, Germany and France were resolved to exact heavy indemnities in addition to the sums required to pay for the damage done to their nationals.

Some years later the American Government recognised the case for revising its claim. The following account is given by Professor Willoughby:

On June 15, 1907, the American Secretary of State, Mr. Root, notified the Chinese Minister at Washington that it was the intention of the United States, when all the claims and expenses growing out of the Boxer troubles

[1] Cmd. 2766, p. 42.

THE BOXER SETTLEMENT

and the American participation in the expedition for the relief of the Legations at Peking had been presented and audited, "to revise the estimate and account against which these payments were to be made, and, as proof of sincere friendship for China, to voluntarily release that country from its legal liability for all payments in excess of the sum which should prove to be necessary for actual indemnity to the United States and its citizens".

The revised estimate of the legitimate claims for American loans and expenses was found to be $11,655,492.69, and President Roosevelt thereupon, in his annual message to Congress of December 3, 1907, asked for authority to remit and cancel all claims upon China in excess of that amount. Pursuant to the request, Congress, by Joint Resolution of May 25, 1908, authorised the reduction of the American Boxer Indemnity to $13,655,492.69, and the difference between that amount and the original sum allotted to the United States, which was $10,785,286.12, to be 'remitted' to China.

The result of this action upon the part of the United States did not release the Chinese Government from the obligation to pay to the United States the amounts called for by the Protocol, but it did provide that, to the extent indicated, these sums, when paid to the United States, should be 'remitted', that is, handed back, to China.

This remission upon the part of the United States was an unconditional one, that is, it was not made dependent upon any formal undertaking upon the part of China to make certain uses of the moneys thus returned to her. However, prior to the final authorisation of Congress of the remission and of the Executive Order making this remission effective, the Chinese Government had indicated that, if and when the remission was made, it was its intention, in appreciation of this generous act, to devote the moneys thus received to the sending of a considerable number of Chinese youths to America for education in American institutions. In order better to prepare such students for coming to America, the Tsing Hua College was founded in 1911, and is supported in large measure from the sums remitted by the United States under the Joint Resolution of Congress of 1908.[1]

The matter is here mentioned because the large

---

[1] Willoughby, *Foreign Rights and Interests in China*, vol. ii. p. 1012.

number of Chinese students who from 1908 onwards have been trained in American universities is a factor of cardinal importance in the subsequent history of China. Of all the results which flowed from the settlement forced on China by the Powers after the Boxer Rising, this was the most profound and the most lasting. It sealed the fate, not merely of the Manchu dynasty, but also of dynastic government in China.

To meet the charges imposed by Article VI. the service organised by Sir Robert Hart was empowered to collect the native as well as the foreign customs at Treaty Ports. Thus, to a greater extent than before, this service assumed the character of an agency to collect money owed by China to the Foreign Powers.

A tremendous burden was thus imposed on the rapidly weakening Government of Peking. At the same moment a blow was aimed at the corps of officials, which was, in fact, the only agency through which the Imperial Government was now able to make its control felt in the provinces. The joint result of these two conditions was little realised by the Powers that imposed them. They had, in fact, sealed the fate of that system of government which in calmer moments it was their policy to maintain.

In the earlier years of the nineteenth century, when China began to feel the impact of Western civilisation in the south, it was ruled by a foreign dynasty from the north. From their fortified capital in Peking, the Manchus controlled the provinces, partly through Tartar garrisons posted in the towns, and partly through the civil officials, who were largely if not entirely Chinese. By the middle of the century the military prestige of the Manchu dynasty was fatally shattered by defeats inflicted by Foreign Powers and still more by the Taiping rebellion, which was only crushed by foreign assistance. Their weakening control of the provinces was thereafter maintained through the great bureaucracy which was closely interwoven with the ancient fabric of Chinese society. Its members were trained in the lore of Confucius and recruited, like our own Civil Service, by boards of examiners. This mandarin hierarchy was a government of Sages—a practical expression of Laôtze's ideal. Its members were posted to the provinces from Peking, but never to provinces in which they were born. But the governments they constituted in the provinces were practically left to themselves so long as they remitted to Peking the contributions required to maintain the Imperial Government.

In the task of raising these revenues, and also the much larger sums reserved for local expenditure in the province, they were aided by their intimate connection with the bankers and merchants who handled the internal trade of China, which from ancient times had depended on credit rather than cash. This trade was closely bound up with the family system.

In the Treaty Ports the foreign merchants were introducing their totally different methods of commerce and industry, which the Chinese themselves were rapidly adopting. One important expression of this change was the foreign customs service, which collected and remitted to Peking large revenues which were independent of the mandarin bureaucracy.

By the end of the nineteenth century the ancient system of banking and commerce through which the mandarins had raised the revenues was seriously deranged. In order to meet the crushing burdens imposed by the Boxer Indemnity, the Imperial Government sought to apply to internal taxation methods which had proved successful in the sphere of customs. The Ministry of Finance tried to impose and collect taxes for itself, instead of leaving the whole business of taxing to the provincial governments as in the past. But the strain was destined to prove too heavy for the slender ties which still bound the provinces to Peking. Meantime, the suspension of public examinations, by the outraged Powers, as a penalty for the Boxer Rising, was weakening the mandarin bureaucracy. In the provinces they were faced by a rapid increase of young men ignorant of the Chinese classics, but trained in the ideas and methods of the West, in matters of trade as well as in politics. The foreign missionaries had established in China thousands of schools, in which upwards of 50,000 scholars were acquiring some knowledge of western science and of the English language. Of those, a few had found their way to the universities of Europe, hundreds more to those of America and thousands to colleges in Japan. There had thus come into being in China a westernised intelligentsia, which exercised an influence out of all proportion to its numbers. After 1908 it was reinforced by students trained in America at the cost of funds drawn from the Boxer Indemnity. The official bureaucracy had done their best to exclude these westernised scholars from the public service, admitting them only to a few diplomatic posts in which knowledge of western methods or language was essential.

It is easy to see that these westernised students were the driving force of the revolutionary movement of which Sun Yat Sen was the recognised leader. As the provinces renounced the control of Peking, it was they who were challenging the claim of the mandarins to control the provincial administrations. They were far, however, from wishing to disintegrate China, and aspired to replace the Manchu Government by a westernised republic.

From these various strands the Foreign Powers had all unknowingly twisted the cord which in ten years strangled the Imperial regime.

CHAPTER XIV

THE LEGATION QUARTER

THE Foreign Powers had accomplished more than the downfall of a dynasty. They had also rendered impossible the maintenance of the great fortress from which foreign dynasties had dominated China as its future capital. Yet so little did the diplomats realise whither their acts were tending that they sought to entrench their own establishments in the city whose fate they had sealed.

We have seen in an earlier chapter how Kahnbaligh, or Canbaluc, was created by Genghis and Kublai as the capital, not of China, but rather of an empire which included most of Asia and part of Europe. When this empire dissolved the native dynasty of the Mings established their court at Nanking in the heart of China. In a few generations they were forced to return to the citadel in the north, in order to guard the Great Wall against tribes in Manchuria whose military prowess was again threatening China. It was at this period that Canbaluc began to be known as Peking, or the Northern Court, as distinguished from Nanking, the Southern Court. The name suggests that the Ming dynasty conceived the idea of two capitals, one a national capital on the Yangtze from which the domestic affairs of China would be ordered, the other a military capital upon which the defence of the northern rampart could be based. When the Manchus eventually broke through the Wall, and ousted the Mings from Peking, they naturally retained it as the capital from which they could dominate China by Tartar armies recruited north of the Wall.

The Treaty of Nanking marks the period when forces which came by sea from the south, more subtle and penetrating than the militant hordes of northern Asia, were beginning to disintegrate the ancient structure of Chinese society. The Manchu dynasty was doomed by the fact that its court was domiciled six hundred miles from the native capital where the treaty was signed. Had their Court been moved to a Treaty Port on the Yangtze as the Japanese Court was moved to the neighbourhood of the principal port of Japan, it would there have come into daily touch with the methods and ideas of the West which were fast transforming those of China. It might even have succeeded like Japan in adjusting its system to rapidly changing conditions. By timely reforms it might have avoided the dangers and throes of a revolution.

The Court, however, understood so little the forces by which it was threatened as to think that provincial viceroys could still be left to deal with the foreign barbarians. Its refusal to admit the envoys of Foreign Powers to Peking led to a second war, at the close of which those Powers dictated their terms in the capital itself. The Imperial Court was forced to accept the establishment of legations in Peking, and to handle foreign affairs directly, and not through the medium of provincial governments.

The principal advisers of the Foreign Powers were thus secluded like the Government of China itself from intimate contact with the problems they were called on to handle. Like Jerusalem, Rome, Constantinople and Mecca, Peking is one of the legendary cities of the world. Its ramparts and palaces, temples and monuments exercise a spell which fixes the mind on the past. In this historic environment the student interpreters destined for the Consular Service, which advises the Ministers, studied the language in the most impressionable years of their life. Their environment was such as disposed them rather to view China through the medium of her past, than to study the factors which were breaking the links with that past and reducing her whole life to confusion. Those factors were mainly operative in the Yangtze valley, where foreign merchants were developing trade with the Chinese, a region which could only be reached by a four days' journey. In point of time, the seat of government was more remote from the principal scene of action than Moscow from London.

The bulk of the trade in the Yangtze valley was British. From the outset the British Legation has been out of touch with the merchant communities of the Yangtze, especially Shanghai, where the trade between China and the rest of the world mainly centres. In Peking there was everything to attract the professional diplomat, and much to repel him in a place like Shanghai, where, as Tawney remarks:

A modern fringe was stitched along the hem of the ancient garment. The furniture of western society, which stands a sea voyage better than its spirit, was unpacked at suitable points on the eastern sea-board. The economic frontier between the West and China was moved inland, so that the traveller who approaches the latter by way of Shanghai is tempted to reflect on the vanity of a pilgrimage which ends in a city so similar in externals to that in which it started.[1]

The diplomats who visited Shanghai could not always conceal their anxiety to finish their business and escape from distasteful surroundings. The remote-

[1] R. H. Tawney, *A Memorandum on Agriculture and Industry in China* (published by the Institute of Pacific Relations, Honolulu, 1931), p. 9.

ness of Peking thus gravely accentuated the social aloofness which is apt to exist between diplomatic and mercantile circles in foreign countries.

The merchants, however commonplace in their tastes and outlook, were none the less a medium through which the dynamic forces of western civilisation were disintegrating China. They were the real factors in the problem, human factors who needed a guidance and leadership, which no British Minister in Peking has ever been able to supply. The British colonies on the Yangtze have never been taught to look to their Minister, as those in South Africa looked to men like Grey, Frere or Milner, or the British community in Egypt looked to Cromer.

When in 1900 the Foreign Ministers and their staffs had to fight for their lives, the head office of the Chinese Customs was in the legation quarter and so was the residence of the Inspector General. This explains why Sir Robert Hart, himself an official of the Chinese Government, went through the siege, and would, no doubt, have perished with the rest if the expeditionary force had not arrived in the nick of time. The moment the siege was raised he started to write a series of letters to an English magazine reminding the Western world of the provocations by which the people of China had been goaded into their recent excesses. These letters written from day to day reflect the thoughts current in legation circles immediately after the siege. In one dated so early as August 1900, he writes:

Some think . . . that partly to meet certain native—that is Chinese not Manchu—wishes and also save the Legations from ever again being thus isolated and thus insulted, the capital of the future ought to be Nanking and not Peking.[1]

Here for one moment glimmers the idea of accepting the welfare of China herself as a rational motive

[1] These from the *Land of Sinim*, p. 58.

of policy. From the subsequent letters we see how quickly the spark was extinguished in the welter of passions which a sanguinary struggle always provokes. The sanctity which all civilised governments accord to the envoys of Foreign Powers had been wantonly violated. After facing the prospect of hourly destruction for a couple of months, they suddenly found themselves surrounded by their own victorious forces, with the capital of China at their absolute disposal. Their power to exact retribution was limited only by the difficulty of settling the terms as amongst themselves. But on matters affecting their own establishments it was easy to agree. The results were embodied in Article VII., which runs as follows:

> The Chinese Government has agreed that the quarter occupied by the Legations shall be considered as a quarter specially reserved to their usage and placed under their exclusive police, where the Chinese shall not have the right to reside, and which may be put into a state of defence. . . . By the protocol annexed to the letter of 16th January, 1901, China has recognised that each Power has the right to maintain a permanent guard in the said quarter for the defence of its Legation.

In Article IX. provision was made for military control by the Powers of the line from Peking to the sea. They also acquired the right to maintain troops in the Foreign Concessions of Tientsin, from which guards to defend the legation quarter could be drawn.

What all this meant in actual practice may be gathered from the following statement by Morse:

> . . . The legation quarter may be considered as the provision of a defensible fortress in the heart of the capital of a hostile power—for which purpose it was much too large; or as the happy grasping of the opportunity to provide spacious quarters for the diplomatic representatives of the powers, in park-like surroundings, free from the old-time insanitary conditions, and at the cost of China—and in

that case it was not justified. The quarter set apart was a solid block, approximately 1200 metres from east to west, and 650 metres from north to south, with an area of about 200 acres; around this was an open space 40 metres wide, carrying the quarter on the north to a distance of 100 metres from the wall of the Imperial City, and on the south including the wall of the Tartar City with its projecting bastions. On the west the ministries of War, Works and Justice were partly, and the imperial Carriage Park was wholly, taken in, but on the north the Hanlin (Imperial Academy) was not included. The British legation was extended to the west, its area increased three-fold, from 12 to 36 acres. The Russian legation was also extended to the west, increased four-fold, from 5 acres to 19 acres. The American area was extended for the guard, but the legation itself was nearly unaltered; it reached, cut into by other premises, from the Tsienmen to the Water Gate, thus—U.S. parade ground, U.S. guard, Netherlands legation, U.S. legation, Russo-Chinese Bank, Banque de l'Indo-Chine, U.S. legation students—and it carried with it the duty of guarding 700 metres of the Tartar City Wall. Germany grasped the opportunity and extended her legation area from $2\frac{1}{2}$ to $25\frac{1}{2}$ acres, undertaking at the same time to guard 800 metres of the Tartar City Wall. The French legation was extended from 6 to 20 acres, being now entirely covered by other legations, and having no longer a front to guard. The Austrian legation exchanged its previous area of less than 2 acres for an area of 10 acres, from which to superintend political and commercial interests in China which were of small importance. The old Italian legation, sufficient for the small Italian interests, measured one acre, and Italy now claimed a new area of $12\frac{1}{2}$ acres. In it were included the offices of the Inspectorate General of Customs and the houses of the Inspector General and of the Inspectorate Secretaries; but some at least of the powers were deeply concerned at this disturbance of a semi-foreign Chinese department, and, on representations being made, the Italian envoy made some abatement of his claim; he still retained his hold on the offices and houses of the staff, but he restored to Sir R. Hart his house and a part of its grounds, giving also for customs use his old legation; but he demanded as compensation some land formerly destined for France. By this readjustment the Italian area was 10 acres. A further portion of the land of the Inspectorate of Customs was taken for the International Club; but within the legation quarter the customs received, in five pieces, a total of about 11 acres. The Japanese legation expanded so as to include the whole of the Suwang Fu, which its guards had so gallantly defended, thereby increasing its area from one acre to $14\frac{1}{2}$ acres. The Netherlands legation remained in its old site, increasing its area fourfold, to 2 acres; it had been suggested that, as it did not share in the defence of the Tartar City Wall, it should be removed from its vicinity, but the suggestion was not acted on. Belgium received a site within the legation quarter, double the size of its old site on the Hatamen Street. The Spanish legation was extended to about 2 acres.[1]

The diplomats thus established for themselves an equivalent of the Settlement created in Shanghai for the purpose of foreign trade. But unlike the merchants they were able to take whatever they pleased, and the real need for security was, as Morse shows, somewhat forgotten in the wish to provide for their future comfort.

This fortified settlement, half a square mile in extent, has become the home of a diplomatic and military society which lives a life of its own, discussing the news of events which reach it from every part of the world. A more entertaining or attractive community would be difficult to find. Around it lies a world of palaces, temples and shops, the paradise of collectors. This legendary city attracts a stream of tourists, mainly American. An hotel exists for their entertainment in the legation quarter itself. Beyond the city are facilities for racing, riding and hunting. The climate is bright and exhilarating except in summer, when the British Legation moves to its summer quarters at Peh Tai Ho on the Gulf of Pechihli. So attractive is the life that those who have enjoyed it sometimes find on retirement that existence elsewhere is unbearable and return to spend

[1] Morse, *The International Relations of the Chinese Empire*, vol. iii. p. 355.

their old age in Peking. The capital of a country torn by political convulsions, the battlefield of Foreign Powers and scourged by famine and widespread natural disasters, has thus come to be regarded in the diplomatic professions as the most desirable of foreign stations. The result has been a silent but continuous pressure on China to keep her government located at a spot fatal alike to its own effective authority and to the unity of the Chinese people.

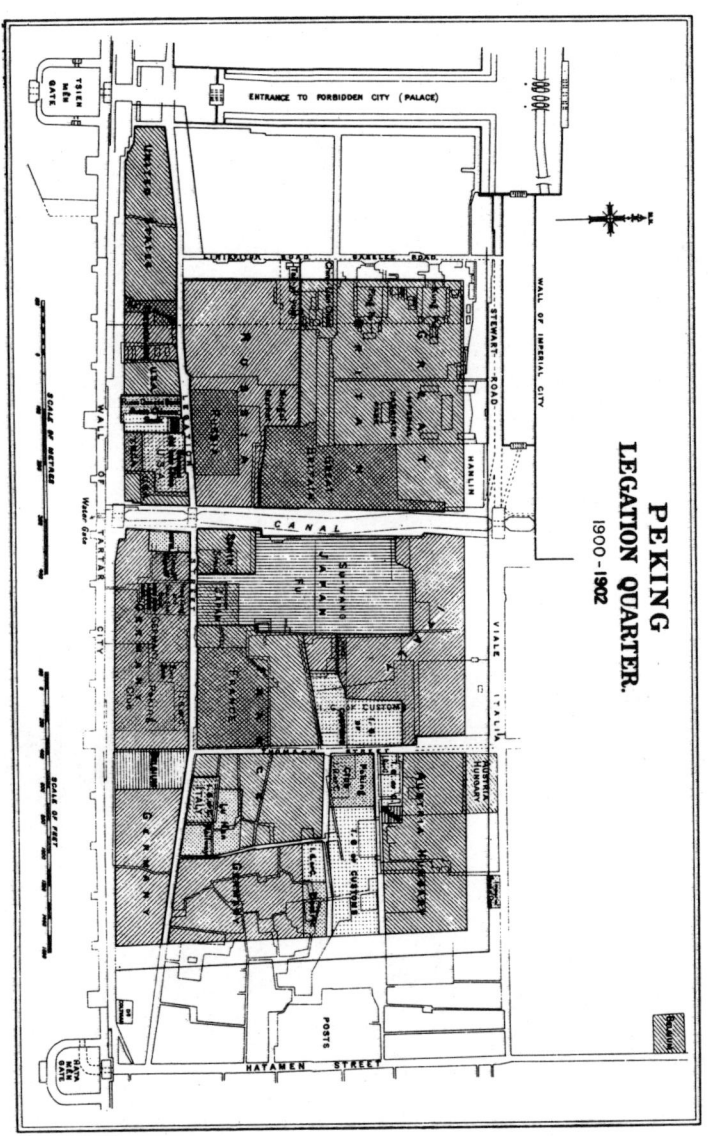

CHAPTER XV

THE RUSSO-JAPANESE WAR AND THE CHINESE REVOLUTION

THE Boxer Rising had enabled Russia to realise her aims in Manchuria. Without using the word annexation she had virtually added these vast regions to her empire and was hastening to absorb Korea by similar methods. In a previous chapter we have seen the close analogy between this unhappy country and Belgium. With Korea in the hands of Russia Japan would have lost all but the shadow of her independence. If a struggle had to be faced it was obviously wiser to fight before rather than after a Russian fleet could be based on Korean ports. She had confidence in herself and was fully prepared for single combat with the Russian Goliath.

To the military rulers of Russia, defeat at the hands of this stripling nation was inconceivable. Obsessed by the weight of the forces they wielded, they chose to ignore the British proposals made at this time for a general settlement of questions at issue in Persia, India and China, especially that of the open door in Manchuria. The two island empires were thus driven to support each other and on the 30th June 1902 signed a treaty of alliance. Each country was to aid the other if attacked by more than one power. In effect, this treaty meant that Japan could no longer be coerced by a combination of Western Powers as she had been in 1895. She was free to settle the issue with Russia alone.

Events moved quickly to an outbreak of war in February 1904. The Russian fleet in Eastern waters was at once swept from the open seas. Until the fleet from Russia under Rodjesventsky arrived more than a year later to meet destruction in the sea of Japan, the war was fought out between Russian and Japanese armies on Chinese soil. By April 1905 the Russians had recognised their utter defeat by land and sea and were suing for peace. On the invitation of President Roosevelt negotiations were opened at Portsmouth in New Hampshire. The Russians were represented by Witte. On the 5th September the Treaty of Portsmouth was signed. The paramount interest of Japan in Korea was recognised. Japan acquired from Russia the lease of the Liaotung Peninsula and the railway to Port Arthur as far north as Changchun. Both Powers agreed to withdraw their armies from the soil of Manchuria.

The moral effects of the Japanese victory were far-reaching. The idea so firmly established in the previous century that Europe was destined to dominate Asia was challenged. The corruption and folly of their own government was rudely revealed to the people of Russia, and the way prepared for its utter destruction by the militant communism which is now seeking to change the whole order of human society. On the people of China the effect was threefold. As in Russia it shattered their faith in dynastic government. It nerved them afresh to resist foreign attempts to exploit their weakness. They began to feel that they also might do what the Japanese had done for themselves.

The old Empress was shrewd enough to recognise that some response must be made to the reformers. In 1905 a system of national education on Western lines was established. In 1906 effective steps were taken for stopping the production of opium in China as well as its importation from abroad. In England the public conscience was now thoroughly roused. An agreement was made which brought the trade to an end in 1917. In the meantime the growth of the poppy in China had largely ceased. The recrudescence of this evil is one of the penalties which China has paid for the subsequent period of anarchy.

On the 15th November 1908 Yehonala died. It was scarcely a coincidence that the Emperor, still in confinement, had breathed his last on the day before. In the hours that remained to her the dying Empress raised to the throne his nephew Pu Yi, a child three years of age, and appointed Yuan Shih-kai and Chang Chih-tung as his guardians. According to Chinese authorities she had hoarded wealth to the value of £16,000,000 sterling. Of her riches she took what she could to her grave. Jewels of fabulous value were buried with her corpse, to become, twenty years after, the spoil of ghouls who plundered her tomb.

In the eyes of the reformers Yuan Shih-kai had betrayed their cause in 1898. The Manchu courtiers were too stupid and reactionary to support a ruler of real ability, and in January 1909 Yuan was obliged to retire. The central government was now in the hands of Manchu courtiers. The reformers made themselves felt in the provinces and there established provincial assemblies which jointly demanded the election of a national parliament within two years. The Court resisted the demand, but eventually summoned a national assembly to meet in Peking in January 1910. The assembly demanded a national parliament and was then prorogued for a year.

Matters were brought to a head by the machinations of one Sheng Hsüan-hwai, who in 1896 had been appointed director of railway constructions. In January 1911 he became Minister of Communications, and proceeded to negotiate loans for the centralisation of all railways in the hands of the Imperial Government, especially in the Yangtze valley.

Sheng, who was thoroughly corrupt, had accumulated a vast fortune for himself. The Yangtze provinces feared that the government at Peking was becoming an instrument through which foreign financiers would secure the same kind of control in the Yangtze valley that Germany had acquired in Shantung and Russia and Japan in Manchuria.

In October 1911 the situation had become so serious that Yuan Shih-kai was recalled to power by the terrified Manchu Court at Peking. He assumed office on the 22nd October and the Second National Assembly was opened there on the same day. On the 27th it demanded that relatives of the Emperor be excluded from the Cabinet, that Chinese should be treated on an equal footing with Manchus, that a Cabinet responsible to a parliament be created and that political parties with freedom of speech should be recognised. On the 30th October imperial edicts were issued conceding these measures in abject terms. On the 7th November Yuan was formally appointed premier by the National Assembly.

In the south a parallel and more violent revolution was in progress. Hankow and the neighbouring cities were in open rebellion, which throughout central and southern China took the form of a general strike. In December a National Assembly was convened by the revolutionists at Nanking which hastened to elect Dr. Sun Yat Sen as "President of the Provisional Government of the United Provinces of China".

On the 1st January 1912, Dr. Sun, in the presence of the National Assembly at Nanking, swore:

To overthrow the absolute oligarchic form of the Manchu Government, to consolidate the Republic of China, and to plan and beget blessings for the People, I, Sun Wen, will faithfully obey the popular inclinations of the citizens, be loyal to the nation, and perform my duty in the interest of the public, until the downfall of the absolute oligarchic

Government has been accomplished, until the disturbances within the nation has disappeared, and until our Republic has been established as a prominent nation on this earth, duly recognised by all the nations. Then I, Sun Wen, shall relinquish the office of Provisional President. I hereby swear this before the citizens.

The First Day of the First Year of the Republic of China.[1]

On the 12th February 1912 Yuan notified Dr. Sun and the Provisional Government at Nanking that the Emperor had abdicated. As Prime Minister he offered to go south to discuss with Dr. Sun the inauguration of the Republic. On the 14th February Dr. Sun replied, inviting him to Nanking and offering to resign the office of President in his favour. He stipulated, however, that a Republic should not be authorised by edict of the fallen dynasty. On the same day he presented his own resignation to the National Assembly at Nanking, and in doing so added the following words:

The abdication of the Ching Emperor and the Union of the North and South are largely due to the great exertion of Mr. Yuan. Moreover, he has declared his unconditional adhesion to the national cause. Should he be elected to serve the Republic, he would surely prove himself a most loyal servant of the state. Besides, Mr. Yuan is a man of political experience, to whose constructive ability our united nation looks forward for the consolidation of its interest. Therefore, I venture to express my personal opinion and to invite your honourable Assembly carefully to consider the future welfare of the state, and not to miss the opportunity of electing one who is worthy of your election. The happiness of our country depends upon your choice. Farewell.[2]

By this utter devotion to the public interest Dr. Sun was hoping to avert a sanguinary struggle between the conservative north and the revolutionary south. The realists of Peking were hoping to establish an executive strong enough to dominate a popu-

[1] MacNair, *Modern Chinese History*, p. 718.   [2] *Ibid*, p. 728.

lar Assembly. The idealists of Nanking desired a parliament strong enough to control the executive. They were too inexperienced to realise the need of a government strong enough to maintain order. As a body young China had yet to attain the standard of public devotion which guided the conduct of Dr. Sun. The Assembly, when it met, went far to discredit itself by fixing the salaries of its members at 4000 dollars a year.

Dr. Sun was right in thinking that at that moment Yuan was the one man able to maintain order in China. He decided to trust his professions of loyalty to the new regime and can hardly be blamed if that trust was misplaced. As events were quickly to show, Yuan had no belief in popular government as a practical system for China. He accepted the revolution as the necessary means for bringing to an end a dynasty which had now "exhausted its mandate". He was looking, not for a new system, but a new dynasty, and merely awaited the convenient moment to appear as its founder. The young, inexperienced, and not wholly disinterested republicans could be trusted to provide it in due course.

It is needless to argue that Yuan Shih-kai had no sympathy with their aims. He was realist enough to see the futility of attempting either to revive the moribund Manchu dynasty, or to control the provinces through the agency of the old mandarin bureaucracy. He believed only in the efficacy of force, and had long been preparing for a crisis which he saw was inevitable. Li Hung-Chang, in whose school he was trained, had appointed him resident-general in Seoul. When China was expelled from Korea by Japan, he was posted to the province of Chihli, where Li Hung-Chang had established a school for the training of officers. He developed this school and reorganised the provincial army on western lines. In 1898 he was charged by the Emperor with the task of westernising the Imperial Army. He used his position to betray the Emperor, and, as his reward, was appointed by the Empress to govern Chihli. He there created a new military school at Pao-ting-fu. It was in these military schools that men like Wu P'ei-fu, Sun Ch'uan-fang, and Feng-husiang were trained, who afterwards became military dictators in various provinces. Yuan was in fact following the example set more than two thousand years ago, when the first Emperor, Shi Hwang-ti, tried to abolish the government of scholars, and forced unity on the provinces by the sword.

On the 10th March 1912 a provisional constitution was proclaimed. An advisory council was established at once to arrange for a parliament. The Council met on the 29th April. The majority were followers of Dr. Sun and a state of extreme tension at once developed between them and the President. In August Yuan executed without trial at Wuchang two republican generals accused of conspiracy against him.

In the parliament, when elected, the Kuomintang were again the dominant party and went to Peking resolved to maintain the republic and thwart the President. On the 21st March their leader, Sang Chiao-yen, was murdered at Shanghai on his way to Peking, and when parliament opened on the 8th April Yuan did not venture to face the Assembly. He was only waiting until he should be able to impose his authority on the south by force. His primary need was money to mobilise his army, and for this purpose he was hoping to borrow on a large scale from foreign financiers.

In the course of the year 1912 he was trying to negotiate with the sextuple group, which consisted of British, American, German, French, Russian and Japanese bankers, backed by their Governments. The parliament tried to thwart him by declaring that a loan raised without their consent would be unconstitutional. In March 1913 President Wilson assumed office at Washington and immediately ordered the American bankers to withdraw from the group. In May he formally recognised the Chinese Republic.

The Five Powers had now decided to put their money on Yuan, and on the 21st May 1913 agreed to provide £25,000,000 for the reorganisation of China. The loan was successfully floated in London, Paris, Berlin, St. Petersburg, Brussels and Tokyo.

In July a rebellion broke out in the Yangtze valley which Yuan with funds at his disposal was able to crush within two months. The Kuomintang began to realise that a republic could only be established in China by force of arms. A number of young Chinese made their way to the military schools of Japan and there began to acquire the knowledge and training which fifteen years after enabled the southern armies to march to Peking.

In October parliament was constrained by Yuan to elect him President for five years and his Government was then formally recognised by the Five Powers. By January 1914 he felt himself strong enough to dissolve the parliament. In May a constitutional compact was promulgated which conferred on Yuan dictatorial powers for ten years. A council of state responsible to the President was to be appointed by him. To this was added an indirectly elected chamber, with merely nominal powers. The provincial governments were to be as they had been under the Imperial regime.

A month later the Archduke Ferdinand was murdered at Sarajevo, and events were rapidly moving to a struggle which was destined to involve a vast majority of the human race. In August China declared herself neutral, and proposed that hostilities should be excluded from her waters and territories, including those leased to Foreign Powers. America supported this request, but Japan was resolved to take the opportunity of seizing the German possessions in the Far East, and feared less China might declare war on Germany in order to regain possession of Kiaochow. An ultimatum was sent to Germany demanding the cession of this territory to Japan. She then informed Peking that the matter did not concern China. On the 23rd August she declared war on Germany and blockaded Kiaochow. Japanese troops landed on the north coast of Shantung and marched through that province to the territory leased to Germany. The protests of China were ignored. Her neutrality was no more respected than it had been when Russia and Japan fought on the soil of Manchuria. On the 24th September a small British contingent arrived to take part in the siege. On the 7th November the Germans capitulated.

On the 18th January 1915 a note was presented to President Yuan embodying the demands of Japan grouped under twenty-one heads. China was asked to agree in advance to any arrangement which Japan might make with Germany as to German rights in Shantung. The leases of Port Arthur and Dalny, of the South Manchurian and Antung railways, and of the Liaotung Peninsula were to be greatly prolonged. In South Manchuria and Inner Mongolia Japan was to have mining and other valuable rights. She was also to share the control of the largest iron works in China, opposite Hankow. China was in future to cede no territory to any Power but Japan. She was to engage "influential Japanese as advisers in political, financial and military affairs". In "important places" Japan was to share with China control of the police. In future the Chinese Government should raise no loans from abroad without first consulting Japan. A warning was added that President Yuan must discuss these terms without revealing them to any of the Foreign Powers. A member of his cabinet, however informed the American Minister as to their contents, which presently became known to the Press in Peking.

For the moment the whole of China, including the republicans of the south, rallied to support President Yuan. But China was helpless. On the 7th May 1915 an ultimatum was served requiring President Yuan to accept most of the demands within two days. On the 11th May the United States notified both Governments that it could not

> recognize any agreement or undertaking ... impairing the treaty rights of the United States and its citizens in China, the political or territorial integrity of the Republic of China, or the international policy relative to China commonly known as the "open door" policy.

On the 25th May two treaties were signed in which China yielded most of the demands but with certain important modifications.

For the moment the insult inflicted on China seemed to strengthen the position of Yuan. Immediately after the Japanese ultimatum, the Chou An Hui Society was formed to foster the idea that China could only recover her position in the world by returning to monarchy. Scholars were engaged to advocate the merits of "Constitutional Monarchy". Dr. Frank Goodnow, Constitutional Adviser to the President, was moved to declare that "the monarchical system is better suited to China than the republican system". On the 23rd October 1915 orders were issued for elections to be held with a view to the establishment of monarchy. England, Russia and Japan, at the instance of the latter, counselled delay. Yuan persisted and on the 11th December it was declared that a large majority of electors were in favour of monarchy. The council of state formally invited Yuan to ascend the throne. After thrice declining he accepted the offer and announced his enthronement for the 1st January 1916.

A rebellion at once broke out in Yunnan which rapidly spread to Kweichow, Kwangsi and Kwangtung. The Japanese Government warned Yuan to desist, and his courage now began to ebb. He first put off the enthronement, and on the 22nd March renounced his claim to the title of Emperor. His death on the 6th June 1916 saved him from further humiliations.

CHAPTER XVI

SINO-JAPANESE RELATIONS DURING AND AFTER
THE GREAT WAR

THE internal system of government established by Yuan may be termed for convenience "the Government of the Major-generals"; for, like Cromwell's regime, its roots were all in the barrack-room. Of the soldiers he trained not one had an instinct for genuine statesmanship. As rulers of provinces they ground from the peasantry and merchants revenues to pay for their armies. The constantly changing governments at Peking were the transitory products of their mutual intrigues, the results of which were determined by the balance of military forces. The names of the presidents and ministers who figured as the Government of China till the Southern armies entered Peking would only confuse a narrative which must be confined to the barest outlines.

The maintenance of a government in Peking after the death of Yuan was largely due to the pressure of external affairs. To keep in existence some kind of authority which could purport to speak for China as a whole was an obvious necessity for the Foreign Powers. For this reason they had recognised and supported the Government of Yuan, and were ready to recognise anyone with a colourable claim to succeed it. Though China south of the Yangtze openly disowned the authority of Peking in domestic affairs, the one sentiment which still united the whole country was a smouldering resentment against the Foreign Powers to whom, not without reason, the humiliations inflicted upon it were felt to be due. But neither of these forces would have sufficed to maintain a government in being in the absence of revenue to meet its expenses. This practical difficulty was largely met by that curious institution the Foreign Customs Service, which continued to remit balances to the recognised Government at Peking, after meeting the charges for the loans secured on it.

England, France, Belgium, Italy and Russia were naturally anxious that China should join them in the war, partly to supply labour, which was sorely needed in Europe, and partly to get control of the enemy ships interned in Chinese ports. But Japan was not of the same opinion, and in November 1915 Viscount Ishii informed the Allies that

Japan could not regard with equanimity the organization of an efficient Chinese army such as would be required for her active participation in the war, nor could Japan fail to regard with uneasiness a liberation of the economic activities of a nation of four hundred million people.[1]

By February 1917 the submarine menace had become so serious that the allies of Japan were prepared to make any terms to secure the aid of her fleet in the Mediterranean. So in March they agreed in secret treaties to support the claims of Japan to Shantung and to the German islands north of the equator. These treaties were not revealed to President Wilson when the U.S.A. declared war on Germany in April 1917. Negotiations were then opened in Washington between Mr. Lansing and Viscount Ishii. An agreement was reached in November in terms of which the principles of the open door and of the integrity of China were affirmed. But the following words were added:

[1] Morse and MacNair, *Far Eastern International Relations*, p. 865.

The governments of the United States and Japan recognise that territorial propinquity creates special relations between countries, and consequently, the government of the United States recognises that Japan has special interests in China, particularly in that part to which her possessions are contiguous.[1]

The Government of China was urged by the U.S.A. to break off diplomatic relations with Germany and her allies, but not to declare war. But China had excellent reasons for going to war. The entry of America into the struggle more than outweighed the collapse of Russia. As events were to prove, China was right in banking on victory for the Western allies, and had everything to gain by securing a place at the Conference which would settle a great deal more than the terms which the conquered would have to accept. She would, as she hoped, be able to discuss the claims of Japan in Shantung on a footing of equality. And the gains were not all in the future; a declaration of war would wipe out the unequal treaties with the hostile Powers. The defence of extraterritorial rights that the foreign Governments had united to maintain would at last be breached. The German concessions would revert to China. Enemy rights to the Boxer Indemnities would be cancelled forthwith. She would also be able to claim some relief from her allies, who, in fact, suspended these payments for five years. So in August 1917 the Government at Peking declared war on Germany and Austria-Hungary. Its action was endorsed by the Republican Government in Canton, and, when in 1918 hostilities ceased, North and South agreed to send a joint delegation to the Conference at Paris. Mr. Lou Tseng-tsiang, Mr. Wellington Koo and Mr. Alfred Sze represented Peking; Mr. S. Y. Wei and Dr. C. T. Wang represented Canton. They seem to have worked in har-

[1] *Ibid.* p. 876.

mony, but were gravely weakened at the Conference by the known fact that in China North and South were in open conflict.

At Paris the secret treaties with England and France which Japan had exacted as the price of naval assistance at length became known. The claims of China to recover control of Shantung were supported by President Wilson till Japan threatened to retire from the Conference and refuse membership in the League of Nations. It was then decided that under the Treaty of Versailles Japan should retain the German rights in Shantung, and, to ease matters, the Japanese delegates declared that:

> The policy of Japan is to hand back the Shantung peninsula in full sovereignty to China, retaining only the economic privileges granted to Germany and the right to establish a settlement under the usual conditions at Tsingtau. The owners of the railway will use special police only to insure security for traffic. They will be used for no other purpose. The police force will be composed of Chinese, and such Japanese instructors as the directors of the railway may select will be appointed by the Chinese government.[1]

The news, which reached China in May 1919, brought into being a movement which has since played a prominent part in Chinese affairs. Students' unions were formed in the chief educational centres and were backed by merchants and bankers. Youth took charge of the situation and age was content to follow its lead. All China was profoundly moved by the agitation. Three members of the Government in Peking, denounced by the students as tools of Japan, escaped to that country. The Chinese delegates at Paris refused to sign the Treaty of Versailles, but secured admission to the League of Nations by signing the Treaty of St. Germain with Austria. As a sop China was given a temporary seat on the Council

[1] *Ibid.* p. 894.

of the League. With Germany she made a separate peace.

The acquiescence of President Wilson in the claims of Japan in Shantung was one of the factors which led the Senate to reject the Treaty of Versailles. In spite of all that had happened in Paris, Japan thus failed to secure the assent of the United States and of China.

CHAPTER XVII

THE WASHINGTON CONFERENCE

IN reviewing this episode in the history of Japan one has to remember the fears which are always present to the minds of its rulers. Within two generations she had passed from the civilisation of the Middle Ages to that of the twentieth century. With amazing facility she had studied and applied the productive methods of the West. Like the British Isles she had learned to support a growing population, far in excess of her natural resources, by importing materials, treating them in factories and selling the finished products abroad. She had none the less awaked from the sleep of centuries to find her natural birthright in the hands of others. Of the three continents washed by the Pacific, two, North America and Australasia, were largely closed to her people and trade. To secure control of the raw materials and markets of China seemed to her statesmen not a question of power or prestige, but literally a matter of life or death. They forgot, however, that trade is a matter of willing buyers and sellers. By a policy of force they brought on themselves the very result they were always dreading. For the people of China had in their armoury a weapon more difficult to combat than fleets or armies. They simply refused to buy Japanese goods. So complete was the stoppage of trade that by January 1920 Japan was approaching China with an offer to reconsider the arrangements embodied in the Treaty of Versailles. She was met with a summary refusal to negotiate on the basis of that Treaty at all.

The relations of America with Japan had been so strained by the episode that the Anglo-Japanese alliance was viewed with anxiety on both sides of the Atlantic. At the Imperial Conference in the summer of 1921 this anxiety was strongly expressed by Mr. Meighen, the Prime Minister of Canada. On the 11th August the United States formally invited the four principal allied Powers

> to participate in a conference on the limitation of armaments, in connection with which the Pacific and Far Eastern questions would also be discussed.

China accepted in the hope that the Shantung question would now be discussed at the Conference. To this Japan was opposed, but the British and American Governments at length persuaded the Chinese and Japanese delegates to meet and discuss the question at Washington. At these discussions Mr. Hughes and Mr. Arthur Balfour were represented by observers friendly to both parties. An arrangement was reached satisfactory to China under which the Japanese were to evacuate Shantung within nine months. It was then to be opened to the trade of all countries.

The Chinese demand that the Treaty accepted in 1915 under compulsion should be cancelled outright was refused by Japan. She agreed, however, to abandon all but four of the twenty-one points, retaining her sole right to share the control of the Han-yeh-ping Iron Company and its mines in the Yangtze valley.

While the delegates of China and Japan were at work on these matters the Powers in conference were discussing the future status of China. On this as on other matters the war had profoundly modified British opinion. It had been in essence a struggle for principles which, since the dawn of history, had been fighting for mastery throughout the civilised world. The great autocracies have always claimed to provide a system of government better than men in the mass can provide for themselves. To this claim is opposed that of ordinary people to decide who their rulers shall be and how they shall rule. A practical method of giving effect to this claim was the product of British civilisation. Neglect of the principles which inspired it had led to the loss of the American colonies and their subsequent organisation as a separate and sovereign commonwealth. Its better observance thereafter had led to the continued expansion of the parent commonwealth. In the empty regions of Canada, Australia, New Zealand and South Africa new British communities sprang into being. But the rule of the commonwealth was also extended to include millions in Asia and Africa who had no experience in the arts of self-government. The tasks of an empire were imposed on a commonwealth. It came to think of itself as an empire, and developed some policies and habits of mind at variance with the principles which had made it possible for the British people to extend their rule to close on a quarter of the human race.

In the crisis of the war the British people were forced to think out for themselves the principles which lay at the root of their civilisation, and to state them to the world. In doing so they saw that these principles could not be reconciled with certain practical developments of their own system. The announcement in 1917 of responsible government as the goal of policy in India, the Act passed in 1919 to give effect to that announcement, the Irish Treaty of 1921, the acceptance in 1926 of the sovereign equality of the great Dominions, are cases in point. Not one of these changes could have been made if the people of England had continued to think as they were thinking before the war. Another conspicuous case in point was the attitude which England had adopted in China. For the reasons given in previous chapters she had studiously avoided any attempt to govern in China as she governed in India. She sought only the right for her merchants to trade and her missionaries to teach the Christian religion, but had thought too little how the means through which she had chosen to assert those rights would affect China itself. The interests of Great Britain, if opposed to those of China, were frankly accepted as the basis of policy.

Here again it needed the shock of the Great War to convince public opinion in England that no policy was admissible unless it enured to the ultimate benefit of the people of China themselves. But the British statesmen who went to Paris had their hands tied by pledges given in the dreadful exigencies of the war.

At Paris China relied on American friendship. Unlike the British the Americans had not developed an overseas empire except in the islands of Hawaii and the Philippines. Unburdened by major responsibilities for maintaining order in vast and distant regions, they were freer than the British to proclaim those principles which lay at the root of their own civilisation. In the matter of opium, for instance, the American Government was free to dwell on the moral issues, while England had always to remember that a stoppage of the trade would gravely embarrass the public finances of the Native States as well as of British India. It is fair to remember also that by virtue of the most favoured nation principle America reaped the fruits of British aggression in China, without incurring the odium which forcible measures brought on the nation which took the initiative.

America had thus been freer than England to champion the cause of non-interference, and by constant insistence on the principle had rendered a service to everyone concerned. As a natural consequence China had come to regard her as the one Power to whom she could look for protection. Her failure at Paris to secure the effective support of President Wilson had seemed to leave her without a friend in the world.

The episode lay heavy on British and American minds, and their common desire to redress an open injustice was one of the motives which had led to the Washington Conference. The result was a Treaty "relating to principles and policies to be followed in matters concerning China" which was signed on the 6th February 1922 by the United States, Belgium, the British Empire, China, France, Italy, Japan, Holland and Portugal. In Article I. of this Treaty the nine Powers agreed:

> To respect the sovereignty, the independence and the territorial and administrative integrity of China; *to provide the fullest and most unembarrassed opportunity to China to develop and maintain for herself an effective and stable government*, to use their influence for the purpose of maintaining the principle of equal opportunity for the commerce and industry of all nations throughout the territory of China; and to refrain from taking advantage of conditions in China in order to seek special rights or privileges which would abridge the rights of subjects or citizens of friendly States, and from countenancing action inimical to the security of such States.

A number of detailed provisions were added for giving practical effect to these principles, and also an agreement that *"there should be full and frank communication between the contracting Powers concerned"* whenever a situation arose which involved the application of the Treaty in the opinion of any one of them. It was further agreed to invite the adhesion of other Powers to the Treaty.

A further Treaty was signed by the nine Powers which provided for the meeting at Shanghai of a

Tariff Revision Commission to bring the specific tariff up to an effective five per cent, and also a commission to report on means for assisting the Chinese Government to effect such legislative and judicial reforms as would warrant the several Powers in relinquishing, either progressively or otherwise, their respective rights of extraterritoriality.

For a hundred years China had been in ever closening contact with peoples whose ideas and manners of life differed from hers almost as much as if they had come from a different planet. Those stronger nations had imposed arrangements for adjusting these contacts which suited themselves, without considering or indeed knowing how far they suited the people of China. The Washington Treaties were in effect a formal and public abandonment of this practice, an acceptance of the principle that in all such arrangements the welfare of China herself must be the first instead of the last object in view.

The existing arrangements, however, could not be altered by a mere stroke of the pen. Their practical reform would require action on the part of a Chinese government, which was really competent to enforce its authority in China. While the whole country was prepared to accept the Washington Treaties scarcely anyone beyond the walls of Peking was ready to obey the Government which signed them on their behalf. The practical realisation of the objects proposed must await the appearance in China of a government competent to execute treaties as well as to sign them. For the moment there was little to show that China was in reach of that goal.

So long as they were able, the Foreign Powers clung to the fiction that whatever government was in being at Peking was entitled to speak for the country as a whole. The various nonentities who, since the death of Yuan Shih-kai in 1916, had figured as the Government of China in Peking were puppets of the

XVII   THE WASHINGTON CONFERENCE

Tuchuns who controlled the provinces of Northern China. Of these Tuchuns the most prominent were General Wu P'ei-fu in Chihli, Chang Tso-lin, a bandit of genius who controlled Manchuria, Yen Hsi-shan whose record as governor of Shansi earned him the title of "model Tuchun", and Feng-husiang "the Christian general" who was dominant in Honan, Shensi and Kansu. As these and less prominent Tuchuns combined, betrayed or out-generalled each other, their nominees figured as presidents and premiers in Peking, or escaped for protection to the foreign concessions of Tientsin. The armies upon which these Tuchuns rested grew to enormous proportions. They were cheaply armed with the weapons which the close of the Great War had let loose in the world. Their means of support was wrung from a famine-stricken people and largely supplemented by encouraging the growth and use of opium. In the closing years of the dynasty, when the intellectuals had gained the upper hand, the native production of opium had been almost entirely stopped. The Tuchuns revived it and found in the national vice the most lucrative source of revenue.

In the South the confusion seemed equally great—on the surface at any rate. When the Parliament at Peking was dissolved in 1917 the Kuomintang members retired to Canton and there established a government under Dr. Sun. They were rent with internal dissensions, and the military party in Kwangsi, the province west of Kwangtung was a constant thorn in their side. Dr. Sun was on various occasions obliged to escape from Canton and take refuge in the French Settlement at Shanghai. It was during these visits that he drew to his side the Student Movement provoked by the treatment of China at Paris. Shanghai was the centre of this movement.

CHAPTER XVIII

SUN YAT SEN AND THE RUSSIAN ALLIANCE

Whilst the Conference of Paris was in session in 1919 the two governments in Peking and Canton had agreed to divide the surplus revenue from customs in the proportions of 86·3 for the North and 13·7 for the South. In the spring of 1920 the Nationalist Government was expelled from Canton by the Kwangsi faction and the Northern Government then appropriated the 13·7 allocated to the South as security for domestic loans it was raising. But the Nationalist Party was presently restored in Canton by the military aid of General Ch'en Ch'iung-ming, and in April 1921 Dr. Sun Yat Sen was elected "President of the Chinese Republic".

The Washington Conference had scarcely completed its work in the spring of 1922 when Wu P'ei-fu attacked and defeated Chang Tso-lin and set up a new government at Peking. Dr. Sun had supported Chang Tso-lin against the advice of General Ch'en Ch'iung-ming, who now turned on him in wrath and drove him out of Canton. He took refuge in Shanghai, where he owned a house in the French Concession, the gift of admirers.

Admiral Mahan has somewhere remarked that no amount of tactical skill will save a leader whose strategy is wrong, while a leader whose strategic conceptions are sound can afford to make many tactical blunders. The career of Sun exactly illus-

CH. XVIII SUN YAT SEN AND RUSSIAN ALLIANCE 143

trates the second part of this aphorism. While his tactical blunders were constant and flagrant, the success of his cause is explained by his grasp on the larger realities. He saw for instance that before China could stand on an equal footing with Foreign Powers, she must first, like Japan, acquire the knowledge which lay at the roots of their power.

Chinese aspirations [he wrote] can be realised only when we understand that, to regenerate the state . . . we must welcome the influx of foreign capital on the largest possible scale, and also must attract foreign scientists and trained experts to develop our country and train us.[1]

Dr. Sun made various attempts to obtain help from Canada, England, Hong-kong, the United States, Germany and Soviet Russia.[2]

In 1911 when the news reached him in London that the dynasty had fallen in Peking he had tried to secure British assistance before leaving for China, and met with little but chilling politeness. To officials, merchants and journalists the man was a futile visionary, and, as after events were to show, British money was staked on Yuan Shih-kai as the genuine realist. A distinguished American had supported his attempt to found a new dynasty, and Dr. Sun never forgot it.

He had long hoped [says Professor Holcombe] that the necessary aid might come from America, which, he used to say, should give the Chinese Revolution its Lafayette. But America continued to disappoint him.[3]

Her Government had always opposed invasions on Chinese sovereignty, but shrank from a positive and constructive policy.

It is not to be wondered, therefore, that Dr. Sun listened with interest to overtures from Russia. In

[1] Holcombe, *The Chinese Revolution*, p. 130.
[2] MacNair, *The Annals of the American Academy of Political and Social Science*, Nov. 1930, p. 219.
[3] *The Chinese Revolution*, p. 159.

January 1923 M. Joffe, who had come to Peking at the head of a Soviet mission, visited Dr. Sun in Shanghai. Dr. Sun had no belief in the application of Communist principles to society in China. He decided, however, to accept the assistance of those who had shown themselves able to replace the Russian Autocracy by a government which was certainly able to govern. He accepted the risks with his eyes open, and a joint declaration was published by him and Joffe that while

> the Communistic order or even the Soviet system cannot actually be introduced into China, because there do not exist here the conditions for the successful establishment of either Communism or Sovietism . . . most cordial and friendly relations existed between them.[1]

Joffe, who was now broken in health, went back to Russia, and his place at Peking was taken by Karakhan, who sent Borodin, with Galens as military adviser, to co-operate with Dr. Sun.

In February 1923 General Ch'en Ch'iung-ming was expelled from Canton by troops hired by the Nationalists in Yunnan and Kwangsi, and Dr. Sun was once more at the head of affairs in that city. His authority scarcely extended beyond it, and he found the greatest difficulty in raising money to pay the mercenaries who were keeping Ch'en Ch'iung-ming at bay. The taxes levied on the city were straining the loyalty of his own supporters, so he now demanded the share of the customs revenue which in 1917 the Government at Peking had agreed to recognise as due to the South. Having been in alliance with Chang Tso-lin, it was clearly useless to apply to the new Government which had just ousted his nominees. He therefore requested the Diplomatic Body at Peking to instruct the Inspector-General of Customs to remit to Canton the proportion of revenue

[1] MacNair, *Annals*, p. 219.

XVIII SUN YAT SEN AND RUSSIAN ALLIANCE   145

due to the South. "This request does not appear to have been taken seriously in the first instance".[1]

When pressed for an answer the Ministers referred Dr. Sun to the Government at Peking as the only authority with power to dispose of the surplus revenues accruing from customs. Dr. Sun declared his intention of seizing the custom house at Canton, but an international fleet of British, French, American, Japanese, Portuguese and Italian warships was sent to protect it. This precedent was reversed when eight years later the forces in rebellion against the Nationalist Government seized the customs at Tientsin. In this second case the Foreign Ministers at Peking abstained from all intervention.

In Borodin and Galens Dr. Sun had, however, secured the kind of assistance which for the moment he most needed. Borodin, whose original name was Grusenberg, as a boy had left Russia for America, where later on he conducted a business school at Chicago. As a revolutionary he served his apprenticeship in Mexico, and appeared in Turkey as representing the Third International in the camp of Mustapha Kemal. The talent for organising the military power which the Nationalists most needed was supplied by Galens. It was now that a military institute was established at Whampoa on an island opposite Canton. The instructors were German and Russian officers, and some Chinese trained in Russia. At the head of the institute was Chiang Kai-shek.

Politicians absorbed in reading the minds of others, are apt to forget the importance of using their own. The strength of the Bolshevist movement lies in aims clearly conceived and lucidly stated. Under Borodin's guidance an institute was created for the training of skilled propagandists. Of the literary material which Dr. Sun had long been preparing much had been lost in the revolution. He was now persuaded by

[1] *Survey of International Affairs*, 1925, vol. ii., p. 312.

Borodin to give the gist of what he had written in the form of lectures which were published under the following preface.

After the three volumes of my *Plans for National Reconstruction*—Psychological Reconstruction, Material Reconstruction, Social Reconstruction—had been published, I devoted myself to the writing of *Reconstruction of the State*, in order to complete the series. This book, which was larger than the former three volumes, included The Principle of Nationalism, The Principle of Democracy, The Principle of Livelihood, The Quintuple-Power Constitution, Local Government, Central Government, Foreign Policy, National Defence, altogether eight parts. Part one, The Principle of Nationalism, had already gone to press; the other two parts on democracy and livelihood were almost completed, while the general line of thought and method of approach in the other parts had already been mapped out. I was waiting for some spare time in which I might take up my pen and, without much further research, proceed with the writing. Just as I was contemplating the completion and publication of the book, Ch'en Ch'iung-ming unexpectedly revolted, on June 16, 1922, and turned his guns upon Kwan-yin Shan. My notes and manuscripts which represented the mental labor of years and hundreds of foreign books which I had collected for reference were all destroyed by fire. It was a distressing loss.

It now happens that the Kuomintang is being reorganised and our comrades are beginning to engage in a determined attack upon the minds of our people. They are in great need of the profound truths of San Min Chu I and the important ideas in The Quintuple-Power Constitution as material for propaganda. So I have been delivering one lecture a week. Mr. Hwang Ch'ang-ku is making stenographic reports of the lectures and Mr. Tsou Lu is revising them. The Principle of Nationalism series has just been completed and is being published first in a single volume as a gift to our comrades. In these lectures I do not have the time necessary for careful preparation nor the books necessary for reference. I can only mount the platform and speak extemporaneously, and so am really leaving out much that was in my former manuscripts. Although I am making additions and corrections before sending the book to the press, yet I realise that in clear presentation of the theme, in orderly arrangement of the discussion and in the use of supporting facts, these lectures are not at all comparable to the material which I had formerly prepared. I hope that all our comrades will take the book as a basis or as a stimulus, expand and correct it, supply omissions, improve the arrangement and make it a perfect text for propaganda purposes. Then the benefits which it will bring to our people and to our state will truly be immeasurable.[1]

CANTON, *March* 30, 1924. SUN WEN.

The book was entitled *San Min Chu I: the Three Principles of Nationalism, Democracy and Livelihood*.

What [he asked] is the Principle of Nationalism? Looking back over the history of China's social life and customs, I would say briefly that the Principle of Nationalism is equivalent to the "doctrine of the state". The Chinese people have shown the greatest loyalty to family and clan with the result that in China there have been family-ism and clan-ism but no real nationalism. Foreign observers say that the Chinese are like a sheet of loose sand. Why? Simply because our people have shown loyalty to family and clan but not to the nation—there has been no nationalism. The family and the clan have been powerful unifying forces; again and again Chinese have sacrificed themselves, their families, their lives in defence of their clan. . . . But for the nation there has never been an instance of the supreme spirit of sacrifice. The unity of the Chinese people has stopped short at the clan and has not extended to the nation.[2]

And so of "Democracy".

Government is a thing of the people and by the people; it is control of the affairs of all the people. The power of control is political sovereignty, and where the people control the government we speak of the "people's sovereignty".[3]

[1] *San Min Chu I*, translation published by Chinese National Council of Institute of Pacific Relations, Shanghai, 1927, pp. x. and xi.
[2] *Ibid.* p. 4.   [3] *Ibid.* p. 152.

But Dr. Sun had moved beyond the rights of man, the individualism which inspired the American and French Revolutions. To him the sovereignty of the people was a means to an end which may best be described in the language of Sir Horace Plunkett as "better living".

Our Three Principles of the People mean government "of the people, by the people, and for the people"—that is, a state belonging to all the people, a government controlled by all the people, and rights and benefits for the encouragement of all the people.[1]

The discourses were naturally coloured by the lecturer's desire to emphasise points upon which he agreed with his Russian allies. But the difference of aim could not be repressed. He rejected the materialist basis of the Marxian system and its methods of class war. His conception of nationalism was bound to conflict with the aims of the Third International—aims, cosmic as those of the Catholic religion or of Islam itself. The Soviet touch in these lectures fails to disguise the Anglo-Saxon ideas which the speaker was voicing.

Under Borodin's influence the party was reconstructed on the Soviet model. Wherever possible local committees or Tang Pu were formed with power to elect an annual congress. The congress appointed the central executive committee, with power to control the entire movement between its sessions. The register of members was purged of those who objected to the Russian alliance. At the congress of January 1924 Borodin succeeded in securing admission to the party of Communist members, on the understanding that they recognised the principles of the Kuomintang. The party as such still rejected Communist principles; but with Communists admitted to its ranks Borodin was willing

[1] *San Min Chu I*, p. 444.

to bide his time. As events were to show, the fanatics who controlled him in Moscow were unable to realise the wisdom of patience.

The constitution which at this period Dr. Sun outlined for China owed little to Anglo-Saxon models, and was deeply influenced by Soviet ideas. It was here that the Russian connection left its most lasting impression. A system, however elaborate in form, can be worked by an autocrat. It is not, however, in the genius of China to produce Lenins and Stalins, and the difficulty experienced by the Nationalists in establishing an effective government in China is largely traceable to the constitution devised by Dr. Sun under the influence of his Russian advisers.

In the autumn of 1924 the merchants of Canton organised a movement to destroy the semi-Communist government of Dr. Sun. The revolt was crushed with considerable slaughter, and a large part of Canton was destroyed in the struggle. It was perhaps in desperation that Dr. Sun now accepted an invitation to discuss with the Northern militarists, Fenghusiang and Chang Tso-lin, the establishment of a central government for China. These overtures with Chang Tso-lin can scarcely have been palatable to Russia, and it looks as if Dr. Sun had begun to distrust his Soviet allies. As a trained physician he probably knew that his end was near. He reached Peking, but only to die there of cancer on the liver on the 12th March 1925.

CHAPTER XIX

THE SHANGHAI INCIDENT

THE death of Sun Yat Sen made it easier for his followers and the Communists to co-operate for the moment. The policy followed in Russia when Lenin died was adopted, and Sun Yat Sen was canonised as the central figure of a semi-religious movement. His Three Principles were recognised as its gospel, and his books elevated to the rank of scriptures in rivalry with those of Confucius.

Meanwhile the hold of Communism, especially over the student movement, was increasing. It served the purpose of Borodin to direct this movement against the foreigners, especially the British. After the war when the British Government was absorbed in the overwhelming task of rearranging the map of the world, Mr. Winston Churchill was in charge of the War Office and so in control of vast stores of surplus munitions. He used these to support the efforts of White Russians under the leadership of Denikin and Kolchak, with the result that Great Britain has since been regarded as the arch-enemy of Soviet Russia. It suited the Russians, therefore, to encourage the students to concentrate their movement against the British as the dominant power in the Yangtze valley. They were also busy fomenting unrest in the labour unions, and strikes broke out in Tsingtao, Canton, Hankow, Hongkong and Shanghai. In January 1925 a strike which began in a British mill

CH. XIX THE SHANGHAI INCIDENT

in Shanghai was settled. But in February far more serious strikes occurred in the Japanese mills, which led to a number of deaths, including that of a Japanese manager.

The students now joined in the movement, and in May a series of attacks were made on Japanese mills, in which some Chinese labourers were wounded, and one died of his wounds. A parade of protest was arranged by the students for the 30th May in contravention of municipal by-laws. The Municipal Council was not at this juncture well equipped to handle the difficult situation. It had at this time an American chairman of outstanding ability—Mr. Fessenden. But in course of years the Council elected by foreign ratepayers had lost effective control of their permanent officials. In spite of specific warnings by the chairman as to what might happen on the 30th May, and as to the far-reaching consequences of serious disorder, the responsible officer was attending races when he should have been controlling the situation in the streets of Shanghai.

On the 30th May the police in charge ordered the procession to disperse, and when they refused arrested three of the leaders. The crowd then got out of control and threatened the station where the leaders were confined, which also contained a store of arms. When the crowd attempted to rush the station the English Inspector of Police, in command of Indian and Russian constables, warned them to desist, and after ten seconds opened fire, with the result that twelve Chinese lost their lives and seventeen others were wounded. In the following week four others were killed and one European was wounded in various disturbances.

These incidents led to an outbreak of resentment against the British which recalled the days of the Boxer Rising. It spread as far north as Peking, to Chungking in the west, and Canton in the south. A demonstration was there planned for the 23rd June, which ended in an open affray with the foreign residents on the island of Shameen, in which a French merchant and fifty Chinese lost their lives and more than a hundred were wounded. A boycott of British trade immediately followed.

The trade of Hongkong was brought to an absolute standstill by a strike, which spread to Swatow, Waichow, Pakhoi, Nanning and other cities in the south.

While these events were in progress there was held in July 1925 in Honolulu a Conference organised by leading Americans under the President of Leland Stanford University, Dr. Ray Lyman Wilbur, who was afterwards appointed by President Hoover as Secretary of the Interior. This Conference was attended by unofficial parties from the United States, China, Japan, New Zealand, Australia, Canada, Korea, the Philippines and Hawaii. The intention had been to bring a number of people bordering the Pacific into personal and friendly relations. But meeting as it did on the morrow of the Shanghai incident, it was found impossible to exclude from the discussion the bitter attacks made by the Chinese members on British policy. A decision was reached to arrange a further Conference in 1927, and members from the British Dominions requested that some suitable body in England might be asked to send spokesmen competent to explain the character and motives of British policy in China. An Institute of Pacific Relations was created to conduct research and collect material for discussion. It thus became possible for other than officials, merchants and missionaries to study Pacific affairs and realise their importance to the rest of the world.

CHAPTER XX

CHINA WITHOUT A CENTRAL GOVERNMENT

WHEN the Washington Conference adjourned in 1922 the intention had been to discuss tariff revision within a few months. A dispute between China and France as to whether the instalments of the Boxer indemnity due to France should be paid in gold or in paper francs had delayed the ratification of the Washington Treaties, which only took place on the 5th August 1925. The Conference on the tariff opened in the following October in Peking. In November an agreement was reached that the new treaty when signed should contain an article conceding tariff autonomy to China on the 1st January 1929, on the understanding that China would by then have abolished likin. But the Conference got little further than this, for the ground was crumbling under its feet. On the 21st October 1925 a statement was issued by Wu P'ei-fu from Hankow that fourteen provinces had asked him to take action against Peking on the one hand and Canton on the other. In Manchuria Chang Tso-lin was engaged in a struggle with a mutinous subordinate, and on the 26th November Feng-husiang occupied Peking. In January 1926 Wu P'ei-fu, now in alliance with Chang Tso-lin, began his advance against Peking. In April Feng evacuated Peking after inviting Wu to take control of the city, which Wu declined to do. The "Chief Executive", Tuan Ch'i-yui, resigned, and with him vanished the last vestige of any authority in Peking which the Foreign Ministers could address as the Government of China. The Chinese members of the Tariff Conference faded away. The foreign representatives, left to themselves, dispersed in July 1926.

It was now open for anyone who could do so to establish an authority which the Foreign Powers would agree to recognise as the Government of China. On the one hand were a number of Tuchuns, the spawn of Yuan Shih-kai, with dreams of a throne never far from their minds. Chang Tso-lin, the dictator of Manchuria, now in control of Peking, Yen Hsi-shan "the model Tuchun" of Shansi, and Feng-husiang the so-called "Christian general", whose power lay in the regions west of Shansi. In the provinces north of Kwangtung the dominant power was Wu P'ei-fu. From Hankow he controlled the province of Hupeh together with Hunan to the south and Honan to the north of it. The country between these provinces and the sea, Kiangsi, Anhwei, Fukien, Chekiang and Kiangsu, was controlled by Sun Ch'uan-fang from Shanghai, who obeyed Wu only so long as he felt too weak to pose as a Tuchun on his own account.

As against these adventurers the strength of the Nationalist Government in Canton lay in the feeling created by its founder that it stood for the people of China. The real issue at stake between the Tuchuns and the Nationalist party was whether China should revert to the old dynastic system, or develop on the lines worked out by the natives of western Europe and America. But this issue was constantly confused by the rivalry of the Tuchuns and the factions which rent the Nationalist party. "The model Tuchun" or the "Christian general" were ready, whenever it served their immediate interests, to join the Nationalists. Their readiness helped to enhance its internal dissensions.

xx CHINA WITHOUT A CENTRAL GOVERNMENT 155

From the nature of the issue the north was the natural stronghold of the Tuchuns, the south and centre of the Kuomintang. Had one of the Tuchuns succeeded in mastering China, he would presently have mounted the dragon throne in the ancient seat of autocracy at Peking. But if ever the Nationalist party should master the Tuchuns, and really essay the task bequeathed them by Sun Yat Sen, of creating for China a government based on the principles enunciated by President Lincoln, that government must move its seat from the Canton river to the valley of the Yangtze—and no further. From Canton no government based on popular suffrage could ever expect to control Peking or the provinces north of the Yangtze. No more from Peking could it hope to control the provinces south of the Yangtze, and that nursery of revolutions, Canton. For reasons of political geography such a government as Sun Yat Sen had projected must centre on the Yangtze, as surely as the founder of a new dynasty would find his natural home in Peking.

The Manchu dynasty had made their capital the centre of its very inadequate railway system. Apart from this one artificial factor, economic conditions imposed by contact with the rest of the world called for the transfer of the capital to the Yangtze. The significance of these factors had already been seen by one trained observer as far back as 1924.

... It is small wonder that these great centers, so remote from one another, should display separatist tendencies whenever the central authority exercised from Peking is weakened and that regional differences of economic interest and outlook should take a political form. But where there is, as in China, an underlying cultural unity, differences due to topographical isolation can be reduced and finally overcome by a systematic policy designed to remove or lessen the isolation. An improved system of inland communication is a prerequisite of Chinese consolidation. In particular the completion of the great Wuchang-Canton

Railway, which would put the Canton Delta into direct continuation with Wu-Han and the Central Basin, is an urgent necessity. It would almost inevitably lead quickly to a much closer industrial relationship through Canton's need of Pingsiang (Hunan) coal, and the establishment of an intimate commercial nexus would greatly reduce the chances of any permanent political separation. Similarly the building of the long-projected Szechwan railway from Wu-Han would tend to bring the great western province into the full stream of Chinese life.

In the task of consolidating China, the Middle Yangtze valley, and particularly the Central Basin, seems marked out by nature to be the link and mediator between the great centers of the north, west, east, and southeast. Probably no other country in the world has such a wonderful nodal region as China possesses in the Central Basin of which Wu-Han is the heart. Here the greatest north-south trunk line (Peking-Hankow-Wuchang-Canton) will intersect the incomparable west-east waterway of the Yangtze at the head of navigation for ocean-going vessels. The great corridor valley routes, from the south by the Siang and the Kan, from the southwest by the Yuen, from the northwest by the Han, converge upon it. It is the point of contact of Szechwan with the rest of China, and the significance of this must soon be immensely enhanced. Moreover, this great nodal or geographical center is nearly the geometrical center also.

Geographical considerations would certainly suggest that this region of the Yangtze below the Gorges ought to contain the organising capital of modern China. In Yuan, Ming, and early Manchu times the appropriateness of Peking to serve this role is evident enough, and nothing need be added here as to the significance of its site at the northern apex of the Plain in relation to the bordering grasslands. The law of inertia will inevitably militate against change, and any proposal to transfer the capital to the Yangtze is certain to arouse the strongest opposition. Apart from vested interests, there is the sense of historical continuity to which the whole atmosphere and setting of Peking make a powerful appeal. Moreover, Peking has been deliberately made the chief railway center of China, and new economic significance is being given to its site by the development of the pastoral northwest through the construction of the Peking-Kalgan-Sui-Yuen line. Again,

xx CHINA WITHOUT A CENTRAL GOVERNMENT

Peking is undeniably the intellectual capital of modern China, and most of the important new movements in the realm of Chinese thought have their center there.

These are strong forces and may well prove too powerful to be resisted. But if the creators of a united China make up their minds that one of the biggest factors in union is a national capital in as effective communication as possible alike with the Northern Plain, the great western province of Szechwan, and the commercial communities of the Yangtze and Canton Deltas, they are most likely to find it on the Yangtze below the Gorges—either at Wu-Han or at Nanking, a city with space relations not greatly inferior to those of Hankow and with historic traditions hardly less appealing, and more distinctively Chinese than those of Peking.[1]

[1] Percy M. Roxby, Professor of Geography, University of Liverpool, "The Distribution of Population in China: Its Economic and Political Significance", published in the *American Geographical Review*, January, 1925, vol. xv. No. 1.

CHAPTER XXI

ADVANCE OF THE NATIONALIST ARMIES TO THE YANGTZE

THE success achieved by the Kuomintang in its march to the north owed much to the military training of its Russian advisers, but more to their skill in the arts of political organisation. Its agents were taught by Borodin how to penetrate the rank and file of the armies opposed to them, and break them up, by appealing to the spirit of nationalism which Sun Yat Sen had evoked. Under Borodin's influence he had copied the organisation and methods invented by Lenin. But his aim was a commonwealth on American lines. It had nothing in common with the goal to which Borodin was trying to guide the Kuomintang, a system of Communism which can only be realised by methods which lead to an absolute autocracy, and away from popular government.

Borodin succeeded in converting but a small minority of the party to Communism. But the personal jealousies which demoralise Chinese politics played into his hands. He was constantly able to draw large sections of the party which did not believe in Communism into open conflict with its ablest leaders.

The sentiment to which all Chinese parties were bound to appeal was resentment against the unequal treaties, the force of which will be understood by those who have followed the previous pages. Boro-

CH. XXI   ADVANCE OF NATIONALIST ARMIES   159

din, hoping to absorb China into the Soviet system, wanted a rupture with the Foreign Powers and had no hesitation in appealing to the Chinese hatred of foreigners. The Nationalists, on the other hand, had always to remember that an open rupture with the Western Powers would involve absorption by Russia and the reconstruction of China on the Communist model.

When Sun Yat Sen died the task of completing his work had fallen to Chiang Kai-shek. Born in 1886 in the province of Chekiang, just south of the Yangtze, he studied military science at Tokyo. In 1911 Sun Yat Sen chose him as secretary, and in 1923 sent him to study the military system in Russia. In 1924 he placed him in charge of the military academy at Whampoa.

In the following year began his official connection with T. V. Soong, brother of the widow of Sun Yat Sen. Born in Shanghai of a notable mother, Soong was educated there at St. John's University, and later at Harvard, where he read Economics. Trained in a bank at New York, he became president of the Central Bank of Canton in 1924, and Minister of Finance in the Nationalist Government in 1925. His able management of the Nationalist finances was largely responsible for the military achievements of Chiang Kai-shek, who married his beautiful and gifted sister, Miss Mei-ling Soong, in 1927. A third sister was married to Dr. H. H. Kung, a descendant of Confucius, educated at Yale, who afterwards became Minister of Industry, Labour and Commerce at Nanking. Both Sun Yat Sen and the Soong family were Christians, and in 1930 Chiang Kai-shek was baptized into that faith. This brilliant and cultured family group are derisively known to their enemies as the Soong dynasty. But the gibe can scarcely include Madame Sun Yat Sen, who, after the death of her husband, maintained the closest connection with

Russia, in open hostility to the government of Chiang Kai-shek. The Soongs, like the English Cecils, are distinguished by that individuality which scarcely admits of strict uniformity in family opinions.

Chiang Kai-shek knew well that Russia was hoping to make a cat's-paw of China. He realised, however, that Borodin and Galens could supply the technical aid in military and political organisation which no other Power was disposed to offer to the Nationalist movement. He therefore accepted their alliance for the moment, knowing that they used it to saturate the members of the Kuomintang with the doctrines of the Third International.

On the 15th of May 1926 Chiang Kai-shek at Canton carried a resolution making Communists ineligible as departmental chiefs, and curbing their activities in various directions. Having thus strengthened his position, he set out in July 1926 on his northward march to attack Wu P'ei-fu and his doubtful lieutenant Sun Ch'uan-fang. These Tuchuns had both underrated the Nationalist movement. Like other Tuchuns they stood for themselves, and failed to realise the strength of a movement inspired by a cause. So little did Wu realise his danger that he had started in 1925 to attack a semi-independent Tuchun in Hunan called Tang Sheng-shih, who in 1926 entered into a defensive alliance with the Nationalists of Canton. In July 1926 the Nationalists were able to capture Changsha and thus to command the railway which connects the province of Hunan with Yochow, its port on the Yangtze. By the middle of August they reached Yochow, and Wu fled to Hankow. Feng-husiang now hastened to announce his adhesion to the Nationalist cause. By the 7th September 1926 Chiang Kai-shek had occupied Hankow Hanyang Wuchang at the confluence of the Han and Yangtze rivers, the triple city (known as the

Wuhan), and Wu was retiring to the north by the Hankow-Peking railway. At this juncture, however, Feng-husiang came in on the side of the Kuomintang and defeated the forces which Wu had sent to invest Sianfu, the capital of Shensi. Feng was thus able to establish communications between the northwestern provinces and the headquarters of the Kuomintang at Hankow.

The Wuhan cities are the largest industrial centre in China outside Shanghai. A number of factories had sought the protection of the foreign concessions at Hankow. At Hanyang were the largest iron works in China. The thousands of labourers employed in these industries were soil ready to Borodin's hand for the propagation of Communist doctrines. If the capital were moved to Hankow he might hope to control the Government, with the proletariat to support him. The workers could also be moved to attack the foreign concessions, and thus precipitate an open rupture with the Western Powers. With these objects in view he succeeded in inducing the Nationalist executive to transfer the Government from Canton to Hankow. At the end of November 1926 a commission of seven, with Eugene Chen as Foreign Minister, left Canton. On the 2nd December 1926 they reached Hankow and announced the establishment of the Nationalist Government there.

Mr. Lampson had just been appointed from the permanent staff of the Foreign Office in London as Minister in China. On his way to Peking he turned aside to visit Mr. Eugene Chen at the Wuhan, which he reached on the 8th December and left again on the 17th. On the 18th, before he had reached Peking, a Memorandum from the British Government was communicated by Mr. O'Malley, the British Chargé d'Affaires in Peking, to the Ministers of the Powers signatory to the Washington Treaties. In this Memorandum the British Government recalled that the

Powers at Washington had contemplated a revision of their treaties with China. But a government competent to speak for China as a whole no longer existed. For the moment they had to deal with regional governments only. None the less, the growth of a powerful Nationalist movement in the south should be noted with sympathy. The British Government, therefore, invited the Powers to affirm their readiness to negotiate treaty revisions so soon as the Chinese themselves had constituted a government with authority to negotiate. In dealing with regional governments the existing treaties should not be interpreted strictly. The Chinese right to tariff autonomy should be recognised, and the surtaxes agreed on at Washington should be granted at once and without conditions. The British Government expressed its regret that it had previously waived its views on this subject, and had joined the other Powers in protesting against the collection of these surtaxes by the Nationalist Government at Canton.

Annexed to this document was a Memorandum which London had sent to Washington on the 28th May 1926, protesting against the proposal to earmark the Washington surtaxes as security for debts not already secured on the customs revenue.

The publication of this note was received with some indignation at Washington and coldly by most of the other Powers. By the British Press in China it was greeted with resentment and cynicism. The long delay, for which France was responsible, in carrying out the Washington policy had led the British communities in China to suppose that that policy had lapsed. Official diplomacy and the trading communities of the Yangtze were now more than ever out of touch with each other.

The result on Chinese opinion was serious. As we now know, the breach between the moderate elements in the Nationalist party and those which

XXI ADVANCE OF NATIONALIST ARMIES

Borodin had more or less converted to Communism was rapidly widening. The Russians and the Russianised left desired a rupture with Great Britain, and the attitude adopted by the British Press in China enabled them to represent the British Memorandum as an insidious attempt to take the wind out of the sails of the Nationalist programme.

An expression of this feeling was the movement to seize the British Concession at Hankow, in the hope of repeating the kind of incidents which had happened in 1925 at Shanghai and Shameen. This attempt was only frustrated by the almost incredible restraint of the British Marines guarding the Settlement in withholding their fire. The women and children were evacuated, and Mr. O'Malley was sent from Peking to Hankow. He there succeeded in making an agreement with Mr. Eugene Chen for transferring the Concession to Chinese control. The rendition created the impression that in future British diplomacy might be trusted to yield to threats of force. On the other hand, British forbearance under very difficult circumstances saved the policy announced on the 18th December 1926 from foundering at the outset. In spite of the chilling reception received at the hand of the Foreign Powers, and the positive hostility evinced alike by the British Press in China and the Kuomintang, the Memorandum was destined to be recognised as the genuine and permanent expression of British policy towards China.

We have still to mention one factor which for the moment helped to neutralise the effect of the British Memorandum on Chinese opinion. The naval officers who have to protect British communities and shipping are from the nature of their task in intimate touch with the facts of the situation on the Yangtze. The cardinal position of the Foreign Settlements at Shanghai, as compared with those at Hankow or the other Treaty Ports, was appreciated in Admiralty circles. The British Government was led to realise that if the Settlements at Shanghai became the battle-ground of the rival armies in China, the pivot of commercial relations with the rest of the world would be destroyed. Amongst other and more catastrophic results, the policy announced in the Memorandum would be rendered nugatory. In January 1927 the British Government therefore decided to send three infantry brigades, one from India direct to Shanghai, and two from Europe to be stationed at Hongkong pending further developments. Smaller forces were sent by France and the United States. In view of this decision, Mr. Eugene Chen threatened to withhold his signature from the Hankow Agreement, but eventually signed it.

CHAPTER XXII

THE RUPTURE WITH RUSSIA

THE intrigues of Borodin at Hankow were no doubt made easier by the fact that Chiang Kai-shek was busy directing the military campaign. But they must have convinced him that the Russian connection was a greater menace to the Nationalist movement than the Western Powers. With T. V. Soong he realised that Shanghai was the key to the situation. The security maintained by the Foreign Powers had attracted to the Settlements the ablest bankers and merchants of China and enormous reserves of wealth. If the Nationalist forces could secure control of Shanghai without colliding with the Foreign Powers, they would henceforward control the Yangtze valley as far as the Wuhan.

When Wu P'ei-fu was driven out of the Wuhan, Sun Ch'uan-fang, whose forces controlled the banks of the lower Yangtze, had failed to come to his aid. He was now in danger of having to face the armies of Chiang Kai-shek alone. His military headquarters were at Kiukiang, the port of Kiangsi on the Yangtze, connected by railway with the interior of that province. On the 5th November 1926 Kiukiang fell to the army of Chiang Kai-shek. Sun Ch'uan-fang then hastened to Tientsin, where Chang Tso-lin had summoned a number of Tuchuns to a Council of War. This Council, at which Wu P'ei-fu was represented, decided to launch expeditions down the two railways, one under Chang Tso-lin to Hankow, the other to Pukow opposite Nanking. The second occupied Pukow on the 27th November 1926; but the first was brought to a standstill by the jealousy of Wu.

Meanwhile, the Kuomintang agents had been doing their work in advance of their armies, and the governments of the two provinces north and south of the Yangtze estuary, Kiangsu and Chekiang, transferred their allegiance to the Nationalist cause. On the 16th February 1927 Sun Ch'uan-fang was heavily defeated in battle before Hangchow by Chiang Kai-shek, and fled to the north. In hope of saving the situation the Shantung troops which Chang Tso-lin had sent to Pukow crossed the river and occupied Nanking. But the movement was too late, for on the 22nd March the Nationalist forces occupied Greater Shanghai up to the limits of the Foreign Settlements, which were guarded by the troops of the Western Powers.

The control of Shanghai and the lower Yangtze by Chiang Kai-shek was fatal to the schemes of Borodin, who was now bent on embroiling him in a quarrel with the Western Powers. This probably explains why a general strike broke out at Shanghai on the 19th February 1927, and why on the 22nd the French Settlement was shelled by Chinese gunboats under Communist influence. A meeting of the Kuomintang, held at Hankow from the 10th to the 16th March 1927, under Borodin's influence decided to depose Chiang Kai-shek from the post of Commander-in-Chief.

The victorious armies of Chiang were moving, meanwhile, from the south on Nanking. On the 23rd March 1927 the northern forces evacuated the city and crossed to Pukow. On the 24th Nanking was occupied by Nationalist regiments, in whom the Communists had inspired a particular hatred against foreigners, especially the British. This force, com-

XXII THE RUPTURE WITH RUSSIA

manded by one Ho Yao-tsu, had seriously threatened the British residents at Hankow, Kiukiang and Wuhu. The same troops and the same leader were responsible in May of the following year for the troubles at Tsinan. In Nanking they started to massacre the foreigners and loot their property. A number of British, American and Japanese were wounded and killed. The rest were evacuated with difficulty to the warships in the river, which opened fire and established a barrage of shells behind which the fugitives were able with difficulty to escape from the city to the river. On the 1st April 1927 General Chiang Kai-shek, while reserving the right to protest against the bombardment, expressed his regret for the outrage and promised to give satisfaction in due course.

The right wing of the Kuomintang led by Chiang Kai-shek, and the left wing under the control of Borodin, were now in open conflict. On the 2nd April 1927 Chiang took measures to suppress the Communists in Greater Shanghai with ruthless severity. On the 15th he convened a meeting of the Kuomintang at Nanking and established a Government in opposition to the semi-Communist Government at Hankow. This Government was now faced by the very condition which Borodin feared, for the moderate Government at Nanking commanded the financial resources of Shanghai and Canton.

His power at Hankow was presently crippled by a blow from the North. On the 6th April 1927 an officer of Chang Tso-lin raided a building used by the Russians at Peking, and seized documents proving that the Kuomintang was riddled with agents paid by the Soviet Embassy to procure the destruction of the Government to which it was accredited and establish a Communist regime. The Chinese as a people were referred to in terms of withering contempt. Diplomatic relations between Moscow and Peking were at once severed.

The documents revealed that Borodin was following the prudent course of supporting the Kuomintang as a Nationalist movement and keeping his Communist aims in the background, until, as he hoped, the Kuomintang was paramount in China. This was probably the policy approved by the Government in Moscow; but the Third International seems to have thought otherwise. On the 1st June 1927 a Hindu member of that body named Roy (now condemned to a life sentence in India) arrived at Hankow. Two influential members of the Government there were Sun Fo (Dr. Sun Yat Sen's son of his first wife) and Wang Ching-wei, arch enemies of Chiang Kai-shek. From Roy they learned that Borodin had received new orders which he had not communicated to them. The Kuomintang was to be replaced by the Communist Party supported by a Red army, and the land was to be confiscated for the peasants without reference to the Hankow Government.

The terrified members of this Government secured the support of Feng-husiang. On the 18th July 1927 Communists were arrested in large numbers. Borodin and Galens were able to escape overland to Moscow, and arrived there in October. They were followed by Eugene Chen and the widow of Sun Yat Sen.

This repudiation of the Russian alliance by the left instead of the right wing of the Nationalists opened the way to a reconciliation in the ranks of the Kuomintang. For the moment it strengthened the hands of the left against Chiang Kai-shek, who had not been prospering in his operations against the North. In August 1927 Chiang resigned and retired to Shanghai and thence to Japan, while the Nationalist Government was consolidated at Nanking. In November 1927 Chiang returned to Shanghai, married the sister of T. V. Soong, and on the 10th

December was requested by the Kuomintang to resume the position of Commander-in-Chief. T. V. Soong succeeded Sun Fo as Minister of Finance, and after an interval C. T. Wang took the place of C. C. Wu at the Foreign Office. Sun Fo, C. C. Wu, Hu Han-min and fourteen other opponents of Chiang Kai-shek went on a long tour to Europe.

On the 11th December 1927 the Communists in Canton made an effort to retrieve their position by seizing the Government, but three days later were suppressed by an anti-Communist force which massacred some two thousand of them. On the 13th December 1927 Chiang Kai-shek announced at Nanking that the Russian consuls would all be expelled from China.

Thus at the turn of the years 1927–28 the Nationalist Government was established at Nanking under control of the right wing of the Kuomintang with Chiang Kai-shek at its head, supported by C. T. Wang and T. V. Soong, who commanded the confidence of the banking and mercantile community in Shanghai. Its treasure was lodged in the International Settlement at Shanghai, which became the financial anchorage of the Government at Nanking.

CHAPTER XXIII

THE NANKING GOVERNMENT RECOGNISED BY THE POWERS

WHEN the first Pacific Conference had adjourned in 1925 its President, Dr. Wilbur, invited the Royal Institute of International Affairs to arrange that members competent to discuss British policy in China might attend the second Conference which was due to meet in Honolulu in July 1927. This Conference was accordingly attended by members from Chatham House connected with all three parties in London. At Honolulu these members formed friendly relations with the Chinese group led by Dr. David Yui, who was closely in touch with Chiang Kai-shek. In the course of this Conference this group awoke to the fact that the policy of the British Government, as announced in the Note of the 18th December 1926, had behind it the support of all three parties in the Parliament of Great Britain. The Chinese group, realising the unwisdom of continuing to boycott the trade of a friendly country, invited members of the British group to return with them to China. The boycott was brought to an end shortly after the return to power of Chiang Kai-shek at Nanking.

About this time the Municipal Council of Shanghai also succeeded in agreeing with the Chinese Ratepayers' Association that three Chinese members should be added to the Council, and six more to the sub-committees. The accession to power at Nanking of Chiang Kai-shek synchronised with a marked improvement of relations between China and the Western Powers.

With Japan it was otherwise. Till the spring of 1927 Baron Shidehara, who had represented Japan at the Washington Conference, had pursued a conciliatory policy since 1924. In April 1927 the Government in which he was Foreign Minister was displaced by another in close sympathy with the military party. At the head of this Government General Baron Tanaka also assumed control of the Foreign Office. At the end of May 1927 Tanaka announced that, as Nationalist forces were now advancing towards Peking, Japanese troops would be landed at Tsingtao to protect Japanese interests in Shantung. In July detachments were moved up the railway to Tsinan, the capital of Shantung, to protect the Japanese colony there, which numbered 2000.

In the spring of the following year three armies were approaching Peking, one from Shansi under Yen Hsi-shan, another from Honan under Feng-husiang, and a third led by Chiang Kai-shek up the Pukow railway from Nanking. Chiang Kai-shek reached Tsinan on the 2nd May 1928. On the 3rd a collision took place between the Japanese and Chinese troops commanded by Hu Yao-tsu, who had been responsible for the Nanking outrages. As to how it occurred the Chinese and Japanese reports are in conflict. On the 8th the Japanese, strongly reinforced from Tsingtao, drove the Chinese 20 li to the south, except for a body which fled to the walled city, out of which they were then shelled by the Japanese. The Japanese occupied the line as far north as the Yellow River and stopped all traffic. The northward advance of Chiang Kai-shek was thus brought to a standstill. A wave of indignation spread throughout China and started a boycott on Japanese goods.

On the 9th May 1928 Chang Tso-lin suddenly

announced his withdrawal from the conflict. On the 18th the Japanese advised both Nanking and Peking that, should the disturbances develop further in the direction of Peking and Tientsin, the Japanese Government might have to take steps for the maintenance of order in Manchuria. Chang Tso-lin was further informed that, unless he withdrew to Manchuria at once, his return would be barred by Japanese troops. In these circumstances Chang Tso-lin on the night of the 2nd and 3rd June 1928 withdrew his forces to Manchuria. As his own train was passing under the bridge which carries the Japanese railway over the Chinese line near Mukden an explosion occurred which killed him.

On the 4th June 1928 Chiang Kai-shek had got back to Nanking, and Yen Hsi-shan was appointed to command the police at Peking and at Tientsin. On the 8th Yen occupied Peking, while Feng-husiang remained outside the gates. On the 3rd July 1928 Chiang Kai-shek reached Peking. On the 6th July with Feng and Yen he attended a ceremony in the Western Hills to announce to the Spirit of Sun Yat Sen the success of the movement which he had inspired.

For the moment the Nationalist flag flew everywhere south of the Great Wall. North of it, Chang Hsüeh-liang, who assumed control of Manchuria on his father's death, was in sympathy with the Nationalist Movement, and greeted the leaders who assembled on the 6th July 1928 at Peking. On the 18th he was cautioned by the Japanese Consul-General against close relations with the Nanking Government. On the 9th August Baron Hayashi, who had come to attend his father's funeral, warned him that the unification of Manchuria with the territories under the Kuomintang might jeopardise Japanese interests.

In answer to questions in the House of Commons on the 13th and 30th July 1928, Sir Austen Chamberlain declared that:

His Majesty's Government regard Manchuria as being part of China; they do not recognise Japan as having any special interests in that territory, other than those conferred by Treaty, and those referred to in Baron Shidehara's statement at the Plenary Session of the Washington Conference on the 4th February 1922. . . . We recognise that Japan has great interest in Manchuria, which has a great Japanese population, and they will have a certain anxiety as to the protection of those persons. But our interest is a united China under one government, which can take obligations and keep obligations and with which we can negotiate a friendly settlement and maintain friendly relations.

On the 9th August 1928 Baron Tanaka announced that the Japanese Government had no intention of opposing the union of the Nanking and Mukden Government, but that they could not endorse it. On the 10th October, when the constitution of the Kuomintang Central Government was inaugurated at Nanking, Chang Hsüeh-liang was appointed one of the sixteen State councillors. On the 29th December the Kuomintang flag was hoisted in all his territories; but the customs collected in Manchurian ports were still reserved for provincial purposes.

The British Minister had now been instructed to proceed to Nanking and present his credentials to President Chiang Kai-shek, and this he did on the 20th December 1928. His example was followed by most of the other Powers. The Nationalist Government was thus recognised by the outer world as the Government to be held responsible for discharging the treaty obligations of all China. The name Peking (Northern Capital) was changed by the Nationalist Government to Peiping (Northern Peace) in order to indicate that in Chinese eyes that place was no longer the capital of China. The Ministers of the Foreign Powers continued to reside there. A member of the British Minister's staff was posted at Shanghai, where a house was taken large enough to accommodate the Minister himself when visiting the port. The procedure initiated when Mr. O'Malley negotiated the rendition of the British Concession at Hankow now became the recognised practice. Negotiations for revising the treaties, and on other matters under discussion, were conducted with the Minister of Foreign Affairs at Nanking and also on his frequent visits to Shanghai by a diplomatic subordinate acting on written or telegraphed instructions from Peiping. A custom was developed that the British Minister should not himself visit Nanking until his subordinate was able to report that negotiations had reached that stage when some important agreement was in sight.

The new American Minister, Mr. Johnson, who reached China at the end of 1929, when questioned by a journalist, replied that for the present the American Legation would be in his portmanteau. To begin with he used the Consulate at Shanghai as his headquarters, and spent his time between that city, Nanking and other Treaty Ports on the Yangtze. In a telegram sent to the *North China Daily News* from Washington it was stated that later on he reported in favour of moving the Legation from Peiping. In a further telegram from the same agency it was stated that the Department of State had declined to adopt his recommendation. The *North China Daily News* referred to the incident as a rebuff given to the American Minister by his own Government. Thereafter he seems to have made his residence at Peiping.

The Japanese Government hired a house for their Minister, Mr. Saburi, in Shanghai, and he said in a private conversation that he would have to spend most of his time there. After his death in 1929 Mr. Obata was appointed to succeed him, but the Nanking Government declined to receive him, in obedience to a public agitation raised by the Kuomintang. For the moment the Japanese Government refused to make a further appointment, and entrusted their relations with China to Mr. Shigemitsu, their Consul-General at Shanghai. He was afterwards promoted to the post of Minister and his residence in Shanghai was purchased by the Japanese Government. At the same time it was made plain in an obviously inspired message to the *North China Daily Herald*, sent by their correspondent in Tokyo, that Japan had no immediate intention of abandoning her treaty rights in the Legation quarter at Peiping. Her Minister was functioning in Shanghai as a matter of convenience only.

Cuba, Norway, Finland and Turkey seem to have transferred their representatives to Shanghai in 1930, and Italy to have followed their example in 1931.

With these partial exceptions the Legations as a body remained where they were. While recognising the Government at Nanking as the Government of China, the Ministers of the Foreign Powers refrained from recognising its decision to make that city the capital of China. Their reasons, which have never been publicly stated, can only be inferred from occasional comments in the Press, which are here appended for reference.

APPENDIX TO CHAPTER XXIII

The following telegram appeared in the *North China Daily News*:

WASHINGTON, *June* 14, 1930.

A recommendation for the removal of the American Legation in China from Peking to Shanghai was received by Col. Henry L. Stimson, Secretary of State, from Mr. Nelson T. Johnson, United States Minister, to-day.

Colonel Stimson expressed himself as undecided on the matter, but was studying all aspects of the situation carefully. He is known to feel that the United States may be doing some harm to the National Government, or at least displaying lack of courtesy, in allowing the Legation to remain in Peking.

Mr. Johnson expressed the opinion, in his message, that

Shanghai was a satisfactory centre from which the Legation business could be transacted.

Nanking has never thus far been considered as a site for the Legation, because it is felt that there is no assurance that Nanking will maintain its present political importance. At present, it is considered, such importance depends upon the ability of General Chiang Kai-shek's troops to defeat the Northern rebels.

Several officials remarked to-day that the removal of the Legation from Peking would relieve the United States of the necessity for maintaining the present U.S. Marine Guard. This guard costs each year an amount equivalent to what would be spent in removing the Legation, it was pointed out.

June 15.

In connection with his recommendation that the American Legation in China be removed from Peking to Shanghai, it was learned to-day that Mr. Nelson T. Johnson, the United States Minister, has recommended that several minor officials be kept in Peking in the event that the Legation is transferred.

It is assumed, however, that the major part of the diplomatic establishment would be shifted and that the American Legation Marine Guard in Peking would be abolished, with considerable financial saving.—*United Press.*

In another part of the paper appeared the following item of local news:

U.S. LEGATION COMING TO SHANGHAI

Information reaches us which we believe to be accurate that the United States Legation is likely to be removed from Peking to Shanghai in the near future.

The approval of Washington is awaited, but it is believed that this will be no more than a formality.

We understand that the old Kalee Hotel has been secured for Legation headquarters.

In the issue of the 21st June 1930 the following article appeared in the *China Weekly Review*, a journal which reflected the views of the Nanking Government:

U.S. MINISTER'S DECISION TO REMOVE LEGATION

The decision of the American Government, following a recommendation of Minister Johnson, to remove the U.S. Legation from Peiping to Nanking is a timely move and a friendly gesture which will be appreciated by most Chinese, particularly at this time when Gen. Yen Hsi-shan and other militarists are exerting their utmost to destroy the only group in China that holds out

THE NANKING GOVERNMENT

some promise of better conditions. When Minister Johnson first arrived in China he announced that his instructions were to maintain close contact with the recognised National Government. Since that time Mr. Johnson has spent most of his time in Nanking, making that city his headquarters while making trips to Peiping, Hankow and Shanghai for the purpose of familiarising himself with conditions at first hand. . . . A despatch from Washington by the United Press on June 14 stated that Minister Johnson had definitely recommended to Colonel Stimson, Secretary of State, the immediate removal of the Legation from Peiping. In reference to Minister Johnson's request, Mr. Stimson expressed the view that the United States might be unintentionally doing some harm to the National Government, or at least displaying a lack of courtesy, in allowing the Legation to remain in Peiping. A further report from Washington on June 15 stated that in the event of the early removal of the Legation from Peiping that several minor officials would be maintained in that city, the intention apparently being to reduce the Legation to the status of a Consulate since all important records would be removed to the South. The Washington message stated that the removal of the Legation would enable the abolition of the Legation Guard of about 500 Marines, thus resulting in a considerable financial saving. Dr. C. T. Wang, Foreign Minister, apparently had not seen the report from Washington regarding the removal of the American Legation when he issued a statement on last Monday morning to the effect that "the persistence of the Foreign Powers in continuing to maintain their Legations in Peiping was to be deplored, due to the fact that the presence of the Legations gives the self-seeking Northern militarists a false hope that a rival government established in Peiping might obtain foreign recognition". Dr. Wang declared that there is no reason under International usage or expediency why the Legations should not be removed to Nanking, or in the absence of suitable buildings, to Shanghai as a temporary measure. The present status of the various foreign Legations on this question of removal from Peiping was explained in the following announcement of the Shanghai office of the Ministry of Foreign Affairs last week.

The Shanghai office of the Nanking Ministry of Foreign Affairs, in a statement made public yesterday, announces that the Legations of Cuba, Norway and four other Foreign Powers have been removed from Peiping and are now located either in Shanghai or Nanking. It is predicted in Chinese circles that other Foreign Powers will shortly move their Legation to Nanking or Shanghai, unless the political situation grows worse.

The announcement states that the British, Japanese, German and Belgian Legations have permanent representatives residing either in

Shanghai or Nanking. It is pointed out that while American Legation has no representative permanently stationed in Shanghai or Nanking, the American Minister to China, Mr. Nelson T. Johnson, spends considerable part of his time either in Shanghai or at the capital, and that he announced upon his arrival in China that his Government had instructed him to remain near the seat of the Chinese Government.

Following is a list of the addresses of the Legation and Legation representatives in Shanghai, as set forth by the Ministry of Foreign Affairs:

>Cuban Minister to China, 604 Rue Lafayette.
>Norwegian Minister, 29 Szechuen Road.
>Finnish Charge d'Affaires, 63 Route de Boissezon.
>Turkish Charge d'Affaires, 191 Route Dupleix.
>Representative of Polish Legation, 111 Jessfield Road.
>Czecho-Slovakia representative, 510 Avenue Foch.
>Japanese Acting Minister, 1 North Yangtze Road.
>Representative of Great Britain, 8 Route Ghisi.
>Representative of Germany, 9 Whangpoo Road.
>Representative of Belgium, 15 Rue Corneille.

The sequel may be gathered from the following telegram to the *North China Daily News* from Peiping:

PEKING, *June* 22, 1930.

The State Department has shelved for the time being the recommendation made by Mr. Nelson T. Johnson, American Minister to China, that the Legation should be removed from Peking to Shanghai, and that the Marine Guard in Peking be withdrawn from China, according to reliable information received here. The Department takes the view, it is understood, that the present chaotic conditions in China do not warrant drastic action of the sort.

The news that the Minister had made the recommendation, carried exclusively by the United Press in China, attracted more attention here than any other news item in months. The news came as a complete surprise to other Legations, none of which have given any indication that they were considering such a move.

The most surprising feature of the recommendation was that the Legation be removed to Shanghai, which is not and can hardly become the capital of China, since it is a group of "foreign concessions" outside the jurisdiction of the Chinese Government.

While some Chinese newspapers here hint that Mr. Johnson intended to support the central government at Nanking, by taking the Legation from Peking, another view is suggested by Dr. Charles James Fox, American editor of the *North China Star*. Dr. Fox asks editorially, "Will not the Nanking government resent the idea of setting up Legations in a city that never has been, and never has made any claim to be, the capital of China?"

A plausible explanation of Mr. Johnson's views, made by Americans here, is that he feels China must pass through a period of political disturbance, in which no single government will be predominant, and that during such a period Shanghai will be the most coveted place from which to keep in touch with all factions. When a strong central government finally has been established, and has definitely fixed upon a capital, then the Legation can be removed from Shanghai to the capital.

The recommendation naturally was distasteful from a purely personal point of view to members of the Legation staff. In Peking they have adequate quarters, and rents are low since the capital was removed. In Shanghai Legation members would have to find their own quarters, and rents in Shanghai are very high, and houses difficult to obtain. Of course this phase would hardly be considered important if the removal was regarded as expedient.

The most vigorous opposition has developed to the Minister's suggestion that the American Marine Guard in Peking be withdrawn from China immediately. Military officers feel that chaos is worse in China to-day than at any time since the Boxer uprising, when the Legation Guard was first established. They feel that it would be short-sighted to withdraw the Guard at such a time.

The argument that a great saving would be effected by withdrawal of the Guard is declared to be specious. The Marines, officers point out, must be maintained in any case, either in Peking or elsewhere, and the chief additional expense of the Guard here is that of transporting supplies, which is not great. The Guard has an elaborate group of buildings here, in fine condition, upon which little money needs to be spent.—*United Press*.

The comment on the above telegram in the editorial columns of the *North China Daily News* on the 27th June 1930 was as follows:

The rebuff from Washington to the American Minister in Peking in respect of his plan to shift the Legation to Shanghai is of great significance. It means that the United States Government is beginning to lose patience with the endless fighting in China, and the time is not far off when the Powers will first tell each other and then say publicly that China has made the execution of their good intentions towards her impossible.

The following references to the subject are also extracted from the *North China Daily News*:

LONDON'S VIEWS ON CHINA
Central Government's Desirable Situation on Yangtze

LONDON, *July* 8, 1930.

In an editorial article upon the Chinese civil war *The Times* says that it would be unjust to blame Nanking alone for a situation which is the natural consequence of civil war, or to deny that personal ambition has played a great part in the rebellion of the Northern satraps, but at least it is arguable that the Russian constitution imposed upon China by Dr. Sun Yat-sen has contributed to the distrust of the Central Authority which has made rebellion so frequent and general.

The principle that the Courts should be independent of executive control, continues the article, has yet to be recognised. There is no public discussion of public affairs and no final responsibility rests with the Ministers for the last word is with the Central Executive Committee of the Party.

The same system is applied to the conduct of local affairs. The "tangpu" (the headquarters of the Kuomintang) wields an autocratic power over officials, and since no lists of their members are published the public does not know who are its real rulers.

All these points, says *The Times*, can fairly be made against the Central Government, yet its position on the Yangtze and its control of the revenues of the great ports of central China make its survival both desirable and probable.

Its imperfections are obvious, but there is no reason to believe that Marshal Feng Yu-hsiang or General Yen Hsi-shan or the Kuangsi generals would have done any better and there are good reasons to believe that the Yangtze Valley is the only possible centre for the Government of China south of the Great Wall.

This granted, is it desirable that the Foreign Legations should remain in Peking as far from the Capital as Madrid is from London when the railway is working, and much farther when the railway is cut.

General Yen Hsi-shan is at present a rebel against the internationally recognised Government of China, but this does not alter the fact that his action must compel the British Legation, sooner or later, to negotiate with him on a matter which is vitally important to foreign traders and bondholders.

The establishment of more frequent personal contact between Sir Miles Lampson and the Nanking Government, *The Times* concludes, is advisable in the interests of both Great Britain and China. The fact that power is in the hands of the Executive Council of the Kuomintang rather than in the hands of the Ministers makes it all the more imperative for the Diplomatic

Body to obtain and maintain contact with the men who matter most, and it is at least possible that the uncompromising attitude that Nanking has occasionally shown in its treatment of foreign rights and interests is due to natural soreness at the retention of the Legations at Peking. "The immaturity of the Kuomintang Government may be admitted, but will it be cured by isolation?"
—*Reuters.*

THE ADVANTAGES OF PEKING

Northern Reply to Suggestion Legations should move

PEKING, *July* 11, 1930.

Mr. Chu Ao-hsiang, the Director of Foreign Affairs for the Northerners, declared to-day that the suggestion of *The Times* that the Legations should move from Peking could not have been made at a more inopportune moment. It would, he said, convey the impression that the Powers were taking sides against the allies in the civil war.

Mr. Chu then criticised the conditions at Nanking and said that at present there were no suitable buildings there to house the Legations and that the sanitary arrangements, drainage and water-supply were inadequate. On the other hand he emphasised that Peking was well off in these respects. It had, he said, an agreeable climate. From the historical point of view its claims were pre-eminent. It had been the capital for more than 950 years through five dynasties and for most of the years of the Republic. It was, moreover, linked up by means of four great railways with the main rivers of the country so that it was a most suitable centre from a commercial and a political point of view.—*Reuters.*

THE LEGATIONS AND NANKING

Dr. C. T. Wang's Proposal to C.E.C. Plenary Session

November 18, 1930.

Numerous proposals have been submitted by various Government leaders to the Fourth Plenary Session of the Central Executive Committee of the Kuomintang, but one presented by Dr. C. T. Wang, the Foreign Minister, relating to the removal of the Legations to Nanking, is of especial interest.

Dr. Wang points out that, in spite of the fact that Nanking has been proclaimed the national capital of China for more than three years, the majority of the foreign Legations persist in their refusal to move south from Peking under the pretext that no buildings are available in the new capital, and he suggests that the National Government should take steps immediately to allocate land in Nanking on which foreign Legations may be constructed.

The National Government, in allocating these places, Dr. Wang says, should mark them out in different parts of the city, instead of placing them all together, so as to prevent the existence of a district similar to the present Legation Quarter in Peking.

As soon as sites have been allocated, the Foreign Minister suggests, roads should be built and every modern facility, such as electricity and water, should be connected, after which the foreign Legations should be invited to move south from Peking.

After the Legations have been moved to Nanking, the Foreign Minister says, the old Legation buildings should be purchased by the National Government and transformed into schools or government buildings, and, with the funds obtained through the sale of their Peking Legation buildings, the Powers will be enabled to construct new quarters in Nanking.

TOKYO, *December* 19, 1930.

There is little likelihood, in the opinion of the Japanese Foreign Office, that the principal foreign powers will remove the seats of their legations in China from Peking to Nanking or Shanghai during the current year, the United Press is informed.

Japan's action in purchasing a residence for her chargé d'affaires, M. Shigemitsu, in Shanghai, should not be interpreted to mean the Imperial Government has any intention of evacuating its legation premises in Peking, a Foreign Office spokesman said. The residence was purchased purely as a matter of convenience and may be used as the residence for her chargé d'affaires, Shanghai in event the chargé d'affaires ceases to make his headquarters in that city and in Nanking.

Japan does not own the building in which her consulate-general is housed in Shanghai, and long had felt the need of a satisfactory permanent residence for her consul-general. In view of increasing real estate values in Shanghai and the depressed value of silver the purchase of the residence was made merely as a business matter.

Well-informed sources in Tokyo believe the principal foreign legations in China are likely to remain in Peking for a long time for these reasons:

The Legation Quarter in Peking has been improved and is regulated by treaty so that it provides a more satisfactory headquarters for foreign diplomatic establishments in China than the National Government of the Chinese Republic can arrange in Nanking for some time. Diplomats generally like Peking and for purely selfish reasons, as well as practical considerations, want to continue their homes in that city.

The Powers also have a considerable financial investment in their Peking properties and probably would be loath to consider

XXIII THE NANKING GOVERNMENT 183

in the immediate future the expenditures which the construction of new diplomatic establishments in Nanking would entail.

Even if the Powers should wish to remove their diplomatic seats to Nanking, China, to date, has not made satisfactory provision for a Legation Quarter in the new capital. It is admitted here that if and when the Legations are moved to Nanking no replica of the Peking Legation Quarter, which is virtually a fortified area within Peking, can be expected. Chinese public opinion, it is realised, would not tolerate a repetition of the walled and loop-holed Quarter in its new capital.—*United Press.*

SPECIAL AREAS DESIGNATED

NANKING, *December* 28, 1930.

It is stated in political circles that sites for the various foreign legations in the capital have been designated in the residential district around the Drum Tower. Each legation will be allotted 100 mow of land. Contrary to the situation at Peking, the legations will not be grouped together.—*Kuo Min.*

LEGATION BEING MOVED

PROMOTION FOR ITALIAN CONSUL-GENERAL

June 16, 1931.

Special to the N.C.S.N.

The *North China Sunday News* was officially informed by the Italian Consulate-General in Shanghai on June 13 that Count Galeazzo Ciano di Cortellazzo, the local Consul-General, who is the son-in-law of Premier Mussolini, will be leaving to-morrow morning by train for Peking in connection with the removal of the Italian Legation from the former Chinese capital to Shanghai. He will be accompanied by Commander Uff. Giuseppe Ros, Consul-interpreter and honorary First Secretary to the Italian Legation, who was one of the Assessors of the former International Mixed Court.

Count Galeazzo Ciano di Cortellazzo, who is expected to be away from Shanghai for about a fortnight, will not be accompanied by the Countess.

Acting on instructions from the Foreign Ministry in Rome, Count Galeazzo Ciano di Cortellazzo will take charge of the affairs of the Italian Legation in China as the Minister, Commander Daniele Vare, is being transferred. It is not yet known where the latter is being transferred to.

According to the information given to the *North China Sunday News*, the Italian Legation is being removed from Peking to Shanghai. After its removal, it will be among the first of the Legations of the big Powers to be removed south.

CHAPTER XXIV

INTERNAL DISSENSIONS

"The Kuomintang of China, in pursuance of the Three People's Principles and the Five Power Constitution of the Revolution, hereby establishes the Republic of China.

"The Party, having swept away and removed all obstacles by military force and having passed from the period of military conquest to that of political tutelage, now must establish a model government based upon the Five Power Constitution to train the people, so that they may be able to exercise their political powers and to expedite the handing over of such powers by the Party to the people.

"Accordingly, the Kuomintang, in the execution of the duty of direction and supervision of the Nationalist Government which devolves on it by virtue of its history, hereby formulates and promulgates the Law governing the organisation of the National Government."

THIS instrument, through which the Kuomintang was to rule China, had at its head a State Council, the Chairman of which (Chiang Kai-shek) was to be President of the National Government and Commander-in-Chief. The State Council was to consist of from twelve to sixteen State councillors, of whom ten were to act as presidents and vice-presidents of five Yuan or boards. Of these Yuan, one was to act as the executive, a second as the legislature, and a third as judiciary. A fourth and fifth Yuan corresponded to the Board of Public Examiners and the Board of Censors under the Imperial regime. The Executive Yuan was to enjoy a certain primacy, and control ten ministries, finance, foreign affairs, war, agriculture, industry, education, railways, internal affairs, communications and health.

Beside the President, one man of outstanding ability was the Minister of Finance, Mr. T. V. Soong. Together with the other ministers his constitutional position was that of an underling under the Executive Yuan, which, in turn, was supposed to receive its instructions from the Council of State. But the Council of State had also to obey the Central Executive of the Kuomintang, which went in fear of the Tang Pu or district lodges of the party, bodies which constantly aspired to act as local governments in their own areas. The wit of man has seldom devised a more effective mechanism for fomenting intrigue, hampering decisions and obscuring responsibility.

Soong realised that everything depended on getting rid of the armies infesting the various provinces, which menaced the authority of the Government and drained its exchequer. He lost no time in preparing the way by a series of conferences of bankers and business men, who announced that loans would not be forthcoming unless the surplus soldiery were disbanded. On the 31st December 1928 a conference of generals was convened at Nanking to discuss disbandment, in which Chiang Kai-shek, Feng-husiang, Yen Hsi-shan, a representative of Chang Hsüeh-liang and generals from the province of Kwangsi, all took part. The conference agreed to reduce the number of soldiers from 1,200,000 to 700,000 and allow the Ministry of Finance to control the expenditure.

It was plain ere long that the Kwangsi generals had no intention of reducing their forces. On the 6th April 1929, by a rapid movement, Chiang Kai-shek ejected them from their stronghold in the Wuhan, defeated their efforts to seize Canton, and by the end of June had driven them over the frontier into French Indo-China.

In the meantime a quarrel had broken out with Feng, over Chiang Kai-shek's refusal to give him control of Shantung, which the Japanese had now evacuated. Feng retreated to the west, destroying the railway bridges and tunnels, and eventually went into retreat as the guest or prisoner of Yen at Taiyüan, the capital of Shansi.

In September another general, Chang Fa-kwei, revolted and tried to revive the Kwangsi rebellion, but was driven to take refuge in Hunan. In October 1929 Sung Chi-yuan, a henchman of Feng, invaded Honan. Some stubborn fighting was ended by diplomacy aided by a payment of money to the rebels, and to Yen who acted as broker. In the south, Chang Fa-kwei and the Kwangsi forces were again threatening Canton, but were beaten back in a pitched battle in December.

The Nationalist forces were also threatened with serious disaffection in their own ranks. The troops at Wuhu, fifty-five miles above Nanking, mutinied in October. On the 3rd December the Government at Nanking was nearly destroyed by a mutiny at Pukow.

On the 3rd April 1930 Yen Hsi-shan, in alliance with Feng, declared hostilities against Nanking. They were joined by Chang Fa-kwei in the south, who seized Changsha on the 4th June. On the 25th June Tsinan was taken by Yen, but on the 15th August he was crushingly defeated by Chiang Kai-shek, south of the Yellow River. A month later Chang Hsüeh-liang demanded an immediate cessation of hostilities, moved with his troops south of the Great Wall, occupied Peiping and sent the remnants of Yen's army back to Shansi. Yen himself took refuge in Dairen. Feng, defeated by Chiang Kai-shek on the 6th October 1930, withdrew with his army to Northern Honan. The Nationalist Government then appointed Chang Hsüeh-liang Vice-Commander-in-Chief with full power in Northern China, on the understanding that the Kuomintang party organisation was not to operate in the area under his control.

The Central Executive of the Kuomintang had failed to control not only the Tuchuns but also its own local committees.

> The really vexatious tyrants were the Tang Pu—the local organs of the Kuomintang, which wielded, and often abused, an arbitrary power unregulated by any effective responsible central control. ... In the hope of safe-guarding the people against these abuses and mitigating the popular resentment against the party to which this situation was giving rise, a group of enlightened statesmen at Nanking had promoted a Bill of Rights in the early part of the year 1930. The Bill had been accepted by the central Political Council, but had then been thrown out by the Central Executive Committee of the Kuomintang, at the instance of Hu Han-min, on the ground that it was inconsistent with "the state of tutelage" to invest the people with rights, which, *ex hypothesi*, they were not yet qualified to exercise.[1]

The right which the Central Executive party thus claimed to control the Government at Nanking was also claimed and exercised by the local committees of Kuomintang throughout China. Everywhere the Tang Pu were interfering with the organs of government, provincial and local. This was possibly one of the factors which had led the 'model Tuchun' of Shansi into rebellion against Nanking. The resistance of Chang Hsüeh-liang to the Tang Pu was widely approved.

While Chiang Kai-shek was engaged in these struggles north of the Yangtze, the regions south of Nanking had largely passed into the hands of Communists or bandits. With the opening of the year

---

[1] *Survey*, 1930, pp. 340-41.

1931 it looked as though Chiang Kai-shek would be free to restore order in these regions and start the Nationalist Government on the path of reform. A National People's Convention was convened for May, to which it was proposed to submit a provisional constitution for China during the period of tutelage. This project was opposed by Hu Han-min, Chairman of the Legislative Yuan, who was set upon maintaining the dictatorship of the central committee of the Kuomintang. The patience of Chiang Kai-shek was exhausted and Hu Han-min was interned at a health resort near Nanking. The National Convention was held in May and approved the provisional constitution. But meanwhile Sun Fo and other adherents of Hu Han-min seceded and formed a National Government of their own at Canton with Eugene Chen as its Foreign Minister. By the summer of 1931 the country was thus faced by the prospect of another civil war in the south.

In every phase of the Chinese disorders two spectres—(brigandage and famine)—seated, like Black Care, behind the horseman's back—had ridden in the rear of the contending armies; and with each recurrence of civil war the attendant scourges had descended upon the backs of the Chinese people ever more heavily, until, during the campaign of 1930, banditry in the provinces south of the Yangtse and famine in Shensi and Kansu reached what was perhaps their highest known pitch of intensity.

. . . . . .

Some notion of the scale on which the brigands conducted their operations in southern China in 1930 may be conveyed by a haphazard selection from the chronicle of their exploits in sacking entire cities. For instance, on the 30th March, 1930, one band sacked the city of Kanchow in Kiangsi and thereafter dealt likewise with two neighbouring cities in Kwangtung. In May other bands sacked Yunhang and Simakow, two cities of Hupeh, in the valley of the Han. In July others sacked Chaoping, a city of Kwangtung to the north of Swatow. On the 27th July the unfortunate city of Changsha, which had received a visitation from Chang Fa-kwei and his 'Ironsides' the month before, was occupied for five days by brigands marching under the banner of Communism; and when these guests were induced to depart in consideration of a gratuity of $1,000,000 (Mex.), it was feared for a moment that they would repeat this safe and lucrative operation at Hankow. In the course of July and August other brigands sacked Chungmiaochen and Hwangmotachen in Anhwei; others Linchwang and Kiuhwashen and Chwenkaichen and Yahchang and Jukao in Kiangsu; others Hanchengchen in Honan; and others Lienchieng in Fukien. At the end of November Changte, in Hunan, suffered the fate which had previously overtaken Changsha.

The outrages in the metropolitan provinces of Kiangsu and Anhwei were particularly significant as an index of the degree to which the Nanking Government, under the stress of a civil war on two fronts, had lost the power to maintain law and order—not to speak of coping with the economic distress to which this epidemic of lawlessness was directly due. In October the Government sent three divisions, released from the Honan front by the cessation of the civil war, to deal with the brigands in Hupeh, Hunan and Kiangsi. At the beginning of December Chiang Kai-shek himself took the matter in hand. He proclaimed an amnesty for all brigands who renounced Communism and laid down their arms, and at the same time let it be known that no less than 300,000 troops, 20 gunboats and 30 aeroplanes had been detailed for a systematic campaign of suppression. He took command of the subsequent operations in person.[1]

Of these operations this much is known, that his army sustained a serious reverse, and that many of the Nationalist troops went over to the Communists. The prestige of Chiang Kai-shek was seriously injured by the failure.

In the course of these troubles the waterways of the Yangtze were kept open by foreign warships, mainly British, which were often in action against the guns mounted by Communists on the banks.

[1] *Survey*, 1930, pp. 342-3. It has proved impossible to locate in the maps of China some of the places mentioned in this extract.

Little or nothing is heard of this constant expenditure of British ammunition, because it is in the interests of all but the Communists that the vital artery of China should be kept open to traffic. The British officer commanding the Yangtze flotilla is entitled "The Admiral of the Yangtze". Citizens of a Western country can realise the significance of this title by thinking how they would feel if a foreign admiral and fleet had come as a matter of routine to be named after their principal river.

As for the famine [the *Survey* continues] it was reported at the beginning of 1930 by a special delegate of the China International Famine Relief Commission, who had been investigating conditions in Central Shensi, that, out of a population of some six million, two million were estimated to have died of starvation during the preceding twelve months and two million more were expected to die before the next harvest. Equally harrowing accounts, also at first hand, of conditions in Kansu were given by an officer of the China Inland Mission who visited that province in the course of the year in order to dispense funds which the American Advisory Committee of the Relief Commission had allocated.[1]

A still more intimate picture of these conditions has since been drawn by Mr. R. H. Tawney, who, during the winter of 1930–31, was commissioned by the Institute of Pacific Relations to report on Agriculture and Industry in China, with the co-operation and under the auspices of the China Council of the Institute. In the course of his report Mr. Tawney observes that:

Over a large area of China, the rural population suffers horribly through the insecurity of life and property. It is taxed by one ruffian who calls himself a general, by another, by a third, and, when it has bought them off, still owes taxes to the Government; in some places actually more than twenty years' taxation has been paid in advance. It is squeezed by dishonest officials. It must cut its crops at

[1] *Survey*, 1930, p. 343.

the point of the bayonet, and hand them over without payment to the local garrison, though it will starve without them. It is forced to grow opium in defiance of the law, because its military tyrants can squeeze heavier taxation from opium than from rice or wheat, and make money, in addition, out of the dens where it is smoked. It pays blackmail to the professional bandits in its neighbourhood; or it resists, and, a year later, when the bandits have assumed uniform, sees its villages burned to the ground.[1]

There is a case, no doubt, for the bandit, though it is seldom stated. He is often a disbanded soldier who, as in the England of More, is driven "either to starve or manfully to play the thief", or a victim of oppression who robs his robbers. Unfortunately, it is easier to shear sheep than wolves, and, though popular sympathy is sometimes with him, the majority of his victims are worse off than himself. It is not surprising that, in certain provinces, the peasants have armed and formed leagues to keep out "bandits, Communists and Government soldiers". Much that the press ascribes to Communist machinations seems, indeed, to the western observer to have as much, or as little, connection with theoretical Communism as the Peasants' Revolt of 1381 in England or the Jacquerie in France. What is called the Communist question is in reality, in most parts of the country, either a land question or a question of banditry provoked by lack of employment. It appears to be true, nevertheless, that in China, as elsewhere, an elemental revolt against intolerable injustices has been organised and given a doctrinal edge by political missionaries, and that certain regions, such as parts of Fukien, Kiangsi and Hunan—the two last areas with an abnormally high percentage of tenants, and acute agrarian discontent—form small enclaves of revolution, where such government as exists is conducted by Communists.

The indirect effects of the chaos are as disastrous as the direct. Expenditure on war absorbs resources which should be spent on elementary improvements, such as roads and primary education. Trade is paralysed, and such communications as exist are turned by the soldiers who seize them from a blessing into a curse. Capital flies from rural districts, where it is urgently needed, to be buried in the

---

[1] R. H. Tawney, *A Memorandum on Agriculture and Industry in China*, p. 58.

Concessions. Population flies with it; here and there whole villages are on the move, like animals breaking from cover as the beaters advance. When human enemies are absent, the farmer must still reckon with a remorseless nature. "What drove you to settle here, so far from home?" a peasant was asked in the presence of the writer. The reply was, "Bandits, soldiers and famine. . . ."

The number of deaths caused by famine has been variously estimated. That of 1849 is said to have destroyed 13,750,000 persons; the Taiping Rebellion, with the widespread economic ruin which accompanied it, 20,000,000; the famine of 1878–79, 9,000,000 to 13,000,000; that of 1920–21, 500,000. In reality, however, to concentrate attention on these sensational catastrophes, as though life ran smoothly in the intervals between them, is to misconceive the situation. Famine is a matter of degree; its ravages are grave long before its symptoms become sufficiently shocking to arouse general consternation. If the meaning of the word is a shortage of food on a scale sufficient to cause widespread starvation, then there are parts of the country from which famine is rarely absent. In Shensi, stated an eminent Chinese official at the beginning of 1931, 3,000,000 persons had died of hunger in the last few years, and the misery had been such that 400,000 women and children had changed hands by sale. In Kansu, according to Mr. Findlay Andrew, one-third of the population has died since 1926, owing to famine, civil war, banditry and typhus. There are districts in which the position of the rural population is that of a man standing permanently up to the neck in water, so that even a ripple is sufficient to drown him. The loss of life caused by the major disasters is less significant than the light which they throw on the conditions prevailing even in normal times over considerable regions.

In the case of famine, in short, as in that of war, the occasion of the breakdown must be distinguished from its causes. The former is commonly a failure of crops caused by drought or flood. The latter, though aggravated at present by political anarchy, consist in the primitive organisation, and absence of surplus resources over daily needs, which turn the misfortune of individuals into a general catastrophe. It is probable that drought, if not flood, is in some measure unavoidable; there are regions in the north-west where, there is reason to believe, the

XXIV INTERNAL DISSENSIONS

desert may be advancing and progressive desiccation taking place. But one reason, at least, for the occurrence of both on a scale sufficient to produce disaster is that nature has not been subjected to control to the extent which, given a settled economic policy, and the means to carry it out, is to-day practicable. Those directly affected by them cannot meet the blow, for they have no reserves. The individual cannot be rescued by his neighbours, since whole districts together are in the same position. The district cannot be rescued by the nation, because means of communication do not permit of food being moved in sufficient quantities. Famine is, in short, the last stage of a disease which, though not always conspicuous, is always present.[1]

These words had scarcely been written when the Yangtze and Yellow rivers began rising to levels unrecorded in previous history. The alluvial regions flooded are as closely settled as any in the world, and in area are equal to the whole of England and Wales. The multitudes drowned are merely a fraction of those destined to perish for lack of the food which cannot be grown in the flooded areas for the coming year.

The one certain source of relief to which this suffering people can turn is opium in all its forms. Increasing misery steadily promotes the consumption of opium, and is fostering an appetite for the drug in forms which have more rapid and deleterious effects than when it is smoked. Coolies can get a morphia injection for ten copper cash, and their arms can be seen covered with marks of the needle.

The old regime, when it fell in 1911, had just succeeded in stopping the growth of the poppy in China; but all the conditions of anarchy have since combined to revive it. Legitimate produce is taxed or pillaged at numerous points between the producer

---

[1] Mr. Tawney's report deserves to be studied by everyone who is trying to grasp the essential condition to which the manifold problems of China are traceable. It is understood that Mr. Tawney is revising it for republication in England. *A Memorandum on Agriculture and Industry in China*, pp. 58-59, 61-62.

and consumer. Opium is more easy to carry and conceal than cotton or grain, and the farmers naturally grow a crop they can market. They are often obliged to grow it by Tuchuns, who depend on the profits derived from it to pay their armies. The Chinese Navy is largely used in carrying it. This "precious bane" is so easily smuggled that the captain's cabin in a British warship, and even the yacht of the Inspector General of Maritime Customs have been used for the purpose. The ships of all nations that ply on the Yangtze are used by the smugglers. As the ship approaches the mouth of the river a splash may be heard as a parcel of opium attached to floats is thrown overboard, to be picked up by boats which presently glide from the shore. British officers admit that they know of the traffic and frankly state that they are unable to stop it. One captain who tried to do so found himself hanging head downwards over the side of his ship with a pistol in his ribs, till he swore to close his eyes to the business.

This organised traffic is a cancer more dangerous even than that which thrives on illicit liquor in America. Its wealth is enormous and its central emporium is the French Concession. Parcels of opium with the French Municipal mark on them have actually been seized in the International Settlement. Vendors of opium imprisoned in the French Concession are those who compete with the agents of the privileged syndicate. Order is maintained there by an understanding with this criminal organisation, which traffics not only in drugs, but in brothels, gambling and every description of vice, and knows how to silence criticism by murder and kidnapping. It can exercise a sinister influence in the counsels of the party which controls the Government. In the French Concession the Chinese residents have more cause for complaint than in the International Settlement. Yet the French Concession is scarcely if ever mentioned when the cry for rendition is raised. When the League of Nations sent a commission to investigate the traffic in the Far East, the Government refused to allow its inquiries in China.

The only effective remedy for this evil will be found in measures to relieve the grinding poverty of the people which is driving them to drugs for relief. No argument is needed to show that orderly government throughout China is the first condition of all such measures. Whatever problem is examined there its roots will be found in prevailing anarchy.

CHAPTER XXV

EXTRATERRITORIAL RIGHTS AND THE FEETHAM REPORT

THE internal struggles summarised in the last chapter must constantly be held in mind, while tracing the relations of China to the Foreign Powers during the same period.

On the 18th December 1926 the British Government had publicly invited the Powers to affirm their readiness to negotiate treaty revisions, so soon as the Chinese themselves had constituted a government with authority to negotiate. On the 20th December 1928 the British Minister had officially recognised the Nationalist Government at Nanking as vested with that authority.

After some hesitation on the part of Japan, the leading Powers agreed to concede tariff autonomy. A modification of the tariff as settled at the Peking Conference of 1926 came into force on the 1st February 1929.

Before the end of 1928 the Government at Nanking had negotiated treaties with Belgium, Italy, Denmark, Portugal and Spain, in which these Powers agreed to recognise China's tariff autonomy, and also to relinquish extraterritoriality, whenever the other Treaty Powers had agreed to do likewise.

On the 27th April 1929 Dr. C. T. Wang addressed an identic note to these other Powers, the United States, Great Britain, France, the Netherlands, Norway and Brazil, demanding that steps might

CH. XXV   EXTRATERRITORIAL RIGHTS

be taken to enable China, now unified and with a strong Central Government, rightfully to assume jurisdiction over all nationals within her domain.[1]

In May 1929 the British Minister visited Nanking, but only to attend the funeral of Sun Yat Sen in the great mausoleum erected under the Purple Mountain.

On the 10th August the United States, Great Britain, France and the Netherlands presented replies in terms which were similar though not identic. The British reply argued in favour of maintaining the treaty port system—"though perhaps in a modified form", until the new Chinese Courts came to

be free from interference and dictation at the hands not only of military chiefs but of groups and associations.[1]

This was a reference to attempts made by military authorities and the local Kuomintang to deflect the course of justice in the Provisional Court at Shanghai. The British Government went on to invite proposals

as to the procedure to be adopted for examining the question of what further modifications in the system of extraterritoriality it would be desirable and practicable to effect.[2]

The American Note was in stiffer terms.

The third Conference of the Institute of Pacific Relations was due to meet in October at Kyoto, and the subject of extraterritoriality was on its agenda. The British attended with Lord Hailsham as leader. The Americans brought in their delegation, Mr. Fessenden, the General Administrator of the Shanghai Municipal Council. After showing the Conference how the International Settlement had grown out of extraterritorial rights, he announced the intention of his Council to appoint a competent and

[1] *Survey*, 1929, p. 316.   [2] *Ibid.* p. 317.

impartial expert to survey the position. At the previous Conference in 1927 Professor Hornbeck had made this suggestion. He was now official adviser to the Secretary of State at Washington, and Mr. Fessenden had recently seen him there. The proposal was also clearly in line with the suggestion made in the British Note of the 10th August 1929, that the question of what further modifications in the system of extraterritoriality it would be desirable and practicable to effect should be examined.

The Municipal Council lost no time in securing the services of Mr. Justice Feetham, a South African Judge who had previous experience of political inquiries in India, Ireland and East Africa. He reached Shanghai in January 1930.

Dr. Wang meanwhile was asking that personal negotiations with the British Minister might be resumed. As nothing resulted, the Chinese Government at the end of November announced their intention of abolishing extraterritoriality by unilateral mandate as from the 1st January 1930. On the 2nd December Mr. Henderson in the House of Commons replied that the proposed action of the Chinese Government would prejudice the prospect of a satisfactory issue. On the 20th December he handed the Chinese Minister in London an *aide-mémoire*, in which he said that the British Government had intended that the British Minister in China should visit Nanking in order to initiate discussions before the end of the year, *but unfortunately the outbreak of civil war over a wide area in China had made it impossible to carry that intention into effect.* He added that

"in view of the prominence which" had "been given to the particular date of the 1st January 1930", Mr. Henderson informed the Chinese Minister that the British Government were "willing to agree that the 1st January 1930 should be treated as the date from which the process of the gradual abolition of extra-territoriality should be regarded as having commenced in principle, and would have no objection to any declaration conformable with that attitude which the Chinese Government may think it desirable to issue. His Majesty's Government are ready to enter into detailed negotiations, *as soon as political conditions in China render it possible to do so*, with a view to agreeing on a method and a programme for carrying abolition of extra-territoriality into effect by gradual and progressive stages to the mutual satisfaction of both Governments."[1]

On the 24th December Dr. Wang replied accepting this suggestion. On the 28th December the following instructions to the State Council were issued by the "Central Political Council":

1. To issue a mandate beginning the 1st January to all foreign nationals residing in China who are now enjoying extra-territoriality rights, that they shall observe all laws and regulations promulgated by the central and local Governments, and
2. To promulgate as soon as possible measures relating to the administration of justice in cases where foreign nationals are involved.[2]

The complications of the system will be realised when we add that the "Central Political Council" is a body consisting of the Central Executive Committee of the Kuomintang party and the Central State Council of the Government.

A mandate in accordance with these instructions was issued accordingly.

On the 1st January 1930 the British Government accepted this declaration, and promised that the British Minister should now come to Nanking and open negotiations. They requested that orders should be issued making it clear to officials that the extra-territorial privileges of British subjects continued until new treaties were signed. This did not, however, prevent the arrest at Hankow by Chinese officials of a British naval officer whose car had killed a coolie. He was only surrendered on the British Consul

[1] *Survey*, 1929, p. 319.   [2] *Ibid*. p. 320.

giving a guarantee to produce him for trial on demand by the Chinese Government. The officer in question still lives under the shadow of that liability.

There were other reasons which called for the presence of the British Minister at the capital of the Government to which he was accredited. In the International Settlement at Shanghai an agreement had been made in 1926 to substitute for the Mixed Court, controlled by the consular body, a Provisional Court, which was to come into operation on the 1st January 1927 for three years. On the 8th May 1929 Dr. Wang pointed out to the Ministers at Peiping that the Provisional Court would lapse on the 31st December, and requested negotiations. The diplomatic corps replied offering to remit the matter to preliminary examination by subordinates. Dr. Wang objected, pointing to the fact that under the agreement of 1926 his Government had the right to open negotiations at any time before the end of 1929. This obviously meant that the Foreign Minister of China felt himself entitled to ask that the Ministers of Powers which had recognised his Government at Nanking should deal with him in person and not through subordinates. The controversy dragged on till eventually a conference met in December, which was joined by the British Minister when he arrived at Nanking in January.

A cessation of justice in Shanghai was prevented by the Chinese Government, which ordered the Provisional Court to continue in session until the conference had reached an agreement, which was in fact signed on the 17th February by all the negotiating Powers but France.

Meanwhile the relations of Chinese and foreigners in the International Settlement were steadily improving. On the 7th February the Chinese accepted $150,000 from the Municipal Council in settlement of all claims arising out of the Shanghai incident of the 30th May 1925. A proposal to increase the Chinese representation on the Council from three to five members was thrown out in a thinly attended meeting of foreign ratepayers on the 6th April. At a special meeting of ratepayers called for the purpose on the 2nd May this vote was reversed and the two Chinese members were added by an overwhelming majority.

In April an agreement was ratified for the return to China of Weihaiwei, which came into force on the 1st October.

The struggle with Feng and Yen seems to have interrupted negotiations during the summer; but in September the British Minister again visited Nanking and a settlement was reached of the Boxer Indemnity question, the further discussion of which must here be reserved for a subsequent chapter.

On the 11th September the British Minister submitted to Dr. Wang definite proposals for the settlement of the extraterritorial question. These were rejected by the Chinese Government, which submitted counter-proposals on the 1st December.

In April 1931 the British Minister again visited Nanking and resumed the negotiations on extraterritoriality with Dr. Wang. As noticed in the last chapter, a National People's Convention was due in May, and Dr. Wang was naturally anxious to announce to its members an agreement settling this contentious question.

Mr. Justice Feetham was now completing his inquiry, the results of which were presented to the Municipal Council of Shanghai in four instalments, together covering more than 700 pages of print. The first and largest instalment was issued to the public in Shanghai on the 25th April, whilst Dr. Wang and the British Minister were discussing at Nanking the terms of a new treaty to abolish the rights of extraterritoriality. In this preliminary survey the Judge showed how Shanghai had become the greatest city in China, its economic centre, and the key to its trade relations with the outer world. Its unparalleled position he traced to "the rule of law" based on security afforded by the Treaty Powers, in contrast to the arbitrary regime and absence of security outside the foreign concessions. In the International Settlement there was freedom from arbitrary arrest. Taxes were collected to meet the requirements of a published budget, and expenditure was subject to a regular audit. Neither lands nor goods were liable to confiscation. There was proper sanitation and efficient police. The Press was not liable to censorship or suppression. The rule of law was really established; but the Judge was obliged to add that none of these conditions had been realised as yet outside the foreign concessions. His comments were naïvely illustrated by the local branch of the Kuomintang, which at once requested the National Government to forbid the Postal and Customs authorities to transmit the Report, or the Chinese Press to publish it.

The banks of the International Settlement were the only place where the National Government could keep their treasure beyond the reach of a mutinous general. To abolish it would deprive the Government itself of this anchorage, and the Chinese inhabitants of their present opportunity of learning what the rule of law and responsible government really mean. It would also prejudice the economic position of China as a whole, and dislocate her trade relations with the world at large. The Report conclusively showed that the Settlement had grown out of extraterritorial rights, and could only continue so far as those rights were maintained in that area.

On the 4th May 1931 the National Government announced that the negotiations with the British Minister had broken down, and that foreigners would be treated as subject to Chinese law on and after the 1st January 1932. It was presently clear, however, that all this was staged for the benefit of the National Convention which met at Nanking on the 5th May. On the 6th May Sir Austen Chamberlain in the House of Commons pressed Mr. Henderson to lay papers showing the course of the negotiations. Mr. Henderson refused, on the ground that he hoped for their early resumption. On the 16th May the Convention closed its proceedings, and the British Minister returned on the following day to reopen his conversations with Dr. Wang.

On the 8th June 1931 Mr. Henderson stated in the House that negotiations had reached a stage which enabled them to be reported to both Governments. He hoped shortly to make a statement. On the 11th Sir Austen Chamberlain again pressed for papers, and was again refused.

On the 17th June the second volume of the Feetham Report was published, containing the Judge's recommendations. He advised that the return of the Settlement to the Chinese should be recognised as the goal.

> The present Settlement regime, as established under the Land Regulations, should be maintained on the basis of increasing co-operation between the Foreign and Chinese communities, and such constitutional changes should be introduced as are necessary for the purpose of enabling the Chinese to participate effectively in the work of local self-government under some modification of the present system, and of thus paving the way to the eventual establishment of a new system based on a Charter granted by the National Government.[1]

He pointed out that the steps to this goal should be settled by the principal Powers concerned together (and not separately) in conference with the Government of China.

He then added an impressive warning against any

[1] *Feetham Report*, vol. ii. p. 140.

attempt to fix in advance the period within which the goal of rendition can be reached. Negotiations for a gradual advance would be rendered abortive if extremists knew that need for negotiations would end automatically on a certain date. The fixture of the date would destroy the sense of security which has made Shanghai the economic centre of China.

Until the rule of law has been established in China in such a way as to safeguard effectively the ordinary citizen in the exercise of his personal rights and the performance of his civic duties, abolition of extraterritoriality would destroy the vitality of the present municipal institutions.[1]

The publication of this Report in the British Press made a deep impression. The *Manchester Guardian* remarked:

Nationalists in a hurry are not always governed by what appear to detached observers to be elementary principles of prudence.

The Times feared that

the negotiations between Sir Miles Lampson and Dr. C. T. Wang have . . . done a good deal to shake the extraterritorial foundation of the International Settlement. Even if Shanghai be permitted a moratorium of five or ten years . . . Mr. Justice Feetham's prescription of "not years, but decades" will not be fulfilled.

In answer to questions in the House Mr. Henderson admitted that a draft of "the proposed treaty" was being submitted to both Governments.

"In the meantime", he said, "Mr. Justice Feetham's Report will be carefully examined." But added: "I cannot see the connection between the agreement on extraterritoriality and the Feetham Report."

He again promised a statement to the House in due course.

Two wholly separate incidents had aroused the

---

[1] *Feetham Report*, p. 149.

anxiety traceable in these articles and questions. Two leading members of the China Association in London had been summoned to the Foreign Office, where the terms of the draft-treaty settled between Dr. Wang and the British Minister had been explained to them. Simultaneously the same procedure had been followed in Shanghai. The British Consul-General had there sent for four prominent British subjects (none of them members of the Municipal Council), and had made a similar communication. In both cases the communications were made under a pledge of secrecy, and the two members of the China Association in London were not authorised to discuss the information vouchsafed them with the China Association.

Such proceedings, of course, gave rise to a crop of rumours. It was generally believed that the draft treaty contained a provision for the unconditional rendition of Shanghai at the end of ten years, a proposal in direct opposition to the major recommendation of the Feetham Report. Hence the reference to ten years in *The Times* leader of the 17th June.

The second incident was as follows. On the 2nd June a young Englishman named Thorburn had disappeared in a scuffle near Soochow, in which two Chinese soldiers were shot. He was known to have been alive on the 11th June in the custody of Chinese soldiers. The military authorities denied his arrest, and the Nanking Government professed to be unable to find out what had become of him. These statements were followed by a series of questions in Parliament and a growing agitation on the part of the British communities in China. On the 27th July Mr. Dalton stated that the British Minister had been ordered to leave Peiping and present the demands of the British Government in person to President Chiang Kai-shek. The case dragged on till the 30th October, when the Chinese Foreign Minister, as the result of further inquiries, reported that Thorburn, after shooting two gendarmes, had been arrested near Quinsan and had himself been shot on the 8th June at Soochow by Colonel Huang Chen-wu, who had suppressed the truth and destroyed the body. The colonel had since been condemned to fourteen years' imprisonment.

Parliament had risen in August without hearing the statement promised by Mr. Henderson, who ceased to be Foreign Secretary shortly after. In October the British Minister was brought for a few days to Nanking by the Manchurian crisis. On a flying visit to Shanghai he interviewed the Chamber of Commerce, and is reported to have said that a treaty must be signed by the 31st December, because after that date extraterritorial rights would have expired. The Chamber declined to endorse these views, and pressed that the whole question of extraterritorial rights should be dealt with by the principal Powers concerned in conference with the Government of China, as advised in the Feetham Report. On the 7th December Sir John Simon, in answer to a question, stated that the draft treaty had not even been initialled.

On the 31st December 1931 the Government at Nanking issued a mandate postponing the abolition of extraterritorial rights.

CHAPTER XXVI

THE BOXER INDEMNITY AGREEMENT

WE have seen in the last chapter that Dr. Wang and the British Minister had in September 1930 reached an agreement for returning the Boxer Indemnity to China.

When China declared war on Germany on the 14th August 1917 the allied Powers, except Russia, agreed to defer Indemnity payments from the 1st December 1917 to the 1st December 1922. On the 20th December 1922 the British representative at Peking informed the Chinese Minister for Foreign Affairs that the British share of the Boxer Indemnity would be applied to projects equally beneficial to China and Great Britain. The monthly payments were henceforward deposited with the Hongkong and Shanghai Banking Corporation, instead of being paid to the British Treasury.

These arrangements were legalised in the China Indemnity (Application) Act, 1925, in which Parliament ordered that these moneys should be applied to such educational or other purposes beneficial to the mutual interests of Great Britain and China as the Secretary of Foreign Affairs might determine after consultation with an Advisory Committee of eleven persons. This Committee, of which Lord Buxton was Chairman, in 1926 sent Lord Willingdon and five other of its members on a visit to China. Their recommendations were adopted and presented to the British Government on the 18th October 1926 as representing the views of the whole Advisory Committee. These recommendations were that expenditure of the fund should not be limited to direct educational purposes, but that a considerable proportion should be invested in some useful *and reproductive* undertakings, directly advantageous to China, such as railways or river conservancy schemes, and that this investment should eventually provide a permanent educational endowment. The word 'educational' should be stretched to include such purposes as agricultural improvement, scientific research, medicine and public health. A number of purposes were examined and scheduled as suitable objects upon which the capital of the fund, or interest yielded by the capital, should be spent. The control and administration of this expenditure should be entrusted to a Board of Trustees sitting in China, with a Chinese majority.

The British Government approved this report, but nothing further was done till September 1930, when Dr. Wang and the British Minister met at Nanking. The agreement they reached was embodied in a note dated the 22nd September 1930, from the British Minister to Dr. Wang, the text of which will be found appended to this chapter. From this document it will be seen that the Chinese Government agreed *"to deal with the funds in harmony with the general views set forth in the report"* of the Buxton Committee. The agreement, however, differed in certain respects from that report, and also from the plan authorised by the China Indemnity (Application) Act of 1925. A Bill was therefore submitted to the House of Commons to repeal this Act and to give effect to the new agreement. On the 20th January 1931 the second reading was moved by Mr. Dalton, the Under-Secretary of State for Foreign Affairs.

Why is it that the Act of 1925 has now become inapplicable? Primarily for this reason, that whereas in 1925

XXVI THE BOXER INDEMNITY AGREEMENT

there was no national government of China recognised by His Majesty's Government, and the Act consequently did not represent a negotiated settlement, there has been since 1928 a national government in China recognised by His Majesty's Government. Consequently, it became necessary to substitute, and we have finally succeeded in substituting, a negotiated settlement for a unilateral decision by His Majesty's Government. . . . *All the moneys covered by this Bill are to be devoted to education, either by direct grants or by the creation of educational endowments."* [1]

He went on to explain that the moneys covered by the Bill consisted of about £3,500,000 on deposit in the bank, and about £8,000,000 still due to be paid by 1945. (The precise sums were £3,515,419 : 9 : 3 in the bank and £7,847,098 : 4 : 9 to be paid by the 31st December 1945; in all £11,362,517 : 14s.) From the £3,500,000 in the bank £265,000 was to be paid to the Hongkong University and £200,000 to a body called the Universities' China Committee in London. The residue, something over £3,000,000, and half the unpaid instalments equal to about £4,000,000, that is to say, about £7,000,000 in all, was to be spent on materials manufactured in Great Britain for the rehabilitation of the Chinese railways. The materials were to be bought by a Commission in London consisting of a Chinese representative of the Ministry of Railways, four Englishmen and the Chinese Minister as chairman. The £7,000,000 so spent would be treated as a loan to the railways, interest upon which would be payable to a Board of Trustees in China. This Board would include a minority of British Trustees.

Interest on the loan will be devoted, at the discretion of the trustees, to educational purposes in China, and will therefore constitute an educational endowment invested in the Chinese railways.[2]

[1] *Hansard*, Jan. 20, 1931, pp. 98-9.   [2] *Ibid.* pp. 100-101.

The other half of the unpaid instalments, equal to about £4,000,000, will be paid direct to the Board of Trustees in China and applied by them to objects mutually beneficial to the United Kingdom and China. *It is the intention of the Chinese Government that this sum also shall form an educational endowment. Consequently, the whole £11,500,000 will be applied to Chinese educational purposes either directly or indirectly.*[1]

In the course of the debate Mr. Arthur Samuel pointed out that no provision had been anywhere made for carrying out this arrangement and hoped that it might be done in the Bill:

At any rate, it must be thoroughly well understood that it is a condition precedent to this House agreeing to the Bill that the Chinese Government must find the interest and amortisation.[2]

The rate of interest to be paid was never mentioned, either in the Agreement or in the Parliamentary debates.

In response to pressure by Captain Eden and other Conservative members an amendment was passed providing that the Board of Trustees in China *must* include British subjects.

The Bill became law early in March 1931. The Purchasing Committee in London at once began to spend the money on railway material. The Board of Trustees was appointed, consisting of Chinese and British members, the latter appointed on the recommendation of the British Minister. When the Board met in Nanking it appeared that the chairman and most of the Chinese members were unable to speak English. The discussions were conducted in the Chinese language. From time to time the secretary explained the gist of the conversations and translated into Chinese any observations that the British members thought fit to make.

[1] *Hansard*, Jan. 20, 1931, p. 102. [2] *Ibid.* p. 123.

XXVI THE BOXER INDEMNITY AGREEMENT

For the present the only funds which the Board has to administer are one-half the current instalments of the Boxer Indemnity as they fall due, that is to say, a sum of over £250,000 a year. According to the Agreement this money is to be dealt with "in harmony with the general views set forth in the report" of the Buxton Commission, and Mr. Dalton had assured the House of Commons that

> all the moneys covered by this Bill are to be devoted to education, either by direct grants or by the creation of educational endowments.

At their first meeting the Trustees were informed that Dr. Wang and the British Minister had agreed that £40,000 should be spent on a new Foreign Office at Nanking, and £2000 as a grant to a hospital at Peiping. The Trustees were directed to ratify these grants, and obeyed. They have since requested the Government of China to issue bonds entitling them to draw interest on the moneys expended on the Purchasing Committee in London, and presumably also on capital expenditure authorised by themselves; for otherwise such expenditure will yield no income available for educational purposes. No response has as yet been made by the Government of China.

On the 26th February 1932 Mr. Macmillan asked the Secretary of State for Foreign Affairs whether he would request the British Trustees to report to him annually what moneys the Board of Trustees has received under the Act and to what objects mutually beneficial to China and the British Empire such moneys have been allocated; and whether such reports will be laid before Parliament. The answer given by Captain Eden, now Under-Secretary at the Foreign Office, was as follows:

> The members of the Board of Trustees, whether British or Chinese, are appointed by the Chinese Government and

can only report to that Government. As regards the moneys due to the Board, I would refer my hon. friend to page 49 of Cd. No. 2766, of 1926. Under the Act the Board will receive one-half of each annual instalment as set down in that paper. As regards the objects on which these funds are to be expended, I would refer him to Cd. Paper No. 3715, of 1930, pages 11 *et seq*.[1]

APPENDIX TO CHAPTER XXVI

Sir M. Lampson to Dr. Wang

NANKING, *September* 22, 1930.

SIR—I have the honour to acknowledge the receipt of your Excellency's note, which reads as follows:

"I have the honour to refer you to the declaration made by His Majesty's Government in the United Kingdom of Great Britain and Northern Ireland in December 1922, that the balance of the British share of the Indemnity of 1901 would be thenceforward devoted to purposes mutually beneficial to China and the United Kingdom, and to express the hope that His Majesty's Government will at once take steps to remit all payments of the Indemnity as from the 1st December, 1922, to the control of the Chinese Government.

"In the event of such remission being effected it is the intention of the Chinese Government to deal with the funds in harmony with the general views set forth in the report of the Anglo-Chinese Advisory Committee published in 1926, to which the attention of the Board of Trustees in China referred to below will be invited. The Chinese Government proposes, however, in the first instance to apply the bulk of the funds to the creation of an endowment to be subsequently devoted to the educational purposes mentioned in the Report of the Committee. It appears to the Chinese Government that the most advantageous plan for providing such an endowment would consist in the investment of the greater part of the said Indemnity funds, namely, the accumulated funds now on deposit and all future instalments, in rehabilitating and building railways and in other productive enterprises in China. For the control, apportionment and administration of the above-mentioned endowment the Chinese Government will duly appoint a Board of Trustees in China, which will include a certain number of British members.

"In view of the urgent necessity, in connection with re-

[1] *Hansard*, Feb. 26, 1932, p. 719.

construction and development in China, of reconditioning the existing Chinese railways in the first instance, the Chinese Government will take the necessary steps to apply a part of the accumulated funds now on deposit and the instalments due for payment shortly in the rehabilitation of the said railways, especially those lines in which British financial interest has been particularly concerned, to which lines attention will be first given.

"In rehabilitating and building railways and in undertaking other productive works from the Indemnity funds remitted or from loans secured on the said funds, the terms of existing contracts will be taken into consideration, but all orders for materials required and purchased abroad out of those funds themselves, including bridges, locomotives, rolling-stock, rails and other equipment, will be placed in the United Kingdom of Great Britain and Northern Ireland.

"In order to carry out these proposals at the earliest date and in the manner most satisfactory to the two countries, the Chinese Government is prepared to agree that the whole of the accumulated funds now on deposit be transferred to a Purchasing Commission in London, to consist of a chairman, who shall be China's diplomatic representative in London, a representative of the Chinese Ministry of Railways, and four other members appointed from time to time by the Chinese Government after consultation with the Board of Trustees from a panel of persons commended to those Trustees by His Majesty's Principal Secretary of State for Foreign Affairs as being persons of standing with wide experience in business matters, for the purpose of purchasing bridges, locomotives, rolling-stock, rails and other materials from United Kingdom manufacturers for the use of the Chinese Government railways and other productive undertakings in China. It is understood that the Commission will be exempt from all taxation in respect of any income accruing to it, whether by reason of the payment to it of any of the moneys specified in this note or from the deposit or investment of any part of such moneys as is not required for its immediate use, and its functions shall be as follows:

"(1) To enter into and to supervise and secure the carrying out of contracts for the supply and delivery in China of such plant, machinery and other articles and material to be manufactured in each case within the United Kingdom as may from time to time be required and ordered by the Chinese Government; and

"(2) To apply all moneys received by the Commission in accordance with the terms of this note in discharging the obligations incurred under or in connection with any such contracts and in defraying generally the expenses of the Commission, and so far as those moneys are not immediately required for such purposes in establishing a reserve fund to enable the Commission to meet similar requirements of the Chinese Government and its own expenses in future years. All future instalments as they fall due will be paid by the Chinese Government to His Majesty's representative in China, who will transfer one-half to the Purchasing Commission in London, to be used in the same way and for similar objects as specified above, and one-half to the account of the Board of Trustees in China.

"Funds spent in the United Kingdom will be regarded as loans, bearing interest and providing for eventual amortisation, from the Board of Trustees to the Chinese Government Railways or other productive enterprises concerned, and strict account will be rendered from time to time to the said Trustees. The amounts attributable to the service of such loans will be paid to the said Trustees and by them applied to educational purposes at the earliest opportunity."

I have also the honour to acknowledge the receipt of your Excellency's note, which reads as follows:

"With regard to the constitution, powers and proceedings of the Purchasing Commission in London referred to in my note of to-day's date on the subject of the disposal of the British share of the Indemnity of 1901, I have the honour to state that it is my understanding that—

"1. The term of office of a member of the Commission (other than the Chairman) shall be three years, subject to reappointment, but a member may at any time resign his office.

"2. The proceedings of the Commission shall not be invalidated by any vacancy among its members, provided, however, that no decision of the Commission shall be taken in the absence of a quorum, which shall be constituted by any four of its members.

"3. The Commission may provide itself with such offices and employ such officers, expert advisers, accountants and agents as it deems necessary for the proper discharge of its functions.

"4. The accounts of the Commission shall be made up to such date in each year and audited by such persons as the Commission may determine and the Commission shall submit to the Chinese Government a summary of those accounts and of its transactions during the year and cause it to be published.

"5. Subject to the above provisions and the conditions set forth in the above-mentioned note, the Commission may regulate its own procedure and make standing orders governing

XXVI THE BOXER INDEMNITY AGREEMENT 215

the conduct of its business, whether by the Commission or by committees of the members thereof."

I have also the honour to acknowledge the receipt of your Excellency's note, which reads as follows:

"I have the honour to acknowledge the receipt of your Excellency's note of to-day's date on the subject of the disposal of the balance of the British share of the Indemnity of 1901, which contained the following proposal from His Majesty's Government in the United Kingdom of Great Britain and Northern Ireland:

" 'That a sum of £265,000 and a further sum of £200,000 be set aside from the accumulated funds now on deposit, to be donated respectively to the Hong Kong University for the education of Chinese students and to the Universities' China Committee in London for the promotion of closer cultural relations between China and the United Kingdom. The grant to the Universities' China Committee will be invested as an endowment fund, the proceeds of which will be used *inter alia* for inviting eminent Chinese to give lectures in the United Kingdom.'

"In reply I have the honour to state that the Chinese Government is in agreement with the above proposal."

I have the honour to inform your Excellency that I duly communicated your notes to His Majesty's Government in the United Kingdom of Great Britain and Northern Ireland, who have instructed me to inform you in reply that they appreciate and approve the proposals suggested by your Government as to the future utilisation of the balance of the British share of the Indemnity, and that they confirm your Excellency's understanding that the proposed Purchasing Commission in London will be exempt from all taxation in respect of any income accruing to it, whether by reason of the payment to it of any of the moneys specified in your first note above referred to or from the deposit or investment of any part of such moneys as is not required for its immediate use, and also confirm your Excellency's understanding in regard to the constitution, powers and proceedings of the said Commission. The Act of Parliament, the enactment of which is required, will be drafted so as to give effect thereto. His Majesty's Government believe that the rehabilitation and construction of railways will not only provide valuable educational endowments but will also in themselves promote trade and prosperity and will thus advance the mutual interests of both countries. They especially appreciate the intention of the Chinese Government to place orders for materials with British manufacturers in the United Kingdom of Great Britain and Northern

Ireland, and they consider the method of carrying out this intention as suggested in paragraphs 5 and 6 of your Excellency's note of the 19th September should prove satisfactory to both countries. They will be glad to avail themselves of the proposals, subject, of course, to the terms of the existing contracts, both those between British firms and Chinese authorities and those between British firms and their foreign partners. His Majesty's Government will, therefore, subject to the necessary legislation being passed in Parliament and upon it coming into force, remit all payments of the Indemnity as from the 1st December 1922, and transfer to the proposed Purchasing Commission in London all the deposited funds, less the expenditure already incurred under sections I. (1) and I. (3) of the China Indemnity (Application) Act of 1925 and subject to the deduction of the two sums of £200,000 and £265,000 set aside for the Universities' China Committee and the Hong Kong University respectively, and will pass future payments to the control of the Chinese Government in the manner and subject to the conditions provided in the notes referred to in paragraphs 1 and 2 of this note.—I avail, etc.

MILES W. LAMPSON.

CHAPTER XXVII

JAPAN AS SUCCESSOR TO RUSSIA IN MANCHURIA

THE relations of the Nationalist Government at Nanking with its nearest neighbours, Russia and Japan, were less easy. In an earlier chapter we have seen how, at the end of the nineteenth century, Russia acquired Port Arthur and the right to connect that ice-free harbour with the Trans-Siberian Railway.

The importance of this to Russia can be seen by a glance at the map of her Empire, which stretched from the Baltic and Black Sea to the Northern Pacific on the east. Beyond comparison the largest continuous area under one government, its sole outlet in winter was, and again is, at the south-western extremity through the ports of the Black Sea, an outlet which Turkey can close at the Dardanelles. It is not without reason that Bowman in his recent work, *The Pioneer Fringe*, has headed his chapter on the Asiatic territories of Russia with the words "Imprisoned Siberia". The largest continuous coniferous forests which remain to the world exist in this area. It is rich in minerals. Its steppes are capable of grazing cattle and producing grain in unlimited quantities.

Siberia is separated from ice-free waters by Manchuria, a country the size of Germany and France, resembling Canada in its physical and climatic conditions, and in the nineteenth century still almost unpeopled. Its virgin forests and prairies were the lure which drew the rulers of Imperial Russia down paths that led to their own destruction.

Had the struggle of 1904 ended in victory for Russia by land and sea, it can scarcely be doubted that Manchuria and Korea would have both been joined to the Russian Empire. Manchuria then contained scarcely 15,000,000 inhabitants, including 12,000,000 Chinese. Its climate and soil were eminently suited for colonisation by peasants from Russia, who were hungering for land of their own. Its ports would have given them a better outlet for their timber and grain than the peasants possessed even in the neighbourhood of the Black Sea. In a few generations Manchuria would have been Russian in every sense of the word.

These possibilities were ended for ever by the Treaty of Portsmouth in 1905, when Russia ceded to Japan all her rights in Manchuria south of Changchun. These included the right to administer the Liaotung Peninsula, that is to say, Port Arthur, Dairen and the territories adjacent thereto. It also gave Japan the right to keep in Manchuria fifteen soldiers for the protection of every kilometre of the South Manchurian Railways. Under this provision Japan was entitled to maintain a force of some 15,000 in South Manchuria.

The subsequent history of this country illustrates the strangely opposite qualities of the Chinese and Japanese characters. In Chapter I. we remarked that the Chinese peasant, accustomed through ages to expect nothing from government and also to endure great natural calamities, has developed a singular power of making a living for himself in the face of incredible hardships and difficulties. He is by the force of necessity a pronounced individualist. In the great floods coolies might be seen bringing the raw cotton from fields above the level of the water in boats up the streets of Hankow, to be pressed into bales

XXVII JAPAN AS SUCCESSOR IN MANCHURIA

on the upper floors of the factories. This amazing tenacity explains why Chinese colonisation advances so surely in Batavia, the Malay Peninsula and Siam. That all these regions will, in course of time, be absorbed by China is far from improbable. Incapacity to subordinate private interests to those of any group larger than a family hampers this process. A marked deficiency in the power of combined action goes far to explain why the Chinese have found it so difficult to establish an effective government for themselves.

In contrast to all this the Japanese greatly excel in their power of acting together. The long discipline of the feudal system developed an instinct for loyalty in their character and a power of regimentation which is comparable only to that of the Prussians. This explains their rapid and amazing success in naval and military organisation, in public administration, and also in transportation and industry, that is to say, in the fields in which China has failed most signally.

The Japanese were thus able to give Manchuria what was most needed to promote its development, an effective system of transportation. They guarded their lines in the lawless condition of a frontier country with a mere handful of soldiers. They were also able to exclude from Manchuria the armies of Tuchuns struggling for supremacy south of the Wall. The pax-Japonica they established attracted the starving peasantry from the war-trodden province of Shantung. Such a movement in masses had never before been seen in history. The population of Manchuria has been practically doubled since 1905. According to *The Manchuria Year Book*, compiled in Japan, the population has risen to 29,198,000, of which 3·2 per cent are made up of 228,810 Japanese, 607,119 Koreans, and 102,198 other nationalities. The Japanese are thus but 0·8 per cent of the population, including soldiers and officials. The position of

Japan as a colonising power in Manchuria is comparable to that of England in Egypt or India. For the Japanese peasant, a gardener rather than a farmer, is unable to cope with climatic conditions in a raw country. They cannot compete with the Chinese on the land, in the factories or mines.

As regards manual labour the Chinese are certainly superior, because of their ability to do strenuous work on very simple fare, and their low wages rendered possible by this cheapness of living, and their docility in accepting longer working hours, make Chinese labour the most satisfactory and profitable in the world.[1]

Manchuria is thus valuable to Japan as an investment, but of none whatever as an outlet for that 15 or 20 millions to be added to her numbers in the next generation.[2]

The problems which confront Japan in Manchuria largely arise from the fact that her situation in that country was not of her own shaping. She inherited a position fashioned by Imperialist Russia to suit the needs and capacities of its people. Japan cannot complete that position as Russia would have completed it, if the Russo-Japanese war had left Manchuria in her hands.

[1] *The Manchuria Year Book*, p. 284.
[2] See Crocker, *The Japanese Population Problem*, p. 205.

CHAPTER XXVIII

SEIZURE OF THE CHINESE EASTERN RAILWAY

WHEN in 1895 Count Witte had secured from Li Hung-Chang a right to connect the Siberian railway with Vladivostok, he founded the Russo-Chinese Bank. The capital was mostly obtained from France, but in 1926 the Chinese Government contributed 5,000,000 taels and agreed that the bank should organise "The Chinese Eastern Railway Company" to construct and operate the railway. When in 1898 the Liaotung Peninsula was seized by Russia, the C.E.R. constructed a branch to Port Arthur and Dairen. Under the Treaty of Portsmouth this line south of Changchun was transferred to Japan.

After the Russian Revolution the Russians on the staff of the C.E.R. were for the most part hostile to the Soviet regime. In 1924 the Soviet Government made an agreement with China for the joint control of the line, as a purely business enterprise. The Board of Directors was to consist of five: including the President, appointed by the Chinese Government, and five, including the Vice-President, appointed by the Soviet Government. The manager was to be Russian. There were protests against the agreement by France, the United States and Japan which China ignored.

The agreement led to constant disputes between the Russians and Chinese, who used the railways for transporting troops without paying the company.

In January 1926 the Russian manager Ivanov refused to transport troops which Chang Tso-lin was sending to crush a rebellion. Ivanov was arrested by Chang Tso-lin, but released under threats of war from Russia.

We have seen how in April 1927 Chang Tso-lin seized documents in Peking which revealed the designs of Russia and led to the flight of Borodin and Galens. Marshal Chang Hsüeh-liang, forgetting what happened when his father arrested Ivanov, seems to have thought that the tactics he afterwards adopted at Peking could be followed up with impunity. The Nanking Government supported him in this view. In May 1929 four Soviet consulates were raided by Chinese police, who claimed to have found proofs that the Russian employees of the C.E.R. were used to foment a Communist revolution. The Nationalist Government justified this action by reference to the following clause in the Agreement of 1924:

> The Governments of the two contracting parties mutually pledge themselves not to permit, within their respective territories, the existence and/or activities of any organisations or groups whose aim is to struggle by acts of violence against the Governments of either contracting party.
> The Governments of the two contracting parties further pledge themselves not to engage in propaganda directed against the political and social systems of either contracting party.[1]

In June a Soviet Consul-General and other prominent officials were arrested. The telephone and telegraph systems of the C.E.R. were seized and the Russian trading offices were closed down. The Russian manager of the railway and a number of his staff were displaced, and their duties transferred to Chinese officials.

[1] *Survey*, 1929, p. 348, quoting from *League of Nations' Treaty Series*, vol. xxxvii.

SEIZURE OF EASTERN RAILWAY

On the 13th July the Soviet Government addressed a protest to the Nanking Government demanding the reversal of these arbitrary measures and citing a clause from the Agreement of 1924 to the effect that disputes should be referred for settlement to the two Governments. They recalled that on the 2nd February they had asked that all outstanding disputes should be brought up for settlement in this way, and had received no answer to their note. An answer was requested within three days, failing which the Soviet Government

> would find itself obliged to have recourse to other means of defending the legitimate interests.[1]

This note was followed by a complete rupture of diplomatic and consular relations between the two countries. The Nanking Government hastened

> to assure the Treaty Powers that they had no thought of carrying on their campaign against the surviving "unequal-treaties" by the high-handed methods of unilateral "direct action", which they had just been employing against the two Sino-Russian "equal treaties" of 1924.[2]

The United States, Great Britain, France and Japan pointed to the fact that the Kellogg Pact had been signed by both China and Russia. China was also reminded of her obligations as a member of the League of Nations.

Russia, not being a member of the League, was able to take her stand on the following clause in the Agreement of 1924:

> The Governments of the two contracting parties mutually agree that the future of the C.E.R. shall be determined by the Republic of China and the U.S.S.R. to the exclusion of any third party or parties.[3]

Negotiations conducted in the course of July between Moscow and the Government of Manchuria at

---

[1] *Survey*, 1929, p. 350.   [2] *Ibid.*, pp. 352-3.   [3] *Ibid.*, p. 355.

Mukden, followed by proposals exchanged between Moscow and Nanking through Berlin, were equally fruitless. When in August the Soviet Government began to apply military pressure it declined to listen to German remonstrances. Russia was determined to exclude the intervention of third parties, and also to exact the terms specified in its ultimatum of the 13th July, no less and no more, if necessary by force of arms. A small and highly disciplined force was placed under Galens's command on the frontier. An account of its operations was written by the editor of the *Survey of International Affairs*, Mr. Arnold Toynbee, who was in Manchuria at the time, after attending the Pacific Conference at Kyoto.

Thus all overtures for a *rapprochement* between the two parties to the rupture proved abortive until the Chinese were brought to their knees by a sudden intensification of the Russian military pressure in the latter half of November 1929. On the 17th of that month, the Soviet forces launched a vigorous attack, in which all arms co-operated, against Manchouli and Jalai Nor simultaneously and captured both places, together with their Chinese garrisons. The Soviet forces engaged were not numerous—it was afterwards estimated by an authoritative neutral investigator that, from beginning to end of these operations, there were never more than 3000 Soviet troops on Chinese soil—but they were well-equipped, efficient and under strict discipline.[1] The Chinese troops, on the other hand, were ill-equipped and mostly out of hand. Only one Chinese force fought well—the force that was entrenched outside Manchouli under the command of General Liang Chung-chia. The troops stationed in Manchouli itself devoted their energies, before surrendering, to looting the town. The Chinese garrison at Hailar (a station on the C.E.R. about 125 miles south-east of Manchouli) likewise looted that town on the 23rd and 24th November before they were put to flight by a Soviet air-raid. Thereafter, Hailar was occupied on the 27th, and was held for about a month by a small Soviet garrison consisting of about

[1] The stories of Soviet Russian atrocities which arrived, with the news of the invasion, at Harbin, afterwards proved to be unfounded.

300 infantry and 200 mechanics and pilots of the air force. This was the limit of the Soviet forces' advance on the ground, but they carried their air-raids as far as Buhetu, a point on the railway south-east of the Khingan Mountains. In the occupied territory the Russians seized all movable property belonging to the C.E.R., but they respected private property; and in every way the conduct of their authorities and the discipline of their troops appear to have been exemplary (as, indeed, they had been on the previous raids which penetrated less deep into Chinese territory and were of shorter duration). Moreover, they repaired the damage which had been done, during the operations, to the section of the railway between Hailar and the frontier.

Meanwhile, the news of what was happening in the frontier zone had caused consternation both at Harbin and at Mukden.[1]

At Harbin, both the Chinese and the Russian inhabitants (of all political colours), as well as the foreign residents, were afraid not of the victorious Red Army—which was not expected to advance so far or to fail in discipline if it did advance—but of the defeated and demoralized Chinese troops, who were falling back south-eastward along the line of the C.E.R. and were consoling themselves for their military discomfiture by pillaging the places *en route* and even robbing the civilian refugees, who were flying neck-and-neck with them, of such scanty belongings as these had managed to bring away from their abandoned homes. On the 22nd November, the Consular Body at Harbin met to consider the advisability of making arrangements for evacuating all foreign women and children. Happily, the avalanche of the Chinese army's *débacle* came to a standstill before it reached the city.[2]

On the 26th November Chang Hsüeh-liang agreed to accept the terms specified in the Soviet ultimatum of the 13th July, and M. Litvinov laid down the lines of further negotiations in a note. He rejected a proposal of the Nanking Government that troops should be withdrawn to thirty miles on both sides of the

---

[1] The writer of this *Survey* happened to be at Mukden on the 17th-20th November and at Harbin on the 21st-22nd.
[2] *Survey*, 1929, pp. 362-3.

frontier; and refused to listen to representations made by a number of Powers at the instance of the United States. By the end of December a provisional arrangement was accepted by China for the restoration of the *status quo ante* on the C.E.R., the reopening of the Soviet Consulates in Manchuria, and the holding of a conference at Moscow for the settlement of outstanding questions, including the resumption of diplomatic relations.

CHAPTER XXIX

OCCUPATION OF MANCHURIA BY JAPAN

In July 1929 the Soviet Government had shown that it meant to insist on its treaty rights, and refuse intervention by third parties. Thereafter Japan held strictly aloof from attempts on the part of the Powers to intervene between Russia and China. She drew the conclusion that Chinese armies could be trusted to collapse when confronted by prompt and vigorous action. So loose was the link between China and Manchuria that force could be used against the Government of Manchuria without involving a declaration of war with the Government of China. It seemed too that the use of force might not preclude a return to the *status quo ante*, modified only in so far as it suited the user of force to alter it. In the light of after events it is plain that the success which attended the Soviet policy made a deep impression on military circles in Japan, and still more on Japanese officers in Manchuria. The fact that Russia, though a signatory to the Kellogg Pact, was not a member of the League of Nations was perhaps overlooked.

In the early days, when the Japanese had recently expelled the Russians and reclaimed Manchuria for Chinese sovereignty, they were naturally regarded with favour by the local inhabitants and authorities. Their rights beyond the leased territory administered by Japanese officials were indeed workable only so long as these friendly relations continued to exist.

But the maintenance of military forces to guard the railways, necessary in a country so disorderly, was bound in the course of years to create friction and provoke animosity. We have only to think what our own position in South America would have been if the railways owned by the British had had to be guarded by British troops. The necessity of maintaining 15,000 soldiers to guard the South Manchurian Railway meant so many thousand points of potential trouble.

Americans are fond of saying that a railway is something more than two streaks of rust and a right of way. No treaty will suffice to secure its many and various needs in a country where officials and government are unfriendly. An illustration of this was given the writer by one of the directors of the S.M.R. which, under the treaties, controls a narrow strip on either side of the track, and wider areas surrounding the stations. At one of these stations no water is obtainable from the ground controlled by the Company for railway purposes, or for the domestic use of two hundred people who are housed there. An ample supply is available within a few miles; but the Chinese authorities refuse to concede the necessary way-leaves. The director added that twenty years ago his Company would have had no difficulty in the matter.

When Japan had acquired the railway from Russia, she realised that its value might be seriously injured by the building of competitive lines. She was trying to provide against this danger when in 1905 she bound China not to build in the neighbourhood of the S.M.R. any lines parallel to it or any branches prejudicial to its interests. In later agreements, notably in Article V. of the Twenty-One Demands, exacted in 1915, China was bound to give Japanese banks the preference in any loans raised for railway construction.

XXIX OCCUPATION OF MANCHURIA BY JAPAN

In accordance with these agreements arrangements were made at various times with the Manchurian Government for the construction of lines by the Chinese which were largely financed by Japanese money. The S.M.R. seems to have thought that these lines would act as feeders to their own; and that, in any case, superior management would secure the Japanese lines against competition. Events in the last two years have falsified those hopes. The fall in prices produced by world-wide conditions converted the profits of the S.M.R. into loss. The value of the yen based on gold operated to divert traffic to the lines where freights were charged in Manchurian currency. The construction of a port at Hulutao proved that the Manchurian Government was designing to divert the traffic of Manchuria from Japanese lines and ports to their own. In addition to all this the Chinese were failing to pay the interest and sinking fund on the money supplied by Japan for building the competitive lines. In these circumstances it is not to be wondered if the civilian directors of the S.M.R., who realise better than soldiers the dangers of alienating Chinese goodwill, should have begun to consider what steps were necessary to hold China to her obligations.

In the meantime the relative condition of order maintained in Manchuria by Chang Tso-lin had deteriorated under his youthful successor. As usual corruption was at work, creating domestic unrest. In their haste to get rich the rulers of Manchuria were buying the produce of the farmers in paper currency, which, printed as required, sank to a nominal value. The goods so purchased by officials lay rotting in heaps at the railway stations or were sold in the world markets for gold, some of which was actually stored in their cellars, though much, no doubt, was placed in the better security of foreign banks. Swindling transactions in real estate, which are always rife in pioneer countries unless carefully watched by government, proceeded without let or hindrance in the hands of officials themselves. All this was helping to enhance the unrest which the general fall in prices is producing all over the world. Large numbers of peasantry were ruined and the country was overrun with bandits, which of course increased the difficulties of the troops and police guarding the Japanese lines. The methodical staff began to compile a schedule of "unclosed incidents" which, when the rupture came in September 1931, were said to have reached three hundred in number.

Meanwhile the boycott of Japanese goods which was started throughout China in 1928, when Japan intervened in Shantung, had developed as it always does into an organised 'racket'. Bosses in control of boycott committees were allowing the sale of Japanese goods on payment of a charge to themselves. Though Japanese trade was proceeding, this blackmail constituted an irritating charge on the business which estranged merchants in Japan, the class normally in favour of friendly relations with China. By 1931 a storm was inevitable, but, as often happens, it arose from conditions of which little was known outside Manchuria.

In 1908 a Japanese Company had been organised under the name of the Oriental Development Corporation, to promote the settlement of Japanese peasants in Manchuria. It failed so signally in this object that it turned its attention to the settlement of Koreans. As Japanese subjects they were granted extraterritorial rights, and were thus exempted from the operation of Chinese laws and taxation. The Koreans were settled in colonies, loans were granted them, marketing facilities and also the protection of Japanese police.

In July 1931 one of these colonies twenty-five

XXIX OCCUPATION OF MANCHURIA BY JAPAN

miles north of Changchun was attacked by Chinese farmers, who complained that an irrigation canal dug by the Koreans interfered with their rights. Japanese police supported by troops were sent to protect the Korean settlers and Manchurian forces to support their opponents.

This incident was presently followed by a massacre in Korea of Chinese residents by a Korean mob. The boycott of Japanese goods was again intensified throughout China.

The Japanese Government was acutely anxious to arrive at a general settlement with China. On the 15th June 1931 *The Times* correspondent in Tokyo announced the formation of a joint committee to settle outstanding questions in Manchuria, and also the appointment of Count Uchida, a former Foreign Minister, as President of the South Manchurian Railway. On the 15th August the *New York Times* published the following telegram from Mr. Abend, its correspondent at Dairen:

> Although still expressing a hope that their policy of friendship and efforts toward co-operation will bring China to a responsive attitude, Japanese authorities in Manchuria are beginning to speculate on necessary steps if the conciliatory program does not bring results, for co-operation is impossible if only one party sincerely evinces a desire to co-operate. . . .
>
> This is the considered statement of Count Uchida and S. Eguchi, new President and Vice-President respectively of the Japanese-owned South Manchurian Railway. These officials here, after less than a month to survey the difficult political and depressed economic conditions, are representatives of the Minseito party which attained power in Tokyo by opposing the "forward policy" of the Seiyukai party. . . . Mr. Eguchi declares that, if necessary, Japan will discipline certain military, merchant and young patriot groups in South Manchuria which are openly advocating abandonment of the policy of patience and demanding that "China be made to account for her trespasses on Japan's treaty privileges".

This significant reference by a Japanese statesman to the need for restraining chauvinist groups in Manchuria cannot be ignored in any attempt to arrive at an impartial estimate of recent events in Manchuria. A widespread impression exists that the task of the directors and also of the Japanese Government in handling these difficulties has been complicated by intrigues on the part of comparatively junior officers of the Japanese army. Under Chang Tso-lin, with his forcible methods, life and property were perhaps better protected in Manchuria than in China south of the Wall. Undoubtedly this strong-willed ruler incurred the hostility of some Japanese officers. As we have seen in a previous chapter, his train was bombed as it was crossing under the Japanese line outside Mukden, and he perished in the explosion. The Tanaka Government subsequently fell, as the result of a debate in the Japanese Diet, in which it was stated that the murder was planned by Japanese officers.

It will help us to keep our sense of proportion in considering this and similar incidents in Manchuria if we recall to our minds the Jameson raid in 1896. No reasonable person supposes that the British Cabinet in London, the High Commissioner, or the Military Staff at Cape Town were privy to the Jameson raid. Rhodes knew of the scheme, but the actual raid was started in direct violation of his telegraphed orders by subordinate civil and military officials, who hoped and believed that the British Government would condone a breach of discipline if it succeeded.

While the theory that the murder of Chang Tso-lin was planned and accomplished by Japanese officers cannot be dismissed, there is nothing to suggest that either the Japanese Government or the general staff were accessories before the fact. His death, however, removed from Manchuria a ruler who declined to follow the rôle assigned to him. He regarded himself as the real bulwark of China against Communism and also the tyranny of the Kuomintang. In pursuit of these objects he made himself master of China south of the Wall and north of the Yangtze. The Japanese Government objected to his meddling with China south of the Wall because they realised that the corollary of such action would be the intervention of the Government of China north of the Wall. He deliberately chose this adventure in preference to the part which Japan wished him to play—that of ruling the three eastern provinces under her watchful eye.

The Government of Manchuria, weakened by the death of Chang Tso-lin, was a prey to still more mysterious intrigues. The two ablest officers of this Government were his chief of staff, Yang Yu Ting, and the head of the railway administration, Chang Yin Huai. They were both summarily executed without trial by the Young Marshal, who was somehow led to believe that these two competent officials were plotting to destroy their own master. A theory is prevalent in China that their removal was brought about by the same chain of causes which led to the removal of Chang Tso-lin himself.

That the management of the Chinese railways in Manchuria gravely deteriorated when the personal and vigorous control of Chang Yin Huai was removed is not in quesiton. Corruption was rampant and relations with the Japanese railways rapidly moved to a crisis. On the Chinese side a double game of evasion was played which ended by exhausting Japanese patience. Manchurian officials would pose as underlings unable to take definite decisions; but when matters were carried to the Young Marshal, he would often refer them back to subordinates. On occasion he would say that the point at issue must be discussed with the Foreign Department of the Government of China at Nanking.

Facts which are not in dispute at any rate point to this lesson, that wherever government in China is weakened its foreign relations become more critical. Unless a Foreign Power is prepared to govern the country itself, the only policy which offers any hope of stable conditions is to strengthen the native government, and not to weaken it.

On the 17th August the Japanese War Office issued a statement reporting the murder of Captain Nakamura, a Japanese officer, on the 27th June, by Chinese soldiers. On the 9th September *The Times* correspondent in Tokyo reported that a squadron of six army planes, in a practice flight round the Japanese Alps, had dropped 100,000 leaflets calling on the nation to awaken to the dangers menacing Japanese rights in Manchuria. The Cabinet were considering this action on the part of the military.

On the 18th September the South Manchurian Railway was cut near Mukden. Whether the act was perpetrated by Chinese, as the Japanese say, or by Japanese soldiers, as the Chinese assert, may never be known, and does not greatly matter. Japanese forces at once occupied Mukden and burned the barracks after killing a number of Chinese soldiers there. Steps for occupying various strategic points in Manchuria were rapidly taken by Japanese troops, obviously in accordance with a carefully pre-arranged plan which was skilfully executed.

The action of the military led to a Cabinet crisis in Tokyo and ere long to a change of Government, which displaced the Baron Shidehara from the Foreign Office. The question whether the army and navy are really subject to civilian control has still to be settled in Japan. For the moment the nation responded to its instinct to present a united front in the presence of an international crisis. The policy adopted was so far as possible that which Soviet Russia had successfully followed. The Japanese

XXIX OCCUPATION OF MANCHURIA BY JAPAN

Government insisted that the matter was one for settlement with the Government of China without the interference of third parties. Japan, however, was a member of the League, which happened to be in session at the moment, and China at once appealed to the Council of which she as well as Japan was a member. The United States reminded both of their obligations under the Kellogg Pact. Japan disclaimed any intention of annexing Manchuria, but none the less proceeded by force of arms to establish for herself in Southern Manchuria the same kind of control that England had acquired over Egypt at the end of the last century. A great deal of sporadic fighting took place, whether with bandits or with Manchurian troops. Marshal Chang Hsüeh-liang remained at Peiping and Japan refused to recognise the continuance of his Government in Manchuria. The Japanese staff are now engaged on the task of organising Chinese authorities in Manchuria under their own control.

The League was thus faced with the problem of preventing a declaration of war between two states, members of the Council itself. Such a failure would weaken if not destroy the faith of the world in the League's capacity to avoid wars, and might render abortive the Disarmament Conference due to meet in a few months. The world's recovery from economic depression largely depends on the outcome of this Conference. The results which followed the murder of an Austrian Archduke are still in men's minds. The efficacy of the Kellogg Pact as well as of the League is at stake. The vast implications of a local fracas in the wilds of Manchuria are becoming apparent. But the world is slower to realise that behind such incidents is a fundamental condition—that anarchy in so large a section of human society as China is a standing menace to the peace of the world.

The Institute of Pacific Relations had accepted

the invitation of its Chinese members to hold the fourth Pacific Conference in China in October 1931. The obviously convenient place was Shanghai, but the Chinese feeling against holding the Conference in the International Settlement had been so decisive that its choice was not even considered. The place selected was Hangchow, at which large and expensive preparations had been made. The delegates from America, Australia, Canada, England, the Philippines and New Zealand were on their way to China when the rupture in Manchuria occurred on the 18th September 1931. It was so clear that the Japanese members could not be asked to come to Hangchow that the Chinese Council boldly decided to change the venue to Shanghai, and to hold the fourth Pacific Conference in the International Settlement, the only place in China to which their Japanese colleagues could be brought with reasonable safety. There, with the two countries on the verge of war, the Pacific Council met on the 13th October and the Conference opened its sessions on the 21st. A general understanding was reached that members should avoid discussing the actual incidents which had led to the crisis. They agreed to confine the discussion to the fundamental and historical causes which had led to a conflict of Chinese and Japanese interests in Manchuria. Avoiding attempts to allocate blame, they examined the facts of the situation and came to realise that nothing but conflict could issue from such conditions as had developed in Manchuria. They applied their minds to the question how these conditions could be modified so as to harmonise the interests of China and Japan, instead of provoking conflicts between them. These discussions soon pointed to the want of such detailed and exact information as would make it possible to answer such questions.

The discussion of the Shanghai question at the

XXIX OCCUPATION OF MANCHURIA BY JAPAN 237

second Conference in 1927 had led to the same difficulty when Professor Hornbeck suggested that a comprehensive survey of the whole question ought to be made by some qualified and impartial authority. The Feetham inquiry was the outcome of Professor Hornbeck's suggestion. At the fourth Conference both Chinese and Japanese members advanced the idea of applying the same procedure to Manchuria. It was even suggested that a neutral person or commission might be asked to survey the whole field of China's relations to Japan. In the groups from either country were members in touch with their Government. Ideas are exceedingly portable, and it was, perhaps, no mere coincidence that Japan proposed to the Council of the League a plan already familiar to the Government of China which led to the appointment of the Lytton Commission. This Commission might produce a report destined to exercise as permanent and decisive an influence on the mutual relations of China and Japan and also on their several domestic policies as the Durham Report has had on the mutual relations and internal policies of Canada and Great Britain in the ninety years since it was published.

CHAPTER XXX

REACTIONS OF THE CRISIS ON CHINA

THE reactions of the Manchurian incident in China remain to be traced. The Government of Nanking, like that of Tokyo, was taken by surprise by the military coup of the 18th September. It at once adopted a course, which was wise as well as correct, of filing an appeal to the Council of the League, at this moment in session at Geneva.

In the great cities of China popular resentment was approaching the flash-point. Relations with Japanese were severed in every department of life. It was more than a boycott of trade. Shops were refusing to sell provisions to Japanese residents. Bankers suspended financial transactions with Japanese firms at a loss to themselves. A public subscription had been raised in Japan, supported by a gift from the Emperor, to send to the flooded areas a ship loaded with food, medical stores and workers. On the 21st September the Chinese Government refused to accept it. As the ship returned with its load to Japan the angels of peace and goodwill amongst men must have wept.

The Chinese Government did everything in its power to protect Japanese subjects, and largely succeeded in doing so. But as usual the students got out of hand. On the 28th September a number of students at Shanghai seized a train, and made their way to Nanking. Combining there with the local students, till their numbers reached 5000, they shadowed by the more serious struggle on the Yangtze to which they directly led. Those struggles will certainly enhance the difficulty that the Japanese Government will find in controlling Manchuria through a Chinese government obedient to its wishes.

No attempt to deal more fully with very recent events would serve the purposes for which this book is written. These events, however, have already fulfilled one of its purposes, which was to convince readers that the state of China cannot be further neglected without risk to the whole structure of human society. The League of Nations has been in continual session for months. In America events in the Far East are filling the public mind no less than the economic depression.

As to the number of combatants and civilians killed in the fighting about Shanghai, no trustworthy figures have been given. The struggle has diverted the funds set apart by the Chinese Government for repairing damage done by the flood last year. The breaches in dykes will go unrepaired, and vast areas of the richest soil in China will be flooded when the river rises again. This only is certain, that a far greater number of people are fated to perish by starvation than the thousands who have lost their lives in the struggle at Shanghai.

PART II
COMMENT

CHAPTER XXXI

OUR OWN RECORD CONSIDERED

THROUGHOUT these years of disaster and humiliation the exports and imports of China, as shown by the maritime customs, have slowly but steadily increased. With unconquerable courage this multitude of men has continued to work when a people less inured to misfortune would have abandoned the prospect of reaping fruits of their labour as hopeless.

On the other hand, as Tawney shows, the *per capita* output of the Chinese worker is deplorably low. In spite of his skill, industry and persistence, he produces less than one-thirtieth of the wealth produced per head by the people of Canada and the U.S.A. His natural industry is probably greater than theirs; but the Chinese worker is hampered by want of equipment, and the absence of almost every external condition that makes for production. If railways and roads alone were extended the output of China would grow by leaps and bounds, and so would her power to consume goods imported from abroad. The people are so many, and their industry so great, that a general improvement in all their conditions would yield a volume of wealth large enough to effect the economy of the world.

The converse is equally true. One-fifth part of the human race cannot continue in a state of increasing anarchy without affecting the entire structure of human society. Reports of Chinese perishing in numbers comparable to those of the Great War have almost ceased to arouse our emotions. Yet, as Tawney brings home to us, the millions destroyed by recurring wars, famines and floods are incidents only of their normal condition—a condition in which most of the Chinese live in sight of calamity. He compares them to men standing in a pool up to their necks and knowing that any disturbance of the water will drown them. It is difficult to think of any other place in the world, or period of its history, at which men in such numbers have faced the shadow of impending catastrophe. The amazing fecundity of the people continues to supply fresh food for a ravenous death-rate. The darkness of the tragedy is relieved only by their natural cheerfulness.

The obvious remedies, which Tawney indicates, are (first and foremost) a rapid extension of railways and roads, the application of science to agriculture, education, co-operative organisation, the prevention of floods and droughts by embanking rivers and by irrigation, control of emigration, the development of industry, and an international loan to finance these services. The need for such measures is not in dispute: all competent observers agree as to their nature, and as to the order in which to apply them. But the practical difficulty of applying any of them is the same in every case, the absence of any government which can govern.

The same condition defeats every attempt to stabilise the relations of China with the rest of the world. The policy adopted by the Powers at Washington was based on the expectation that China would create for herself a government able to execute as well as to negotiate treaties. Her failure to do so has rendered that policy abortive. The real obstacle to cancelling the unequal treaties is the patent inability of her government to protect life and property, or fulfil the terms of new treaties made to replace them. Inability to control its own officials, to maintain order, or observe treaty engagements, is largely responsible for the troubles in Manchuria. The difficulty which the League of Nations has in handling those troubles is explained by the fact that the Covenant presupposes in its members a power to govern. China as a member of the League lacks that essential qualification. It is time to recognise the broad fact that friendly relations with any country are possible only in so far as its government is able to discharge the duties imposed on it by treaties and international law. The appalling social conditions in China, the insolvency of her government, the unequal treaties, the aggression of Japan, are symptoms only. Experts differ as to their treatment, which at best would relieve local irritation. The radical disease which underlies them is not in dispute.

As to this all competent observers are agreed; but the point is too often discussed as though the people of China alone were to blame. We are apt to forget that her present condition is directly due to our own insistence on trading with her. Our duty in the matter is not discharged by constantly reading her lectures. The question for us is what we ourselves have left undone, and ought to be doing. Our official answer to that question is the Treaty signed by the nine Powers at Washington in which we pledged ourselves

> to provide the fullest and most unembarrassed opportunity to China to develop and maintain for herself an effective and stable government.

Subject to this condition the nine Powers were pledged to revise the unequal treaties.

As seen in a previous chapter, this policy was not at the time acceptable to many of our own fellow-countrymen in the Treaty Ports. It must here be added that this statement does not apply to a number of men in the great banks and mercantile houses whose responsible positions compelled them to take a wider outlook. The change of policy effected at Washington was in fact partly due to the influence of leaders in the business world. But the great majority of British residents in the Treaty Ports regarded the new policy with cynicism. Concerned in the task of earning their own living, they naturally felt that more business could be done if only existing treaties were enforced by gunboats as in the days of the Manchu dynasty. They did not sufficiently realise how fruitless such a policy must prove where a government no longer exists which is competent to execute the treaties. Opinion, as crystallised in the clubs of the Treaty Ports, was openly hostile to the policy of their own country, and, as we have seen, our system provides no kind of political leadership for our own people. The views current in these circles were expressed and emphasised by their own Press, and reflected in the papers at home, whose news of China largely originates in the offices of papers in the Treaty Ports. In recent years a marked improvement has taken place in the attitude of our Press in China, both as regards British policy and towards the Chinese. But still much of the news which comes from China is coloured by the chronic irritation which Europeans who are trying to earn their living in the difficult state of that country can scarcely avoid. When the man in the club saw Japan enforcing her claims, in what he felt was the good old style, he could not but rejoice that the world was at last getting back to realities. This attitude reflected in the London Press has had its effect in encouraging Japan to believe that the Washington Treaties could be safely ignored. The long-standing failure to reconcile British opinion in China with official policy is not without serious results.

The officials to whom the conduct of our policy has long been entrusted are men of ability with a real sympathy for China, a little wanting in the attitude they sometimes assume to their own nationals in that country. They saw clearly enough that in this century the gunboat policy of the last generation was certain to defeat its own objects, and must be discarded. Their contempt for the views of the man in the club was undisguised. The unilateral note of December 1926 reaffirming the Washington policy was issued as much for his benefit as for the Foreign Powers, and rightly so. But between political and commercial circles in China the personal factor has always been wanting.

There is no great difficulty in agreeing with any government in China to abolish unequal treaties, if British negotiators are really able to ignore the views of their own people in the country. It is even possible to negotiate new treaties which must be ratified before the old ones can be cancelled. But what is to happen, when all this is done, if it should prove that no government in China exists which is capable of executing the terms of the new treaties, or even of protecting the persons and property of foreigners resident in the country? These questions point to the fact that revision of treaties was only the secondary condition of the Washington policy. The first condition was "to provide the fullest and most unembarrassed opportunity to China to develop and maintain for herself an effective and stable government". It behoves us to consider what we have done in recent years to fulfil this essential pledge. Our best answer will be found in the stand we made to secure tariff autonomy for China. The additional revenue secured to the Nationalist Government at Nanking, largely at the instance of British diplomacy, was the main factor in enabling that Government to exist as long as it did.

In 1928 there was real hope that Chiang Kai-shek and T. V. Soong, unquestionably the ablest leaders in China, would establish a government competent to execute as well as negotiate treaties. The Powers decided to recognise them as such, and, for the moment, their position was immensely strengthened by this recognition. The effect, however, was rapidly destroyed as China realised that the Powers had no intention of moving their Ministers to Nanking. The conclusion was naturally drawn that they did not really believe in the Government they had recognised. The interest of the Tuchuns in seizing and controlling the ancient seat of Imperial power began to revive. No act on the part of the Powers could have done more to deprive a new and inexperienced government of prestige in a country where "face" is of primary importance.

The British and American Governments are both in the habit of insisting on non-interference with China's domestic affairs. But to recognise a government and then to ignore its choice of a capital, was to challenge a decision which rested with the Government of China and with no one else. An ostentatious refusal to act on the part of one government may at times derange the internal affairs of another to a more serious extent than positive action. "A froward retention of custom is a more turbulent thing than change itself."

Except for one article in *The Times* on the 8th July 1930, a great silence has existed with reference to the subject on this side of the world. It has not often been raised even in papers published in China. Such references as I have been able to find are appended to Chapter XXIII. From them the reader can judge for himself the reasons behind this policy. The official reason for not sending the Foreign Ministers to reside at Nanking, so far as I have been able to ascertain it, is the cost of providing them with suitable establishments, which would all be wasted if, as might well happen, the seat of government were again changed. Such establishments in the primitive wilderness of Nanking would take years to construct. But must we accept the position that the functions of diplomacy in a country like China cannot be conducted in Legations less imposing than those of Peiping? When in 1924 Tokyo was reduced by an earthquake to a wilder desolation than exists in Nanking, it was not suggested that ambassadors should be housed at Kyoto, Nara or wherever some dignified residence could be found at a distance from the capital. In the case of the British Embassy, a building of corrugated iron lined with wood was provided by the Office of Works. Till September 1931 the British Ambassador and his staff lived and worked in these flimsy buildings, just as for many years the Viceroys lived in temporary structures when the capital of India was moved to Delhi. The cost of clearing the site and erecting the temporary buildings was approximately £23,000. The ruins left by the earthquake had of course to be cleared in any case; so the cost of housing the British Embassy during this period cannot have cost the British taxpayer more than about £3000 a year. The cost of acquiring the existing Embassy in Moscow was £40,000 in addition to an annual rent of £4500 per annum. The building at Leningrad previously used was held only on a lease which was not renewed. Had the British Government owned this house, one wonders whether it would have been thought advisable, when the Soviet Government was recognised at Moscow, to keep the Ambassador at Leningrad 400 miles from the Government to which he was accredited.

Had similar steps been taken at Nanking when the Government there was recognised, an actual saving might have been realised by the British Treasury. The maintenance of the British Legation at the inland city of Peiping involves also the maintenance of a whole battalion at Tientsin, the nearest point on the coast. The cost for 1932, which appears on the estimates of the War Office, is £170,000. The transfer of the Minister and his staff to Nanking would render this safeguard superfluous; for at Nanking the Legation would lie under the guns of British battleships, which its occupants could board if serious danger threatened.

When the Government was recognised at Nanking the Foreign Powers would certainly have refused to express any view as to where the capital of China should be fixed. In Legation circles, however, a definite view was taken that the choice of Nanking was an error which time and experience would correct. Importance was attached to the fact that Peiping is nearer to the centre of the whole area, including Manchuria and Mongolia, which the Government of China purports to control. The Government at Nanking might be overthrown by some leader north of the Yangtze who would take the capital back to Peiping. By remaining there Ministers could preserve an attitude of detachment in viewing the whole situation, avoid too close a connection with any one party and escape the influence of "the Shanghai mind". For the British Legation to take the initiative and move to Nanking, would diminish its contact with other Legations, so long as they stayed at Peiping, and so impair the united front to which the greatest importance was attached. That the British Minister himself was not brought into personal contact with the Foreign Minister at Nanking till subordinates there were able to report that agreement was in sight, was considered a positive advantage.

Answers to which these arguments are open will occur to those who have read these pages. The first condition of unity in China is effective unity south of the Wall, and can anyone now conceive a government located in Peiping really controlling Canton and the provinces south of the Yangtze?

The argument that at any moment some Tuchun might overthrow the Nationalist Government and bring the capital back to Peiping, and that Foreign Powers must avoid close connections with any "party", shows how little the recognition of the Nationalist Government was felt to mean. As to fear of "the Shanghai mind" and its influence, one can scarcely conceive a Cromer or Milner asking to be kept aloof from Cairo, Alexandria, Kimberley or Johannesburg on grounds like these. They recognised that to educate and lead their compatriots, domiciled in the country, was their primary duty. When peace was declared in South Africa, Milner could easily have proved on paper that his future duties could best be discharged in the comfortable and dignified surroundings of Cape Town, through Lieutenant-Governors in the Transvaal and the Orange River Colony. He saw clearly, however, that his presence was needed in the north. He chose as his residence a private house in Johannesburg, for the reason that, even in Pretoria, he could not properly lead and control the great commercial and mining community of his own fellow-countrymen on the Witwatersrand.

The argument that the British Minister should remain at Peiping, and not visit Nanking until his subordinates had arranged some settlement of matters in hand, suggests a confusion between the position proper for a Minister accredited to a foreign government, and that appropriate to a Secretary of State. It is generally agreed that before members of two or more foreign governments should meet in conference, the matters at issue should be brought near to agreement by permanent officials. It has not elsewhere been suggested that ambassadors must delay visiting the governments to whom they are accredited till minor officials have completed all but the formal negotiations. Since the Government was recognised at Nanking, the Legation at Peiping has tended to become a secondary foreign office.

As we have seen, Sun Yat Sen realised how difficult it would be for China to establish a government for herself, unless she had foreign advice and assistance. Progressive members of the Nanking Government were eager to obtain it, and advisers were engaged from America, Germany, England, Geneva and even Japan. Their reactionary colleagues resented the presence of these advisers, especially those from the League of Nations. The secession to Canton was partly due to this feeling.

The advisers produced a number of admirable plans for financial, agricultural, industrial, educational and sanitary reform. The advice most needed, however, was in matters of high policy. An initial mistake, which led to the present crisis, was the seizure of the Chinese Eastern Railway. The young inexperienced Government imagined that any rebuff administered to the Communist Government of Russia would be welcomed by the great capitalist Powers. Had the Foreign Ministers been in close personal touch with the members of the Government at Nanking they must have known their intentions in time to correct this mistaken idea and dissuade them from making so dangerous a blunder. It is hard to believe that things could have come to so desperate a pass as they now have if through these three critical years the Government of China had been in daily and personal touch with the Ministers of the leading Powers.

In countries like France, Italy or America, the duties of a foreign representative are mainly to inform his own Government, and act as the vehicle of communications from them to the Government to which he is accredited. But a country undergoing a crisis so violent that its foreign relations are affected has at times found in a foreign representative its best friend and wisest adviser. I once had the privilege of meeting Mr. Dwight Morrow, and asked him to tell me what he did as Ambassador to Mexico and how he did it. The story which he told me in two hours might provide the most interesting chapter in his biography, and show what one government can do to help another to restore internal order if both are advised by a representative who can rise to the occasion. Dwight Morrow never lost sight of the fact that in Mexico the supreme interest of his own country was a government that could govern. He realised that the profits to be made by selling munitions to Mexicans to destroy each other were, as a mere matter of business, of little value compared with the trade which America might do in a country at peace with itself, and realising its full capacity for production. He was able to convince leaders of business of this in America as well as his Government. His attitude on the subject impressed me, for I had lately crossed the Pacific with the agent of a great American oil company who asserted with confidence that a certain Tuchun was about to attack the National Government. When asked why he felt so sure, he explained that he had just sold to this Tuchun a vast quantity of motor spirit. In negotiating the order he had learned the number of military lorries which American firms had sold to the Tuchun. On arriving at San Francisco we learned that the agent's deduction that this preparation of military transport was meant to be used in attacking the Government of China was correct.

It seemed to me strange that Governments pledged "to provide the fullest and most unembarrassed opportunity to China to develop and maintain for herself an effective and stable Government" should allow their nationals to assist military leaders in mobilising armies against the Government they had recognised. The answer given to this question, when I put it both in Washington and London, was decisive. No munitions were allowed to be sold by American or British nationals in China, except on certificates signed by the Chinese Ministers in Washington and London. Motor-lorries and spirit to drive them were not munitions. One felt that a Dwight Morrow would have found some way of convincing, not only the Governments concerned, but the dozen men on each side of the Atlantic who control the production of motors and oil, that to make money by equipping rebels to devastate China was not business in the true sense of the word. There are no limits to the oil and vehicles which China could buy if once peace and order were established and her highly industrious people were allowed to produce the goods to pay for them.

One incident lives in my memory which Mr. Dwight Morrow mentioned, an incident which, on the surface, seems to tell in the opposite direction. A time came when, in his judgement, the Government of Mexico was strong enough to deal with the rebels without any sort of assistance from outside. He felt that by doing so their position would be far stronger than if the support that America was giving them were continued. He therefore persuaded the Government of Mexico to ask the United States to lift the embargo on arms. His advice was taken, and justified by the results. What impressed me in this incident was the influence he must have acquired with the Mexican Government. In accepting such advice the Mexican Government showed infinite confidence not only in the judgement but also in the friendship of this foreigner.

Incidentally he mentioned that he could not remember a single day during his tenure of office in Mexico when he had not spent at least two hours with one or other of the Mexican ministers. In thinking over this conversation I felt that one with the gifts of Dwight Morrow might leave a deeper mark on history as American Minister to China even than as President of the United States.

It is common knowledge that the German Government, in the darkest period after the Treaty of Versailles, constantly relied on the sympathy and advice of Lord D'Abernon and Mr. Houghton. We ourselves have reason to know how a great ambassador, by helping the government to which he is accredited, may render the best service to his own. In the early days of the Great War the danger that British Orders in Council might bring the United States into the struggle against England, as in 1812, was a very real one. The danger was increased by the fact that cotton was a necessary ingredient in high explosives, and the party in power at Washington drew its strength from the cotton-producing states. Had America been represented in London by a pedant obsessed with the technicalities of international law, American feeling might easily have been inflamed to the point of a war. Page realised that the freedom of the world was at stake, and would presently be threatened in America itself if England, France and their allies were crushed by the Central Powers. He set himself to teach the British Government how to handle his own Government and people. No American ambassador has ever rendered a greater service to his own country than Page in averting a war between the British and American Commonwealths.

The most apposite instance of all, perhaps, is Townshend Harris. His single-handed achievement in persuading Japan to open her doors to trade was greater than Admiral Perry's with his fleet behind him; greater far than if Perry had used his guns to shell Yokohama into submission. As sure as the day follows the night, a time will come when the people of Japan will look on her present policy[1] as we in England now look on the policy pursued in America by George III. and Lord North. She will realise her destiny in sending to represent her in China a statesman chosen for his fitness to do for that country what Townshend Harris did for Japan in the crisis of her fate. This will happen when England and America have learned to send statesmen to China with explicit instructions to seek first, last and only the interests of that vast section of human society, knowing that as they achieve that end the interests of England and America will be added unto it.

[1] When this chapter was already in print I noticed in the *North China Daily News* the summary of an article written by Mr. Gyokujo Hanzawa, editor of the *Diplomatic Review* in Japan. The correspondent of the *North China Daily News* evidently thinks that this article reflects the view of those who are for the present directing the policy of Japan. I have decided to print his summary as an Appendix at the end of this book. (See p. 305.)

CHAPTER XXXII

THE CONSULAR AND DIPLOMATIC SERVICES

THE machinery through which effect is given to our policy in China must now be examined a little more closely. British subjects were exempted, by the Treaty of Nanking, from the laws of China, and rendered amenable to those of their own country as administered by their consuls in the Treaty Ports. This led to the establishment of a special Consular Service, recruited by competitive examination. Vacancies in this Service are open to the most successful candidates, for whom there is no room in the Home Civil Service and the Indian Civil Service. They are youths of more than average ability so far as ability can be tested in this way. For several years they are sent to Peiping to learn the language as student interpreters, and are then posted as assistants to consuls to learn their administrative duties. Thoroughly versed in the language and literature of China, they often acquire a deep affection for its people. Unlike the members of the Indian Service, their principal task is not to govern, but rather to administer highly technical treaties. Though paid on the same scale as the rest of the consular service, they are seldom if ever promoted to the more desirable posts outside China, because their knowledge of the language is needed in that country. They are thus penalised by reason of their special qualifications, with the result that in later life the abler members of this Service often resign and accept more lucrative appointments under the wealthy firms and syndicates which do business in China.

It is only in exceptional circumstances that consuls are promoted to responsible posts in the field of diplomacy, which are somewhat jealously reserved to members of the Foreign Office. Sir Harry Parkes, Sir John Jordan and Sir Sidney Barton are exceptions which prove the rule. But the Foreign Office cannot afford to dispense with the special knowledge of the Consular Service. One of its senior members is posted as Chinese secretary to the British Minister at Peiping, another to the Far Eastern Department at its office in Downing Street. Their knowledge as experts is often the dominant factor in Government decisions. The status and rewards accorded to this Service have no proper relation to the burdens imposed on it, or to the influence it wields.

Like the Indian Civil Service, the Consular Service in China is scrupulously loyal to the Government it serves. As highly trained and intelligent men, they cannot avoid having views of their own, as do members of the I.C.S., and their view as a body unquestionably is that the present disorders in China are destined to continue indefinitely. Towards the close of his life, this view was held by Sir John Jordan himself, whose outstanding ability raised him from the Consular Service to the post of Minister at Peking.

This view of the situation implies the conviction that nothing effective can be done to help China to establish a government for herself; and no one is greatly interested in trying to do anything unless they believe that it can be done. None the less, action of some kind has to be taken to justify the Washington policy and give effect to the promise of treaty revision offered to China. Treaties, with all their

XXXII CONSULAR AND DIPLOMATIC SERVICES 261

technique, are a field more familiar to Diplomatic and Consular Services alike than the structure and working of government. Treaty revision is, moreover, the constant and urgent demand of the Chinese Nationalist, and a genuine sympathy with Chinese Nationalism exists in official circles. The upshot has been an attempt to express the Washington policy in treaty revision without reference to the question how far there is likely to be any government in China competent to execute as well as to negotiate treaties.

Our policy has thus developed in a gathering atmosphere of unreality, the essential product of China and its ultimate curse. On p. 21 of his pamphlet, *Chinese Colonization and the Development of Manchuria*, Mr. Walter Young refers to "a characteristic weakness of administrative methods in China", and adds these pregnant words:

> The form having been executed, the fact, ostensibly to be achieved thereby, is assumed to have been achieved.

The instinct to study appearance and ignore reality, the importance attached to 'face', lies at the root of much trouble in China. Her warmest friends are agreed on this point. It is this more than anything which impedes her in establishing a government competent to maintain order at home and stable relations abroad. If we really intend to help her, it can only be done by keeping realities in the foreground in all our relations with her. An instinct for realities, stronger than exists in most nations, explains, I believe, the place which the English have filled in history. For that reason alone we can help China in her difficulties if we only remember that just as a fuller sense of realities can be gained, so also it can be lost. I have in mind a word spoken to me by a wise Englishman who held a responsible position in India. "The mistake", he said, "that we English too often make is in thinking we can manage the Indians by adopting their ideas instead of our own. We think to command their respect by pretentious establishments, uniforms and ceremony. The real contribution which the English can make to India is in trusting to those qualities for which we stand, and in which the East through its past history is wanting—directness, an instinct for truth, simplicity."

These words were lately recalled to my mind in conversation with an Indian friend who was speaking with a passionate reverence of a certain Viceroy. I asked him why this particular Englishman inspired these feelings. "I can answer your question best", he said, "by telling you a story which is typical of the man. The Viceroy was to meet a number of distinguished Indians at the Government House of a certain province. When he entered the reception room he found himself and his staff in a vacant space marked off from the rest of the room by a red cord. Beyond the cord the guests were collected with the intention that one by one they should be brought to converse with him. The Viceroy glanced round the room, then walked to the red cord and, stooping, passed under it, to mix and converse with the Indian gentlemen waiting to meet him, as though they were friends in his own house."

In religion ritual develops as the spiritual faculty of its hierarchy decays. In government the growth of ceremony betrays in rulers an unconscious distrust of their own capacity to command authority.

In China, as in India, our standing danger is a subtle tendency to adopt a Chinese habit of mind. Do we or do we not believe that China can be helped to govern herself? If we do believe it, is it really in the interest of China to abolish the Settlements in which some leading Chinese are learning by actual practice what the rule of law and self-government means? In India we have laid the foundations of self-government by establishing the rule of law, till the people have learned to understand it and count on it. Our greatest achievement is the judiciary, in which there are Indian judges whom members of the English Bench would be proud to recognise as colleagues. No Chinese judge has ever sat on the Bench in Hongkong. Had we faith in the future of China, that little colony might have been used as a school of self-government and have given to China leaders experienced in its methods. As it is, our position in Hongkong remains one of the greatest opportunities which the British Commonwealth has missed.

To do anything effective in China we must get down to the facts and build on the facts. The Feetham Report was a real contribution to that end. A flood of light was thrown on the very centre of the whole situation. The *Manchester Guardian*, the English paper most friendly to China, recognised that unqualified rendition before China had established effective self-government for herself was not in her interests. The Report was the first authoritative survey of conditions in China ever given to the public in England, where it made a profound impression. But why was a task like this left to the Council of the International Settlement? Why, years before, had the costly official machinery in China done nothing to reveal the situation or suggest the appropriate treatment? On the contrary, this machinery, of whose long inaction the Chinese Government had complained, was mobilised just as the inquiry was nearing completion. The text of a treaty containing provisions in direct opposition to the larger conclusions of the Feetham Report was actually settled when its findings were known in China, but when only one of the four instalments had reached England.

CHAPTER XXXIII

BRITISH POLICY REVIEWED IN THE LIGHT OF THE BOXER INDEMNITY SETTLEMENT

INTERESTS so large and permanent as those of Great Britain in China are inseparable from those of China. In advancing her welfare we advance our own. But in order to do this we must form clear and definite conceptions of her real needs, and how we can help to meet them. By adopting the Chinese habit of putting appearance before reality, we are doing a greater mischief to China than to ourselves. The settlement of the Boxer Indemnity needs to be brought to the test of these principles.

Deficiency of power in the Government of China to make treaties really effective is not the only factor which vitiates their relations with the rest of the world. There is still in the Chinese mind a conception of laws, contracts and treaties which differs from ours. This difference has upset the balance of their ancient civilisation, and we might have done more to restore it if we had better understood the distinctive nature of our own. Our financiers and missionaries familiarised the people of China with our knowledge of physical forces. We showed them how to build and operate mechanism moved by steam and electric energy. The missionary colleges taught them chemistry, physics and mechanics, and the science which underlies the practice of medicine and agriculture. The merchants taught them how to organise business and industry on Western lines. In doing all this their ancient system of government was rendered obsolete and fell into ruins. Not even the missionaries seem to have realised that the oldest and greatest achievement of Western civilisation was in the sphere of human relations, in the science and art of controlling the position in society of one man to another and of one group to another. A better knowledge of how this is done in the West would have helped China to adjust her system to the changes which Western methods of business and mechanical knowledge were forcing upon her. In the schools and colleges established in China too little was done to acquaint the rising generation with the methods and standards of justice applied in the West, or to make them realise that popular institutions must rest, and can only rest, on the rule of law.

The reader may remember how this subject was mentioned on an earlier page.[1] In the West a steady advance (though with frequent retreats) has been made in legal precision, in the art of expressing statutes and agreements in such manner as to make clear what is to happen under their provisions. The idea has also developed, especially with ourselves, that laws and agreements are to be carried out as they stand, and therefore that laws and agreements should enjoin only that which can in practice be rendered effective.

In the history of Chinese civilisation, so much older than our own, and at certain periods so much more advanced, there was nothing to develop these conceptions. To the British mind a law or contract prescribes what is to be done, and therefore what can be done. To the Chinese mind laws or contracts present an ideal to which all parties should try to approach, but which no one is really expected to attain, at any rate for the present. The Municipal

[1] See Chap. I, p. 15.

Council of Shanghai was anxious to enforce in the area under its authority laws promulgated by the Government of China. But the factory laws framed by the Legislative Yuan were designed for conditions such as exist in countries like Switzerland, England or the United States. If enforced in Shanghai the factories would have to be closed, just as the British laws of to-day, had they been applied a century ago, would have brought industry to a standstill, instead of reforming it. The Municipal Council shrunk from recognising laws as operative until their actual enforcement was possible.

These impressions were gathered in conversation with Chinese friends anxious to make me see how the legal conceptions of China differed from those of the West. They naturally felt that both conceptions were entitled to respect—that their own, at any rate, was appropriate to China.

On this latter point I am unconvinced. I have no more hope for a system of medicine that ignores the principle of metabolism than I have for a polity which fails to recognise even in principle the importance of confining law to what is enforceable, and of then enforcing it. A society can exist which ignores these principles, but not happily or well, especially when in contact with peoples who recognise them; and such is the present condition of China.

In commercial life contracts present a similar difficulty. When a Chinese merchant has failed to perform a contract he will point with sincerity to the fact that things have happened which were not foreseen when the contract was signed. He has not realised that the object of a contract is to assure all parties to it that certain things will happen, whatever else does or does not happen in a future which cannot be wholly foreseen. Contracts are intended to reduce the element of uncertainty in human affairs, and lose their virtue unless all parties can count on their willing execution or enforcement by the State. The knowledge that contracts can and will be enforced usually renders their enforcement by courts unnecessary. In societies where contracts are not enforceable, the standard of honour which rules in business declines. Foreign merchants in China are now refusing to engage in business if the contracts involved are likely to bring them into the Chinese courts.

This vagueness as to the obligations imposed by contract, which Western nations have been slowly unlearning for two thousand years, some more slowly than others, applies also to international treaties. In the Western view a treaty should be worded as precisely as the subject matter admits. The obligations it imposes should be executed punctually and exactly; and for that reason its terms should include nothing which the parties who sign the treaties cannot in fact perform. That is, at any rate, the standard which Western nations assume, and which in matters like naval disarmament is somewhat nearly approached. In such treaties, tonnage, the calibre of guns and such like technical matters are stated with mathematical accuracy, and no serious complaint has been made that provisions so stated have not been observed. The Locarno treaties, those relating to the open door in China and such like matters do not admit of exact statement. The terms they impose are none the less such as the parties are expected to perform, and which they are thought to be capable of performing.

In the Chinese mind a treaty is unconsciously viewed as a law or contract is viewed. Like the factory laws, it is taken to represent an ideal standard towards which the parties should try to approximate. It is viewed as a contract the efficacy of which may be greatly modified by a change of circumstances.

We can help the Chinese only in so far as we can

help them to change these views, to the same extent that we are changing their views as to medicine, chemistry or physics. This cannot be done merely by lecturing; still less by nagging. These pages are written for English and not for Chinese readers. I believe that much might be done in schools and colleges by enabling Chinese scholars to know what the legal conceptions underlying Western society are. But in changing the ideas and habits of whole communities, precept avails nothing unless there is also practice. In our international relations with China the best service we can do her is to stick courteously and patiently but persistently to the principle of exactitude in word and deed which lies at the root of all that is best in our own institutions. We inflict the deepest injury on China in making agreements which we know that she cannot discharge and indeed does not intend to discharge. Our treaties should be stated with the utmost possible exactitude, and confined to what we believe that the government of China can fulfil if it really wishes to do so. So long as it fails to fulfil these terms we should courteously but steadily refuse to open negotiations for further treaties. We can thus, and thus only, help the statesmen of China to the habit of making no treaties except such as they feel they can keep and intend to keep.

The Boxer Indemnity Settlement shows how easy it is for us to forget our own methods and standards and adopt those of China. We had made up our minds that we ought not to keep this money. In the light of the Buxton Report we had even made up our minds how it ought to be spent for the benefit of China. No final arrangement was possible until we had recognised a government with which to make the arrangement. But why did we then wait close on two years before discussing the matter with the government we had recognised? It was given no urgency till someone conceived the idea of having the money spent, in the first instance, in British factories. The idea was certainly not one likely to enhance British prestige. It does not stand the ideal test of taking the interest of China as the first object to be sought in our dealings with her. The British factories were in desperate need of orders, and all political parties as such supported the proposal. It is difficult for empty bags to stand upright.

This idea having once been adopted, the efforts of everyone seem to have been concentrated on getting an agreement settled in the easiest possible way. And the easiest way was to accept Chinese methods and standards. The Agreement, never reduced to legal form, was expressed in a series of notes exchanged by Dr. Wang and the British Minister. The grants to be made to the Hongkong University and to the Universities' China Committee are specified in a note drafted by the British Minister. Otherwise the terms of this intricate settlement have to be gathered from the notes drafted by Dr. Wang, as the reader can see by reference to the document appended to Chapter XXVI. When the Bill required to implement the settlement was before a standing committee, Mr. Dalton refused an amendment on the ground that the settlement embodied in the notes "can only be altered with the consent of both parties". To all intents and purposes the notes were presented as an international agreement or treaty, and Parliament was certainly invited to regard them as such.

The grave doubts expressed in the House of Commons as to whether this £11,000,000 of British money would in fact become an endowment available for educational purposes in China, as approved in the Buxton Report, have been fully justified. The spending of the money proceeds apace, but the Government of China continues to ignore the request made by the Board of Trustees, that documents entitling them to the interest and amortisation, as specified in the Agreement, should be put in their hands.

At the instance of Captain Eden and others, Parliament insisted on requiring the appointment of British Trustees. But what was the meaning of this insistence unless Parliament expected to be told how far the terms of the Agreement approved in the Act were fulfilled by the Government of China? Captain Eden was fated to announce the decision of the Foreign Office that such information could not be given to Parliament by the British Trustees appointed in accordance with the terms of the Act. The word 'report', as used in the answer quoted at the end of Chapter XXVI, is, of course, equivocal. In the official sense of the word, the Trustees must, of course, 'report' to the Chinese Government which appointed them, and not to the British Government which required the appointment, as a statutory condition of the settlement. But what hinders the British Minister from asking the Trustees he selected to inform him in writing whether the terms of the Agreement are being fulfilled, and from forwarding their answer to the Secretary of State for submission to Parliament? In reply to the question whether the money is being expended on the purposes approved by Parliament, the Foreign Office refers the questioner to the terms of the Agreement, as though in China what was agreed must be assumed to have been fulfilled.

The value of the British Trustees whose appointment Parliament required was largely destroyed by the fact that they cannot understand the language in which the proceedings of the Board are conducted. They are only given the gist of the discussions, to much of which they have no clue. If the Chinese Government would not agree to conduct the proceedings in English and appoint members who could speak that language, then no British members should have been appointed unless they could speak

Chinese. Of the British members one has already resigned. If a member of Parliament should ask what were his reasons for resigning he will doubtless be told that they cannot be divulged, because his appointment, though required by Act of the British Parliament, was formally made by the Government of China. If the reader should feel that in these pages the tendency of officials to devise reasons for withholding information from Parliament and the public has been overstated, I would ask him to consider the answer given to Mr. Macmillan by Captain Eden on the 26th February 1932.

No words more exactly describing the so-called Settlement of the Boxer Indemnity question by our own Foreign Office can be found than those of Mr. Walter Young applied to the schemes for promoting migration into Manchuria.

> They bear a characteristic weakness of administrative methods in China. The form having been executed, the fact, ostensibly to be achieved thereby, is assumed to have been achieved.

A considerable part of the money will be spent in British workshops, but at present there is no sign whatever that any of this money will yield an endowment for educational purposes in China. The disappearance of this £11,000,000 and the consequent frustration of the promises long held out in the Buxton Report will enure to the lasting discredit of England, especially in those educational circles in China where confidence in British sincerity is most important.

The remedy is simple, and also one conformable to the principle that in all transactions with China we should think only what is the ultimate interest of China herself. A Joint Committee of Lords and Commons should inquire whether the conditions under which the Boxer Indemnity was remitted in terms of the China Idemnity (Application) Act, 1931, and the undertakings given to Parliament when that Act was passed, are being fulfilled. By such an inquiry Lords and Commons will begin to acquire the same kind of knowledge of Far Eastern affairs as once Parliament acquired through committees appointed to investigate Indian affairs.

Should the Joint Committee report that steps are not being taken in China to secure that the money will in fact be available for the purposes contemplated by the Act, the course to be followed will be clear. The failure of the Chinese Government to fulfil the terms of the Boxer Indemnity Agreement should be pointed out in courteous terms. That Government should be told that no further negotiations for treaty revision can be considered until the terms of the Boxer Indemnity Agreement are being fulfilled in the letter and spirit. If the Government of China cannot be trusted to fulfil those terms of an Agreement which now affect only the interests of their own people, with what reason can they plead that the terms of the new treaties for which they are asking— terms which affect foreign interests—will be any better observed? This principle should govern our whole policy of treaty revision, which ought to proceed only in so far as reasonable effect has been given to agreements made since the Washington Conference. Such an attitude will really help the Chinese. Our present policy of yielding to demands for treaty revision, but yielding as slowly as we can, is an injury to China as well as to ourselves.

NOTE.—*It is necessary to state that Chapters XXVI and XXXII were both completed before I had seen a confidential report on the same subject made after a visit to China by Sir Reginald Johnston, Prof. Adams and Prof. Roxby for the information of the Universities' China Committee, of which I am a member. Since reading this report I have not altered these chapters, which contain the results of my own inquiries in China.*

CHAPTER XXXIV

THE PRIMARY QUESTION AND HOW TO ANSWER IT

In considering the question whether the radical disease from which China is suffering is capable of treatment, let us be clear that we are seeking to instruct, not China, the world at large, nor even the League of Nations, but first and foremost ourselves. The danger of allowing our thoughts to wander in this matter is increased by the League of Nations, by its constitution and even by its English name, which suggests a government common to the nations, rather than a society of nations, as the French more properly call it. We are somewhat in danger of ceasing to think out for ourselves major political problems which confront us, and of looking to the League to provide solutions. The League can only evolve solutions in so far as its several members are able to bring into conference clearly conceived plans of their own. The question to be considered in these pages is what can be done in the matter of China by the British themselves, and the British Government acting on their behalf. It is not for one moment suggested that England can help China out of her plight by her own unaided efforts. Yet, before we address ourselves on the subject either to the Foreign Powers or the League of Nations, we must have clear ideas in our minds as to what should be done and how to do it.

The Washington policy as at present applied is no policy at all so long as we shrink from facing the major premise upon which it depends. Is China capable of emerging from anarchy within any period worth considering for the purpose of a practical policy? In putting that question to experienced officials, we do not receive encouraging answers; for few of them seem to believe that any conditions other than those of the present disorder are in sight. Having spent their lives in China they can claim to be competent judges. Their views on a subject like this cannot be lightly dismissed. But if we accept them as decisive, we must also have the courage to recognise that the policy officially accepted at Washington is a house founded on sand. To persist in a policy based on a view of the facts we no longer accept is an easy road to certain disaster. If in truth China is doomed to continual disorder no policy worth the name is possible. We can only deal with the incidents as they arise from day to day; which is, in fact, what the experts mostly advise.

In India we have handled a situation which is somewhat similar, despite the fact that we are actually responsible for governing that country. Our government there is entrusted to disinterested officials of the highest ability, trained to the service from youth upwards. The people of India have yet to realise what they owe to these men in accustoming them to the rule of law, if only for the reason that no real system of responsible government is possible for people in whose minds that idea has not been established. Yet long training in the East has rendered it difficult for members of the Indian Civil Service to believe that Indians could govern themselves within measurable time. As experts they naturally claim to be better judges of the question than the great mass of their fellow-countrymen who have never visited the East. They can scarcely be expected to realise that because they know more of India, they know less of the forces beyond it than those whose business it is to direct the policy of the Commonwealth from its centre. For that reason Viceroys are selected from men with this wider kind of experience. The policy which commands the assent of public opinion in England is based on the views of men of affairs, and not on the view taken by officials whose more intimate but narrower experience is limited to India. These policies have, none the less, been accepted and forwarded with the utmost loyalty by the Indian Civil Service, whose knowledge, ingenuity and courage have alone made workable reforms enacted by Parliament.

Our responsibility for the people of India is too heavy to ignore, and we choose to be guided by men of affairs rather than by experts. In China, where we never attempted, and will never attempt, to govern, we have acted on the dangerous theory that our interests are limited to matters of trade. We have failed to realise how profoundly the situation we there created for the purpose of trade has reacted on China. It has altered the life of her people, and deflected the course of their history. The changes we have wrought, in conjunction with others who have followed in our wake and adopted our methods, will in the long run react as decisively on us and the rest of the world as those we have wrought in the smaller field of the Indian peninsula. The present situation in the Far East is evidence of a fact too long concealed by the extreme remoteness of China. The result is that we have never, since the days of Lord Elgin, thought of sending to China a minister with the qualifications which are deemed necessary for the Viceroy of India.

Our experience in handling problems of this magnitude is by no means confined to India. It may help us to recall some other situations in which methods of statesmanship have yielded results the importance of which is not in dispute.

In 1837 the British Government in Canada was faced by two rebellions, one in Quebec—the other in

Ontario. To de Tocqueville, as to many also in England, it seemed that the time had come when British colonies in North America and elsewhere would inevitably follow the path set by the United States. Lord Durham was commissioned, not only as Governor, but also to report on the whole situation. In spite of official opposition the Report was published by Lord Durham himself, but for some years had little effect and seemed doomed to oblivion. It none the less introduced a policy which determined, not only the future structure of Canada, but also that of the British Commonwealth.

When the Suez Canal was opened in 1869, Egypt became the most vital point on the route which connects the eastern and western dominions of the Commonwealth. The affairs of that country were in growing disorder, and the British Government had the good fortune to select as its agent a man who could certainly have ruled India with distinction. Lord Cromer developed in Egypt a regime the like of which had never been seen in the world before. He established order, and created such an era of prosperity as the peasants of the Nile had never enjoyed in their long history. He realised that, in order to accomplish a task so novel and immense, he must have behind him the support of his own country, and was careful, therefore, to see that the people and Parliament of England understood his object and methods. His annual reports on Egypt were masterly expositions of his policy, and supplied the material for public opinion at home. He was also fortunate in the co-operation of a great journalist, Moberly Bell, who through the columns of *The Times* explained and interpreted his measures to its readers.

The third case is that of South Africa. In the middle of the nineteenth century Sir George Grey had shown that the country was a natural unit, the peculiar problems of which could only be handled by a government able to deal with it as a whole. In 1881 the British Government ignored these counsels by agreeing to recognise the Transvaal as an independent republic. A few years after, the discovery of gold and the growth of a vast industry in the Transvaal created in South Africa social, economic and political problems on a scale which Grey himself had never foreseen. It rapidly became the storm centre of the world, and in 1897 Sir Alfred Milner was sent to deal with the situation. The issues were far more contentious than those which Durham had handled in Canada or Cromer in Egypt. In the light of after events it is difficult to see how they could ever have been solved except by war, and the British public was deeply averse to war. Like Cromer, whose pupil he was, Milner realised that the people of England must understand what he was doing and why; and this he was able to do, partly in his speeches, but still more by writing despatches which were published and laid before Parliament. Here again he was helped by two eminent journalists on the spot, Edmund Garrett in Cape Town, and Moneypenny, the special correspondent of *The Times* in Johannesburg. In result, South Africa was united as a self-governing dominion of the British Commonwealth on the same basis as Canada.

In all these cases the policies adopted were effective and led to far-reaching results, because they were studied, not merely by permanent officials, but also by Parliament and the British electorate. A bureaucracy cannot originate policies. Where public opinion is not interested, the conduct of foreign affairs develops in the hands of officials on the lines of opportunism. But public opinion cannot be interested unless it is informed. The last generation of Englishmen cared more about China than the present one, because they were suffered to know what responsible men on the spot thought of events in that country. In the crisis of 1898, when Kiaochow was seized by the Germans and Port Arthur by the Russians, the despatches of Sir Claude Macdonald, the British Minister at Peking, were published and laid before Parliament. In those days the men who were actually dealing with difficult situations abroad were expected to write despatches or reports for the information of the nation at large as well as of the Foreign Office. The despatches, for instance, of Colonel Chermside on the troubles in Crete in 1897 were published. This practice which required the man on the spot to write despatches for the information of people who, unlike the Foreign Office, knew little of the details, compelled him to view the situation in outline, and to think out a policy for dealing with the problem as a whole. It afforded a valuable antidote to the opportunism into which men in official positions so easily drift.

In this century, or at least since the war, the practice has been silently dropped, except in the case of India, where the situation compels the Viceroy at any rate to make speeches on occasion. This change is a symptom of the growing power of the permanent bureaucracy, to which Lord Hewart has drawn attention. A bureaucracy can never understand that the power of governments to govern, in foreign no less than in home affairs, depends upon public opinion, that the power of a government to act is determined by the force and character of the public opinion behind it. Its natural instinct is against publicity. It normally opposes the reference of a question to public inquiry or the publication of official reports. This tendency is natural to men who spend their lives secluded from public notice, studying papers which are confidential, and to whom reticence is the first law of their profession.

The concentration of public attention on Europe and America has given free rein to this tendency in

XXXIV THE PRIMARY QUESTION

Far Eastern affairs. Since the days of Lord Curzon, till recent events compelled Sir John Simon to give personal attention to the Far East, an understanding existed in the Foreign Office that the time of the Secretary of State was to be left free to deal with the problems of Europe and America. When a public statement on China was necessary he became the mouthpiece of the permanent officials. How far such statements reflected the views of the men on the spot is unknown, because such views have seldom if ever been given to the public.

The degree to which publicity has been suppressed can be gauged by comparing the footnotes to books on Far Eastern affairs in the nineteenth century with the footnotes to the chapters on China in the *Survey*. Books of the last generation teem with references to despatches and papers laid before Parliament. The *Survey* has now mainly to rely on references to telegrams in *The Times* and *Manchester Guardian* and quotations from statements made by the Secretary of State in the House of Commons. When a definite incident happens like that at Shameen or Nanking, the consular report narrating the actual facts is sometimes published. But the public is seldom allowed in these days to know what ambassadors or governors think of the situations they are handling. They are treated as if they were officials in the Foreign or Colonial Offices. Their identity is merged in a corporate control, which can in practice decide what the Secretary of State is to say, or not to say, in the House of Commons. Parliament and the public are now given the least possible access to original documents, and are only allowed to think of a situation what permanent officials think they should think.

The general result is that in England in the twentieth century there has been no effective public opinion so far as China is concerned. The absence of interest in the subject has been gravely enhanced by the fact that Morrison, the journalist who really instructed public opinion in the last century, left no successor. The result is that public opinion, with no foundations in genuine knowledge, is, in the present crisis, blown this way and that by press correspondents ignorant of the language of the country, whose messages too often reflect little more than conversation in clubs.

China itself is the native home of bureaucracy. The tradition of secrecy which the mandarins founded has outlived their fall to bedevil the present regime. As Mr. Justice Feetham observed, the Settlements are the only place where facts distasteful to those in power can be published without physical danger. The smoke screen which envelops the whole country is the greatest obstacle to the real followers of Sun Yat Sen who mean that their country shall develop on constitutional lines. It stifles the growth of a wholesome public opinion. The reports of a British Minister written for publication would go far to enlighten and strengthen public opinion in China itself. The state of the country is one of advanced political insanitation. It needs, before anything, light and air.

A definite answer can now be given to the question proposed in this chapter. The people of England cannot know how they should act in respect of China until they have recognised the magnitude of the issues at stake and adopted the course successfully followed in other fields of similar importance. They must send to the capital of China as their Minister a public man whose estimates of the facts, and whose methods of handling these facts, will, when explained by himself in reports and despatches, convince not merely the Secretary of State and the Cabinet, but Parliament also and the public opinion it represents. In great matters no policy is effective unless it is continuous, and no policy is continuous unless it is backed by an interested and instructed public opinion.

In such matters, the nation at large cannot be properly instructed and convinced until it has heard what the man on the spot thinks of the matter. The need for this cannot be met by special commissions of inquiry. The advice of men like Durham, Cromer, Milner or Irwin would scarcely have been what it was, nor would have commanded the authority it did, if they had not been weighted with the burden of responsible office.

CHAPTER XXXV

SOME SECONDARY QUESTIONS

IF a Minister of the type outlined in the previous chapter were accredited to China, the primary questions he would have to consider are whether we can hope for a stable government in that country, and what we can do to promote that end. There are, however, a number of secondary questions upon which his views should be heard.

The British Minister is more than the mouthpiece and adviser of his Government. He has amongst other things to control the Consular Service in China. Can this Service, as now paid and organised, hope to attract and retain men adequate to the duties they have to perform? Is it trained to give British enterprise the same measure of support as American, German or Japanese Consuls give to the trade of their country? Can any saving be effected on the present costs of the British Legation, and could those savings be used to strengthen the Consular Service? An answer to questions like these should clearly be framed by a Minister drawn from neither of these services, whose position in public life would command the attention of Parliament.

In controlling the relations of China to Great Britain such a Minister would also find that his power is not commensurate with the problem he is sent to handle. The Foreign Office has long known that its representative cannot control foreign policy in the

Far East unless he can also control the Government of Hongkong. When that island was annexed by Great Britain under the Treaty of Nanking, it became the basis from which the British representative controlled the interests of his country in China until Great Britain had exacted the right to establish a legation in Peking. The minister at Peking then ceased to control the administration of Hongkong, the governor of which was appointed by, and responsible to, the Colonial Office. The island has now been swept into the vortex of Chinese politics. The decisions of its Government constantly affect our relations with China. Control of those relations is thus divided between the Foreign and Colonial Offices, and so weakened to a dangerous degree. To cite one instance, the punitive raid on the pirate villages at Bias Bay, in 1927, was planned and ordered by the Government of Hongkong in conflict with the lines of policy prescribed by the Foreign Office.

The relations of Hongkong and Peking were at this period strained. The Foreign Office had decided not to resist the increased duties which the Government of Nanking had decreed. This increase led to a serious development of smuggling, and Hongkong is the entrepot of this lawless trade. The smuggled goods were largely run into China in small boats registered under the British flag in Hongkong. Under the treaties these boats cannot be searched in Hongkong waters by the revenue cutters of the Chinese customs. In order to prevent this, the Chinese asked permission to post customs officers in Hongkong to inspect the loading of these ships, just as they already had officers in Kowloon to inspect the trains which run to Canton. They were also asking that the traffic might be reserved under inland waters regulations to Chinese boats which they could inspect. This raised the wider question of China's claim to reserve her coastal trade to ships under her own flag. Commercial opinion in Shanghai was divided on that question. The largest firm of shipowners was in favour of meeting the Chinese views. The next largest was in favour of meeting them; but only in return for some valuable concession in another direction on the part of the Chinese Government. Meanwhile separate negotiations were started between the Government at Hongkong and the head of the Chinese customs.

The inability of the British Minister to dispose of questions like this is ill calculated to strengthen his position with the Government of China. A change in personnel has since operated to improve the relations of Hongkong with Peiping but the danger of divided counsels remains so long as the Minister responsible for British relations with China has no authority in Hongkong.

In some measure the same conditions apply to Singapore and the Straits Settlements. In Singapore the Chinese colonists are now in an actual majority. They are prosperous, and, as we have seen in an earlier chapter, it is from oversea colonies like this that the sinews of revolution in China were drawn. The Kuomintang, the ruling power in China, has a powerful branch in Singapore and an influential Press. The action of its Government directly affects the delicate issues which have to be handled by the British Minister in China. As I write these words the news is arriving that events in Shanghai have led to a riot in Penang.

In the last century the British Government had to deal with a similar position in South Africa, which was then divided into various colonies and protectorates under British rule, with two independent republics. The difficulty was met by making the Governor of Cape Colony High Commissioner for all South Africa. In this latter capacity he controlled

XXXVI PERSONAL CONCLUSIONS

This suggestion ignores the essential unity which economic conditions have imposed. It suffices only to mention customs and railways. Over these matters the separate units would be constantly at war with each other, and order would not be established. This suggestion also ignores a sense of unity which underlies Chinese civilisation, incomparably stronger than anything in India. Wherever the Chinese are in the majority they will look to China and seek for unity with it. The strength of this feeling is in curious contrast with the weakness of their power of united action. It is not in the least likely to weaken, whereas their capacity for united action can be improved, and it should be the first concern of everyone to improve it.

The policy which Japan is now pursuing in Manchuria is partly the outcome of this view, and will certainly come to grief. In any country a conqueror can find natives prepared to enjoy the sweets of power under the protection of foreign bayonets. Such people were found even in the Rhine territories. But men of this type have not in them the stuff of which rulers are made. They become the objects of fanatical hatred by their own countrymen. They are of all governments the most unstable and difficult to maintain. Japan will presently be found trying to rule 30,000,000 Chinese in Manchuria as she now rules 20,000,000 in Korea, with the same results. Her position there will be fatal to friendly relations with China. She can live only as a military state with inevitable consequences to her own constitutional development. Trotsky is said to have remarked that the Japanese dynasty, like that of Russia, will find its grave in Manchuria. There is still time for Japan to avert the terrible import of this ominous prophecy.

Again and again I have heard this idea, that order will only be restored to China by breaking her up, soberly advanced by those whose long residence in the country entitles their views to respectful attention. But never as yet have I met one who could answer the difficulty that fragments of China, however governed, but especially by military despots, would be constantly at war with each other. This again is a policy which all foreign governments should not only discard from their minds, but show the Chinese that they have discarded it. Effective order in China can, I am sure, only be based on the union of China.

We have seen how the Foreign Powers, other than America, decided to back Yuan Shih-kai against the republican movement organised by Sun Yat Sen. This decision was based on the advice of officials familiar with the history of China. When a dynasty had exhausted its mandate a period of anarchy had often followed. Order was restored when a native leader or conqueror appeared to lay the foundations of a stronger dynasty. Disorder in China was contrary to the interests of Powers seeking to trade with that country. In the light of history, the obvious way, when a dynasty had fallen, to bring the ensuing period of chaos to an end, was to strengthen the hands of the ablest leader. That the people of China were unfit for self-government would soon be evident. The strongest leader could then be recognised as emperor and become the founder of a new dynasty. Then everything in China would go on as before.

All this might have happened if the policy of limiting our relations to trade had really succeeded; but the train of events familiar in Africa, where missionaries opened the door to traders, was reversed in Asia. The traders had opened the door for missionaries, and to China American missionaries came in even greater numbers than the British. Their schools and colleges introduced Western ideas to thousands of young Chinese. Of these a considerable number passed to universities in America and Europe.

Their number was largely increased when America decided to appropriate a large proportion of the Boxer Indemnity due to her for the purpose of bringing Chinese students to her universities. Scholars in the missionary colleges, and especially the students who passed to foreign universities, lost the ideas upon which dynastic government in China had rested for ages. Graduates of a modern university seldom believe that the government of a whole nation is divinely entrusted to a single family.

In matters like this a few thousand intellectuals wield more influence than millions of illiterate peasants. The natural impotence of a peasantry in a vast agricultural country can be seen in the case of Russia. As Professor Hoover observes:

> The Russian peasantry is an immense inert force, which is of tremendous importance negatively. But the peasants are quite incapable of working out any constructive program, or of effectively fighting for such a program by themselves, if such were actually in existence. . . . The support of the peasantry definitely tipped the scales against the Whites and in favour of the Bolsheviks. But when once the Bolsheviks had overthrown the Whites . . . the peasants were as helpless against the determined policy of nationalization and collectivization of the Bolsheviks as they had been against the oppression of the Tsarist landlords or against the raids of the Tartars in still an earlier day. When driven to the wall by unbearable oppression the peasant will rise as in the days of Pugachev or of Stenka Razin and will commit acts of savage brutality which show him as the semi-Asiatic which he is, but a determined government can always drown such risings in blood or still them by temporary and unimportant concessions, or by a combination of both, as has been the Russian custom. Apart from these wild and planless outbursts, the Russian peasant is rivalled only by the Chinese coolie in his ability to bear the misfortunes which an inscrutable Providence sees fit to inflict upon him.[1]

In India the westernised intelligentsia brought into

---

[1] Hoover, *Economic Life of Soviet Russia*, pp. 69-70.

being by the educational system founded by Lord Macaulay were described as a "microscopic minority". This expression shows how easy it is to allow quantity to obscure quality. Bacteria are microscopic, and vitamins too minute to be visible even through the highest magnifiers, but their size is no index to their power of disintegrating or vitalising masses incomparably larger than themselves. A comparison of Russia, India or China with a country like Switzerland would, indeed, suggest that the impotence of peasant masses is rather increased by their size. In such countries the mere handful of educated people who are breaking away from the past are the vital and dominating factor.

It is this which falsifies the view, so natural to officials whose whole training has been in the East, that order will be restored and China again be united under one government when a new dynasty has been found to sit on the vacant throne at Peking, and not otherwise. To men so trained it is scarcely possible to conceive that the people of China will ever be able to govern themselves on the lines of a commonwealth.

The difficulties are hard to exaggerate, and no one who has had personal experience of working self-governing institutions can be blind to them. Yet none of the alternatives proposed offer any real hope of effecting the object in view, that is to say, of establishing order on permanent foundations. By a process of elimination we are driven back on the system which alone in the world as it is gives promise of an order at once stable and progressive. The only practicable course I can find is to look the difficulties in the face, and see whether we can help to overcome them.

It is for that reason, amongst others, that the British representatives sent to China should be men of wide political experience. A man of that type would, I believe, agree with Sun Yat Sen in thinking that government is the necessary basis of self-government; that before any real progress can be made some sort of effective authority must be established in an area however limited. In the Nationalist Government recognised by the Powers at Nanking in 1928 there was real promise. The mere presence of the Foreign Powers in the persons of their Ministers at Nanking would have gone far to strengthen its prestige and discourage the Tuchuns from attacking it. But more than prestige it needed advice, and was conscious of the need. The greatest of all needs was advice how to establish a government for a country so vast as China, accustomed only to methods admittedly obsolete. It is just this kind of friendly advice which foreign Ministers with wide political experience could give if once they established the kind of intimate relations with the Government of China which Mr. Dwight Morrow established with the Government of Mexico, or Mr. Page with our own in the war period. Nor do I think that this contact would be limited to the British Minister. If two insulated wires are coiled together, an electric current run through one of them will induce a current running through the other. The principle of induction operates also in human affairs. If England once adopted the practice of sending to China Ministers drawn from the first rank of public life, and also of allowing them to speak their minds, it is scarcely likely that Americans would remain content to be represented less influentially. I am bold enough to think that the Japanese Government would follow suit.

The best way of studying the future is to look at the past, and to ask ourselves what different results would have followed if certain conditions had been changed. It is worth considering, therefore, what might have been done to help the people of China if since December 1928 the Government at Nanking had been in daily intercourse with men selected, so far as possible, to reproduce the qualities of Lord Elgin, who introduced responsible government in Canada, and was afterwards Viceroy of India, of Mr. Dwight Morrow, and of Mr. Inouye, the late Japanese Minister of Finance. Such men, surrounded by staffs who shared their outlook, would have changed the atmosphere of Nanking, and have helped it to pass from mediaeval to modern ideas. An improvement in the foreign relations of China will depend upon how far the Government we have recognised there can adjust traditional machinery to meet conditions as they now are. The organisation of a government is not entirely different from the organisation of a business enterprise. The Chinese have established railways, factories, banks and shipping lines by watching how foreigners do these things and taking their advice. In constructing a government on modern lines, experience counts as much as in business, and experienced advisers are harder to find. Had foreign Ministers trained as statesmen been on the spot in Nanking, and had seen what the Government there was trying to do, their informal advice would certainly have been listened to with attention. It would not, perhaps, have been followed in every instance, but the constant presence in Nanking of detached, informed and experienced Ministers would have led to a state of opinion at the capital strong enough to prevent many of the obvious mistakes that were made.

I believe such opinion would have led the Nationalist Government to realise the primary importance of first establishing their authority, in the provinces they were able to reach from the Yangtze, instead of wasting their resources on asserting a power, at best nominal, over distant regions. Such an area could have been defended on interior lines at comparatively small expense. Their exchequer would not have been drained by subsidies to placate potentially dangerous Tuchuns whose armies they helped to sustain. Commanding the customs revenues as they did, they might have balanced their budget, and what is of even greater importance, published a budget and properly audited accounts. Such a budget might have also been submitted to some kind of public assembly, the existence of which would have paved the way to a gradual extension of popular government. They might have improved the public service, and, most important of all, introduced the beginnings of popular government in the towns and even in the hsien, the basic rural areas about the size of a small English county. They could also have restored and developed the railways in this smaller area. Had this been done their revenues would have increased by leaps and bounds.

A government on the Yangtze, visibly improving and broadening its basis, would have done more to destroy the power of the outlying Tuchuus than the treasure lavished on subsidies or campaigns. As the process continued the people in the outlying provinces would have prayed to come under the new regime.

One cannot visit Nanking without seeing at a glance how, for lack of political experience, the Government there has increased, not only its own difficulties, but those of its successors. The difficulty of all governments other than those based on some kind of autocracy is to hold together. In the case of China this difficulty is extreme; but it is not confined to China. To watch the machinery of government in Whitehall is to realise the constant difficulty of a British Cabinet in holding together. The difficulties largely arise in quarrels between departments. Most of these quarrels are settled between the permanent officials. Only where such settlements fail do they come to the Minister at the head of the department.

If he sees that the matter is serious, he walks over to the other office involved and has a talk with the Minister there. Departmental disputes are usually settled in this way, but where two Ministers are unable to agree, the matter is then taken to the Prime Minister or the Cabinet, which meets several times a week. When this last expedient fails, resignations follow, and perhaps even a collapse of the Government. In plain words, the strongest influence in holding a British Government together is the fact that all the important Ministers do their work within five minutes of each other. The working of great constitutional governments depends as much on physical factors like this as on the written provisions of the laws under which they operate.

As the offices are now distributed in Nanking, one cannot imagine that the unity of a government could be long maintained, even if its members were experienced Anglo-Saxons. In the time which it takes to reach one government department from another there is all the difference between five and twenty minutes. The enormous amount of money spent in building these widely distributed offices is a serious factor.

One's sense of the pity of it all increases as one passes beyond the walls to the vast Mausoleum of Sun Yat Sen, constructed on a scale greater than the monument to Lincoln at Washington. The money and labour there spent could have been, under better advice, devoted to the construction of buildings in which the work of a central government could have been done on effective lines. Such buildings would have been a better expression of the work which Sun Yat Sen outlined for his followers, and a fitter memorial, therefore, for the man himself. He was no transmitter of the past, like Confucius, but a maker of things to come.

These are typical mistakes such as men new to the

PERSONAL CONCLUSIONS

business of government are apt to make through no fault of their own. A British Minister in constant intercourse with the leading members of the Government, who commanded their friendship and confidence, would have no difficulty in letting them see in conversation across the dinner table how essential it is for a constitutional government to build its offices in close contact with each other. His advice on common-sense matters of this kind would be probably followed.

In a country so vast as China, an American Minister, with his knowledge of a federal system, has a special contribution to make. People who have not lived under federal institutions are slow to realise how the system works, or how necessary it is in a great country. In the earlier stages of the Indian Round Table Conference, members who had spent their lives in British politics had a difficulty in understanding discussions which anyone who had lived in America, Canada, Australia or even South Africa would have followed with ease. The National Government was right in thinking that a strong central government was needed in China. But they made the mistake, so natural in the circumstances, of supposing that this could be done by concentrating all power in the central government. A Minister like Mr. Dwight Morrow could have easily shown them that, if all the powers of the States could be concentrated in the Government at Washington, the federal machinery would break down in a week. A government consists of human beings who, as such, are limited by the factor of time. In a vast country the main problem is to find time for the central government to do those things which cannot be done except by a central government. This problem can only be solved by devolving on states or provinces every vestige of power which it is not absolutely necessary for the central government to exercise. For this the protectorates, and handled the questions at issue between the Transvaal and the British community in that republic.

The relations of any two offices in Whitehall are better than those between the Foreign and Colonial Offices, despite the fact that they live upon opposite sides of the same party-wall. Such a question as whether the authority of the British Minister in China should not be extended to include control of the Governments in Hongkong and Singapore is one that permanent officials cannot decide. It can only be settled on the advice publicly given of a Minister of high authority, who brings a fresh mind to bear on the subject after actual experience of the duties imposed on him.

CHAPTER XXXVI

PERSONAL CONCLUSIONS

WHEN discussing Far Eastern affairs with friends I have often been asked to say what I myself think should be done about China. My reply has always been the extremely commonplace answer given at the end of Chapter XXXIV. Before this country can really know what it should do about China, it must send to that country a representative whose judgement commands its confidence, and insist on knowing what he himself has to say on the matter. The fact that we send a Minister to China and not an Ambassador in itself betrays our failure to see the problem in its real proportions.

From this commonplace answer it follows that my own personal views as to what such an envoy would say are of minor importance. As some of them, however, are implicit in what I have written, I must not scruple to state, or restate them, as clearly as I can.

As to the main issue, I do not accept the view that China is doomed to a period of anarchy which precludes any constructive policy on our part, and that nothing we can do will help to restore order in the country. The magnitude of the task is difficult to exaggerate, but so are the consequences of continued disorder in so vast a section of human society. With issues so great calling us to face them, we should not admit the word 'impossible' to the English political dictionary. What Foch taught in the crisis of the war is truer far of the years which follow it. Defeat is the product of a mental state in the minds of defeatists. But certainty of success is possible only to those who have really made sure that the object for which they are striving deserves to succeed. In great national adventures our plans less often miscarry because they are wrong in themselves, than because we have failed to consider whether the goal at which we are aiming is right.

In our dealings with China we have always insisted in terms, as Japan is now insisting, that we have no ulterior object beyond trade. In the light of our own experience we can see that a policy which looked only to forcing the doors of China open to trade has ended in reducing the country to chaos, and is now threatening to cripple her capacity to produce or to trade at all. A realist policy usually ends by proving that its authors were blind to the nature of genuine realities. Apart from economic conditions, a long-continued state of disorder in a whole wing of human society is a standing menace to the main structure. In the light of events passing before us it is scarcely necessary to labour that point.

A policy which seeks, in a country like China, trade and that only must end by utterly destroying the thing which it seeks. The time has surely come when no real statesman need shrink from asserting that a foreign Government, in dealing with a unit so vast as China, will be wiser to ask itself first what is the true interest of that country, and then only to consider, in the light of the answer it finds to that question, what is the particular interest of its own. Cynics are further from realities than saints, and their cant is more subtle and therefore more dangerous. The dominating facts in this situation are the magnitude of China, the vast number of her people, and also their high individual worth, concealed as it is by curable deficiencies. A Foreign Power is not getting down to the bedrock of realities until it is able to recognise that nothing contrary to the welfare of China can in the long run benefit itself or anyone else. We shall fail in all our dealings with China until we recognise that our own interests are misconceived wherever they seem to conflict with hers. The first interest of China is admittedly the establishment of orderly government. The question whether a policy, or a step taken to implement policy, will in the long run help or hinder China in the attainment of orderly government can be safely taken as the practical touchstone of all questions which call for decision in the Far East. I submit it frankly as the only criterion.

Having cleared our minds as to the goal to be sought, and as to the principle which should guide us in seeking it, we have next to consider the way in which it can best be attained. Can order be established in China as in India, tropical Africa or the Dutch East Indies, by her undergoing a period of rule by a foreign Government? It is needless to spend much time in discussing this particular expedient for cutting the knot. Such a task will never be undertaken by the British or American Commonwealths. If attempted by Russia or Japan it will end by ruining either of those countries, and leave China in greater disorder than before. In a word it provides no kind of solution of the problem. Foreign Governments should make it their first object to convince China that no such solution will ever be attempted. Their power to solve the real problem will increase only in so far as they succeed in doing so.

A common opinion amongst those who have spent their lives in China is that government for the country as a whole is impossible, except under a new dynasty. If China is to achieve self-government, whether on Western lines or under dictators, she must be broken up into a number of smaller units.

reason alone the best advice which American statesmanship can offer is indispensable to the Government of China. Such advice is far more effective if offered by the representative of the United States, who enjoys a position of detachment, and knows how to establish personal relations with Chinese Ministers, than if it comes from some professor of constitutional history retained by the Chinese Government as a technical adviser.

A Japanese Minister instructed to follow in China the example set by Townshend Harris in Japan would have special contributions of his own to make to the task of strengthening the Government. The Japanese Government has again and again insisted that China's troubled relations with herself and with other Powers are due to the absence of effective government. As the reader will have seen, I entirely agree with that diagnosis, and a time must come when Japan will realise that lashes are no cure for a patient suffering from physical or even mental debility. The course which has led to military operations in Manchuria and Shanghai will end by demonstrating the futility of the gunboat policy, after which some of our own people are still hankering. As Machiavelli wrote, with imperishable truth, when you go to war with a people, you must be prepared either to destroy them or else to make friends with them. Experience since his time has taught us that to govern a conquered people is, in the long run, no alternative. In attempting to govern China, Japan would certainly end by destroying herself. It is no more possible to destroy a continental people like China than it is possible to destroy Russia or the United States. It is far easier to destroy a nation like our own, and from the outset of the present struggle my own anxieties have been for the future of Japan. Her achievements since she emerged from seclusion stand out in the landscape of history by themselves. She has shown how an Eastern nation can master and use the knowledge of natural forces, and the keys to that knowledge worked out in the West, and yet retain her own personality and civilisation. The greatest of all contributions she has made to the Western nations has been in establishing her own undisputed equality with them. She has made us realise that we are but men, and as other men. The most certain cure for a European who suffers from the Western complex of racial superiority is to visit Japan, and to make for himself Japanese friends.

The spectre which haunts Europe is fear—not of France, but of Germany. The nightmare which troubles the Far East is not fear of Japan, but fear of China. At the root of all tragedy lies an obsession which drives men to action contrary to reason. While Japan has divined with penetrating insight that anarchy is the cause which vitiates China's relations with herself, her policy is constantly distracted by fear of a strong government appearing in China. In the long run nothing can prove more dangerous to Japan than a state of continued anarchy in her great neighbour. No nation can do so much to help China to redress her natural weakness, if once she could summon her courage to follow hope rather than fear as her counsellor. By a change from coercion to active sympathy Japan can still win her way back to friendship with China. Friendship with China is of all Japanese interests the greatest. One must not shrink from uttering platitudes, so long as the truths they contain are ignored.

Such a change of outlook as would lead Japan to apply the remedies which her own diagnosis prescribes, will scarcely be effected by counsels offered from abroad. The Japanese people will learn wisdom, if they learn it in time, when they are taught it by statesmen of their own. England and America can, I believe, by a process of political induction bring it about that the Powers chiefly interested in China will adopt the practice of sending to the capital of that country representatives whose estimate of the situation will command authority with their own people. I know too little of Japan to suggest what particular side of her special experience such a Minister could bring to the task of helping the people of China on to their feet. My instinct tells me that her contribution could be more valuable than any which Western countries can make, if once the people of Japan are resolved to essay the task. The first thing is to change their minds, the second to tell them how it can be done. As in England and America, the people of Japan will discover what should be done, and how, only from a man of sufficient authority, who is representing his country on the spot.

The goal of all human activity is a growth in the sense of duty which men feel to each other. That growth is the product of freedom and order, two different aspects of the same condition. Material prosperity is a by-product of freedom and order, and also their index. When the era of order is really beginning in China an increase of prosperity will proclaim the fact. The time will have come when a practical decision will have to be made whether China can be lent the capital she needs to develop the vast resources of her industry. No investment would be more remunerative to the world as well as to China than money spent on mobilising the productive capacity of this vast and industrious people, especially on transportation, when once they attain a certain standard of government and order and show promise of being able to improve it. The market they can offer is the greatest in the world, if once they are able to produce the goods to give in exchange for those they need.

The task of judging when the right moment has come to lend China the capital she needs, and which in the interests of the world she should have, is of vital importance. The wisdom with which it is made will largely determine the future progress of China towards stability and also the prosperity of the world at large. The advice of Ministers stationed six hundred miles from the main artery of Chinese production and the Government of China itself would be almost worthless. A decision like this should be based on advice given by men of affairs, whose lives have not been spent in government offices, but face to face with the economic and political factors which have to be weighed.

I close this book with a sense deeper than when I began it that to write the political history of China and discuss its collective problems is to present the largest section of the human race on its weakest side. To have written so many pages discussing that weakness would, indeed, have been waste of time, unless I believed that we ourselves can contribute to its cure. To me the people of China are important, less by reason of their vast numbers, than for what they are, and, still more, for what they are capable of becoming. They can, and they will, make of themselves as noble a commonwealth as the world contains; but, as Sun Yat Sen realised, the time which it takes them to reach that goal will depend on the help they receive from outside. No greater adventure awaits human endeavour, and none in which we are fitter to partake. It cannot be achieved through armies and navies, and does not call for the expenditure of money, factors in which we were once strongest, and are no longer. It can only be achieved by the knowledge of free institutions, and how to create them—a knowledge more potent than silver and gold, and wider in range than the heaviest guns. This is the treasure for which China is waiting, and which, if lent her now, in the hour of her need, by those who have it and know how to bestow it, will hasten her redemption perhaps by ages. We, better than anyone, can take the lead in extending this knowledge to China, if once we can see it as the greatest task which has ever come to the hand of this Commonwealth, entrust it as such to the best of our statesmen, and follow their counsels.

POSTSCRIPT

AFTER this book had gone to the printer there came to my hand some notes prepared for the information of a public man who had undertaken to speak on the present crisis in the Far East. The author of these notes is Mr. Patrick Young, who has just retired from China, where for many years he managed the Kailan Mining Administration with conspicuous ability. As his estimate, written in ignorance of what I had said in these pages, broadly agrees with my own view that means for ending the present chaos in China can be found, I have asked and received his permission to append his notes to this book.[1]

His suggestion as to the means to be chosen may seem to differ from mine, but only on the surface. I think he is probably right in advising that the Powers should act through the League of Nations, and that means must be found of co-ordinating the action of America with that of the League. I do not, however, believe that public opinion in England can reach decisive conclusions on so vital a matter without having before it the considered advice of its own representative in China.

A tendency to treat the League as if it were a government and not, what it really is, as a joint committee of governments, creates the most serious obstacle to the growth of its influence and utility. The capacity of the League for effective action will depend upon how far its principal members are severally

[1] See p. 309.

able to arrive at the facts and, in doing so, harmonise their policies on the common foundation of reality. In order to do this they must have on the scene of action Ministers whose judgement the countries they represent are prepared to trust, and whose views, when known, will form the basis of a stable opinion. I think it likely that such Ministers would advise that the Government of China should be moved to request the League to send them a representative of its own, perhaps an American, of equal standing with the Ministers of the Powers, and also to seek his advice in choosing technical experts. Such a representative would be better able than any one person now is to harmonise the action of the Ministers accredited by the Powers. But of this I am convinced — the capacity of Geneva in co-operation with Washington, to help China in the task of establishing an orderly government for herself, will, in the final analysis, depend largely on the wisdom and authority of the Ministers accredited to the Government of China by the leading Powers.

APPENDICES

A

LETTER TO THE *NORTH CHINA DAILY NEWS* FROM THEIR OWN CORRESPONDENT

TOKYO, *February* 21.

THAT Japan is utterly opposed to the permanent presence of Western nations in the Far East and their imposition of their will on China is the significant contention made by Mr. Gyokujo Hanzawa, editor of the *Diplomatic Review* (Gaiko Jiho), a monthly which has a very large circulation and to which even ex-Cabinet Ministers and the like often contribute. Mr. Hanzawa, in an editorial article in the current issue of this periodical, maintains that, if the will of anyone must be imposed on China, it must be that of Japan alone, and that Japan must seize the present opportunity to secure recognition of this on the part of the Powers. It is quite possible that Mr. Hanzawa's views are inspired, for he is known to be in close touch with the higher-ups. It was Mr. Hanzawa who, months before the Manchurian Incident occurred, with a strange prophetic vision, foresaw in significant detail what was going to happen and the aftermath. It is now an open secret that he was in the confidence of what is known as the "shadow cabinet" of the Army, a matter that invests the Manchurian affair with a new significance. Mr. Hanzawa's "Vision" was printed in the *North China* long before the Manchurian Medley started.

Mr. Hanzawa's article, which is called "The Significance of the Shanghai Affair", maintains that the Shanghai affair is not an extension of the Manchurian incident, though it was occasioned by similar causes. He maintains that the fundamental policy of the Nanking Government is to close the doors of all opportunities to foreign nations in China and to trample on and repudiate treaties, on the ground that they are "un-equal", this policy being carried out by instigating and encouraging Chinese to acts of hostility against foreigners. The forcible seizure of the

British concession at Hankow, he says, was one manifestation of this anti-foreign policy, and Japan, he maintains, has suffered most recently as a result of China's anti-foreignism. While he admits that, fundamentally, the Shanghai affair is of the same texture as the Manchurian incident, he insists that there is this great difference between the two—the Manchurian affair must be settled between Japan and China, all interference of a third party, even in the way of mediation, being resolutely rejected; while a solution of the Shanghai affair must be sought in co-operation with the Powers having interests in that region.

Stupendous Sacrifices

The editor of the *Diplomatic Review* maintains that Japan's sacrifices in Shanghai have been "stupendous" and makes the significant admission that not even the Japanese themselves know exactly the nature and extent of these sacrifices.

"That does not matter much," he writes. "We have come to the conclusion that nothing short of severe military chastisement will awaken China to the folly of her conduct, and we must see matters through with determination."

He attributes China's present chaotic condition to the removal of foreign pressure on the freedom of her actions, following the Great War, that being, he says, the commencement of China's resorting to the old game of playing one nation against another, and violating treaties with impunity. The rest of the world, he says, in a moment of "spiritual uplift" after the Great War, paid little or no heed to China's excesses and the result has been the existing chaos in the domestic as well as the foreign affairs of China.

"The effects of disturbances in China are not limited to her," he goes on. "They will prove a potential threat to this country and a conflict in the Far East may endanger the peace of the whole world. We cannot, therefore, stand idly by when China's peace is disturbed on the ground that such is an internal affair. We must wake China up and help her to solve her various problems; at the same time, we must seek again to establish friendly Sino-Japanese relations in order to stabilise the Far East. This is Japan's fundamental policy. It cannot perhaps be effected through diplomatic negotiations: we should, therefore, be ready to oppose the entire world in pushing that policy forward, for that is our national policy and on it depends the future of the empire."

He thinks that China must, by this time, have realised the futility of coping with the military power of Japan or of expecting the foreign Powers to intervene; while he believes that the Powers, too, must now have realised the need for revising their China policies in the light of actual facts.

Joint Restrictions Wanted

China is not the same China that the Powers thought her to be, he proceeds, and he advocates that the Powers jointly put restrictions on China and compel her to observe peace and order within her domains. For this purpose, he contends, the Powers should abandon their present policy of courting the good will of China, which, he says, is "evanescent", and should revive the old policy of acting in concert.

"Japan is now taking the chestnuts out of the fire in Shanghai," he continues, "but her sacrifices will be amply atoned for should the Powers co-operate with one another in solving Chinese problems. The Shanghai affair has brought forth a splendid opportunity for making a beginning in this direction. The Japanese Government, despite which party is in power, should not budge one jot or tittle from this policy, however great the sacrifice necessary to carry it out."

Mr. Hanzawa sees the only way to bring about a fundamental rehabilitation of China in the Powers insisting that all important districts in China in which the Powers are interested should be de-militarised, commencing speedily with the Shanghai area which has been the bone of contention of Chinese militarists because it is a treasure-house for whoever controls that region. If this area is de-militarised, he holds, it will see a wonderful development in the future and dangers to foreign property and lives will be "for ever eliminated".

"Its de-militarisation", he proceeds, "will further result eventually in the decline of the militarists in China, and in order to maintain the de-militarisation of the area, the Powers will have to station some forces for the purpose of inspection, while the peace and order of the district should be maintained by Chinese police. The de-militarisation of the Shanghai area would redound to the benefit of both the Powers and China, and it will not be difficult to accomplish if the Powers willingly co-operate with one another."

Japan's Duty in China

The same system of de-militarisation, Mr. Hanzawa says, should be applied to other parts of China, such as Tientsin, Tsingtao, Hankow, Amoy and Canton, where the Powers have economic and trade interests. "If these districts are de-militarised," he contends, "the *raison d'être* of the Chinese military cliques will disappear, and China will enjoy prosperity and peace, while China's domestic policies will undergo a radical transformation with the result that local autonomy will be expanded and national progress effected."

Japan, however, he says, must not be content merely with the de-militarisation of these areas. It is the duty of Japan, he declares, to take an active rôle in leading China.

"If the plan for de-militarised zones means dividing up China into spheres of influence," he continues, "then we are strictly against it. In reality, however, the plan proposed has no such motives behind it. We want China to realise the importance of her rôle in preserving the peace of the Far East in co-operation with Japan and not with others. We are utterly opposed to the presence of Western nations in the Far East and to the imposition of their will on China. Japan must play the rôle of private tutor, mentor and guide to China, and if any outsider has to impose his will on China, it must be only Japan. We have not attacked China because we hate her, but to reprimand the militarists and to avenge the numerous injustices that China has inflicted on us. The Chinese now understand that the League of Nations was primarily created to deal with European problems and not with Far Eastern affairs. That is why China dare not declare war on us, in spite of the bellicose utterances of some of her politicians. At first blush, Japan's military action may appear unreasonable; our conscience, however, is clear. The protests of Great Britain and the United States contain a measure of truth, but do not suit the existing state of affairs in the Far East."

B

NOTES ON THE CHINESE SITUATION

When we read in the reports received from Shanghai that there is a lull in the fighting since the Japanese called a halt on reaching the 20-kilometre line, we may feel inclined to draw a breath of relief. There is, however, nothing in the situation now brought about which we can regard with complacency.

If events are allowed to take their course, though there may be much further bloodshed before the Chinese are persuaded that material and discipline must prevail over unorganised valour, in the end some settlement of outstanding differences between the Chinese and the Japanese will no doubt be reached. The Chinese will agree, with the mental reservation that, since acquiescence in terms which they cordially detest has been wrung from them under duress, they have a moral right, when opportunity offers, to set these terms aside. That opportunity they will await, embittered not only against the Japanese but against all foreigners, since they will blame the apathy of all other nations for their humiliation.

Furthermore, the prestige of what China has by way of a central government will have been weakened by reason of its failure to avert a national calamity, while its strength will have been diminished by military losses, if not by the transfers of allegiance which so frequently occur at a moment of crisis. Other aspirants to power and the spoils of office will see their opportunity. Civil wars will continue. The vicious circle in which China revolves will remain unbroken—a central government without adequate financial resources and so too weak to discipline contending War Lords; without control over those War Lords and so too insecure to command financial resources.

Clearly, it is in the interests of the Chinese people to find a way of escape from this vicious circle. What the Chinese people want is to be peaceful that they may be prosperous. Given peace, their own industry and capacity, irrigated by the new capital which will then flow, assure prosperity.

But the matter does not end there. Nothing is more important for the world to-day than a peaceful and a prosperous China.

This vast country numbers not less than one-fifth of the population of the globe. Western ideas have impinged upon her ancient civilisation. While this, as many aver, may be the underlying reason for the social and political unrest which has brought some three million mercenaries into the field ready to sell their services for the prospect of loot, its consequences have not all been evil. The Chinese people to-day, awakened from traditional fatalism, are hungry for an improved standard of living. Chinese industrialists and men of business are eager for the organisation and the capital development which will make that standard attainable. That development has been arrested for a generation by political chaos, leaving long arrears to be overtaken. Meanwhile millions perish from starvation; tens of millions live in daily dread of it, though elsewhere people talk of burning surplus stocks of grain. The industrial world complains of lack of orders, not because people do not want to buy, but because they have neither the means to pay nor the credit to borrow. Restore confidence in the political stability of China and you restore the basis of credit; give the necessary purchasing power and you bring one-fifth of the world's population into active business not only as consumers but as entrepreneurs with a great programme of development, demanding iron and other metals, machinery and equipment, bringing orders for the heavy industries that all over the world are starving for want of work.

The moment has arrived when there is at length an opportunity of breaking into the vicious circle in China. Many reasons might be given for thinking that this is the appropriate opportunity. Here are two.

The Chinese as a nation have unquestionably suffered from an inferiority complex brought about by the idea, whether it be correct or not, that a European or an American considers a Chinese a less virile and capable individual than himself. Now, whatever we may think about the rights and wrongs of the deplorable conflict at Shanghai, there is one thing about which we all agree—that the Chinese, ill-equipped, ill-disciplined and ill-organised as they are, have displayed as individual fighters a courage, a tenacity and a capacity which has won our admiration for them as men. If an armistice is imminent it is not because the Chinese have been defeated, not because they have shown themselves incapable of standing up to hammering from the land, the water and the air. Far from losing "face" the Chinese have gained it. A Chinese has every right to hold his head high, proud in the proof which his countrymen have afforded that as individuals the Chinese are a virile and a capable race. The inferiority complex, for the time being at any rate, is in abeyance. A chance has come of offering help from outside China with greatly diminished risk of hurting Chinese susceptibilities.

Again, whatever may have been the attitude of the Government in Nanking and the slogans of politically minded Chinese, there is no doubt that in recent years a large number of responsible Chinese, men concerned in the commerce and industry of the country, have come to hope for such foreign aid as will enable China to break out of the vicious circle. It may be that there are some among the members of the present Government in Nanking who would still think it derogatory to the dignity of China to accept any measure of foreign help in connection with the domestic affairs of that country. There can, however, be little doubt but that a government of responsible Chinese could be called into being who would be not only willing but eager to accept foreign assistance if offered in a way which was consistent with the sovereign dignity of a great country.

The League of Nations is the only suitable instrument through which such help can be offered to China. Two arguments, out of many, may be adduced in support of this contention.

In the first place, any temporary armistice is, on the face of it, the opportunity to settle differences between China and Japan. It is not the business of any other particular Power to intervene. It is only the people of the world—the League of Nations acting in consonance with the United States of America—that have the right to say that there is something more important at stake than the settlement of a dispute between those two nations, an issue affecting the peace and prosperity of the whole world.

Again, any offer of help from a particular nation is clearly liable to hurt the pride of a great nation. There can, however, be nothing derogatory in the offer to China of help from an instrument representing the whole world. Other peoples represented on the League of Nations are sitting on a raft of comparative security, the planks of which are political stability. China, though she has withstood a battering from seas in which any less vigorous swimmer would have been submerged, has failed to climb upon the raft by her own unaided efforts, and is still struggling in deep and turbulent water. She need not be ashamed to accept the helping hands stretched out to her.

It may be premature even to sketch a plan whereby the help of the League of Nations may be offered to China in an acceptable form. One thing is, however, very evident—the League of Nations is not a financial house, and, consequently, it cannot break into the vicious circle by lending money to the Government of China in the hope that by its wise use the required political stability and security will be produced. The League's efforts must be directed towards helping China to break into the circle at the diametrically opposite point and aim at affording security—security in the two senses of the word, first as meaning freedom from the risk that government, law, order and established institutions will be overthrown by violent means, second as meaning that assurance of a steady and adequate income which gives confidence to prospective lenders.

Here, then, is a problem, at once urgent, important and difficult, awaiting the consideration of the League of Nations, a problem which it is possible that the League may fail to solve, but which it is certain that no other instrument in the world can solve. It concerns immediately the welfare of a fifth of all mankind; its successful solution will do more than anything else can to promote the economic recovery of the whole world. Can the nations address themselves to any more worthy endeavour? Can our country supply the leadership in any more noble crusade?

P. C. YOUNG

March 10, 1932.

INDEX

Abend, Mr., 231
Acre, 20
Adams, Professor W. G. S., 272
———, Will, 43, 44, 85, 88
Africa, 21, 137, 288, 290
———, East, 198
Ajunda, 34
Albuquerque, 30, 31
Alexander VI., 29
——— VII., 52
Alexandria, 253
Almeida, 31
Amboyna, 48
America, 32, 33, 39, 48, 49, 61, 85, 86, 135, 154, 276, 278, 279. (*See also* United States of America)
Amoy, 58, 96, 307
Amur, 74
——— R., 18
Andrew, Mr. Findlay, 192
Anhwei, 25, 154, 188
Annam, 83
Anne, Queen, 53
Antonines, 6, 14
Antung Railway, 127
Arabia, 19
Araki, 44, 45
Armenia, 20, 21
Arrow, 71
Ashikagas, 35
Asia, 4, 5, 11, 12, 19, 29, 32, 42, 59, 60, 111, 112, 120, 137, 290
Atlantic, 29, 49, 86, 136, 256
Attila, 12, 18, 19
Augustinians. *See* St. Augustine
Augustus, 12
Australasia, 135
Australia, 49, 85, 98, 137, 152, 236, 297
Austria, 102, 133
Austria-Hungary, 132

Bagdad, 27
Baikal, Lake, 18
Balfour, Arthur (afterwards Lord), 136
———, Captain (afterwards Sir George), 63
Balkans, v
Baltic, 217
Baptiste, Father, 39
Barton, Sir Sidney, 260
Batavia, 17, 219
Behring Straits, 86
Belgium, 39, 42, 96, 117, 119, 131, 139, 196
Bell, Moberly, 276
Bellarmine, Cardinal, 44
Bengal, 54
———, Bay of, 30
Berlin, 126, 224
Bias Bay, 283
Black Sea, 217, 218
Blagovyeshchensk, 102
Bogue, 53, 59
Bokhara, 19, 20
Bonaparte. *See* Napoleon
Bonin Islands, 87
Bordeaux, 240
Borneo, 49
Borodin, 144-146, 148, 150, 158, 160, 161, 163, 165-168, 222
Boston, 59, 86, 87
Botany Bay, 86
Bowman, 217
Bowring, Sir John, 71
Brazil, 78, 196
Bristol, 70
British East India Company. *See* East India Company
——— Empire, 87, 139, 211
——— Isles, 39, 49, 135
Brooks, 101
Bruce, Sir Frederick, 79

Brussels, 126
Buddhism, 13
Buddhists, 21, 35, 37, 43, 51
Buhetu, 225
Burma, 17
Buxton, Lord, 207
Buxton Report, 268, 269, 271
Byzantium, 84

CABRAL, 30
Caesar, 12, 36
Cairo, 253
Calicut, 29, 30
Cambaluc. *See* Canbaluc (now Peiping)
Canada, 136, 137, 143, 152, 217, 236, 237, 245, 275-277, 294, 297
Canbaluc, 20, 26, 111 (now Peiping)
Cantlie, Sir James, 99
Canton, 31, 53-58, 62, 66, 70, 71, 99, 132, 141, 142, 144, 145, 147, 149-151, 153-157, 159-162, 167, 169, 185, 186, 188, 239, 253, 254, 283, 307
—— R., 31, 37, 50, 155
Cape Colony, 284
—— of Good Hope, 29, 31, 85-87
—— Horn, 35, 85, 87
—— Town, 232, 253, 277
Caspian Sea, 19
Cathay, 21, 31
Cecils, 160
Chamberlain, Sir Austen, 172, 203
Chang Chih-tung, 121
Changchun, 120, 218, 221, 231
Chang Fa-kwei, 186, 189
Chang Hsüeh-liang, 172, 173, 185-187, 222, 225, 233, 235
Chang Ing Huan, 95, 96
Changsha, 160, 186, 188, 189
Changte, 189
Chang Tso-lin, 141, 142, 144, 149, 153, 154, 165-167, 171, 172, 222, 229, 232, 233
Chang Yin Huai, 233
Chaoping, 188
Chapdelaine, Père, 71
Chapei, viii, 240
Charlemagne, 34, 83
Charles V., 31, 32
Chatham House. *See* Royal Institute of International Affairs

Chekiang, 20, 154, 159, 166
Ch'en Ch'iung-ming, 142, 144, 146
Cheng-sze, 18
Chermside, Colonel, 278
Chiang Kai-shek, 145, 159, 160, 165-173, 176, 184-189, 205, 239, 240, 249
Chicago, viii, 145
Chichester, Admiral, 97
Chihli, 101, 102, 124, 125, 141
——, Gulf of, 19
China Weekly Review, 176
Chinese Colonization and the Development of Manchuria, 261
—— Eastern Railway, 221-226, 254
Ching, Prince, 104
Chingis, 23, 24
Chinkiang, 19
Chosiu, 89
Chou An Hui Society, 128
Chu Ao-hsiang, 181
Chungking, 151
Chungmiaochen, 189
Chungtu, 18, 19 (now Peiping)
Chung Wang, 68
Churchill, Winston, 150
Chu Yuan-Chang, 25
Chwenkaichen, 189
Clement IV., 20
—— V., 26
—— XI., 52
Co-hong. *See* Hong
Columbus, Christopher, 28, 29
Commercial Press, Ltd., The, Shanghai, viii.
Confucius, 9, 11, 12, 40, 109, 150, 159, 296
Constantine, 51
Constantinople, 83, 84, 112
Cook, Captain, 85, 86
—— Archipelago, 86
Cornwallis, H.M.S., 58
Cortes, 32
Coster, 27
Crete, 278
Crimea, 20
Cromer, Lord, 114, 253, 276, 277, 281
Cromwell, Oliver, 130
Cuba, 96, 175, 177
Curzon, Lord, 279
Cushing, Caleb, 59

INDEX

D'ABERNON, LORD, 89, 257
da Gama, Vasco, 29, 30
Daimyo, 35, 37, 38, 90
Dairen, 186, 218, 221, 231
Dalny, 127. (*See also* Dairen)
Dalton, Mr., 205, 208, 211, 269
Da Motto, Antonio, 34
Dardanelles, 217
Davis, Sir John, 66
Davys, 48
de Lagrené, 59-61
Delhi, 251
de Marinas, Don Gomez, 38, 39
Denikin, 150
Denmark, 44, 196
de Sousa, Martin Alphonso, 34
de Tocqueville, 276
de' Vesconti di Piacenza, M. Tebaldo, 20
Dewey, Admiral, 97
Diaz, Captain Bartholomeu, 29
Dickens, 54
di Cortellazzo, Count Galeazzo Ciano, 183
Diedrich, Admiral von, 97
Diplomatic Review, 305, 306
Dnieper, R., 19
Dominicans. *See* St. Dominic
Dowager Empress. *See* Yehonala
Durham, Lord, 276, 277, 281
Durham Report, 237, 276
Dutch, 43, 44, 47-49, 53
—— East Indies, 98, 288

EAST INDIA COMPANY, 43, 53-56, 58, 86
Eden, Captain, 210, 211, 270, 271
Eguchi, S., 231
Egypt, 27, 30, 94, 114, 220, 235, 276, 277
Elgin, Lord, 73, 74, 275, 294
Elliot, Captain, 57
England, 18, 44, 49, 50, 56, 59, 60, 66, 71, 74, 86, 87, 91, 96, 102, 120, 128, 131, 133, 137, 138, 143, 152, 191, 193, 220, 235, 236, 254, 257, 258, 263, 266, 271, 273, 275-277, 279, 280, 299, 300, 303
Eugene Chen, 161, 163, 164, 168, 188, 239, 240

FEETHAM, MR. JUSTICE, 80, 198, 201-204, 237, 280

Feetham Report, 202-206, 263
Feng-husiang, 125, 141, 149, 153, 154, 160, 161, 168, 171, 172, 180, 185, 186, 201
Ferdinand, Archduke, 126, 235
—— of Spain, 29
Fessenden, S., 151, 197, 198
Finland, 175
Foch, Marshal, 286
Foochow, 58, 71, 96
Formosa, 53, 87, 92, 93
Fox, Dr. Charles James, 178
France, 52, 59, 60, 71, 74, 83, 87, 93, 96, 102, 105, 106, 117, 131, 133, 139, 153, 162, 164, 191, 196, 197, 200, 217, 221, 223, 254, 257, 299
Franciscans. *See* St. Francis
French Indo-China, 186
Frere, Sir Bartle, 114
Friendly Islands, 85
Froez, Father, 37
Frozen Sea, 19
Fu-hsi, 6
Fukien, 26, 154, 189, 191
Fusang, 41

Gaiko Jiho. *See Diplomatic Review*
Galens, 144, 145, 160, 168, 222, 224
Garrett, Edmund, 277
Geneva, 238, 254, 304
Genghis Khan, 18-20, 24, 26, 36, 111
Genoese, 21
George III., 56, 258
Germany, 35, 44, 45, 93, 96, 105, 106, 116, 122, 127, 132-134, 143, 217, 254, 299
Gibbon, 3
Goa, 30, 37
Gobi, 12
Goodnow, Dr. F., 128
Gordon, General, 75
Graeco-Roman, 12, 84
Grand Trunk Canal, 20, 57
Great Britain, 40, 53, 86, 92, 96, 105, 106, 138, 150, 163, 170, 180, 196, 197, 207, 209, 212, 213, 215, 223, 237, 264, 282, 283, 308
—— Wall, 11, 12, 18-20, 25, 111, 112, 172, 180, 186, 219, 232, 233, 240, 252

316 THE CAPITAL QUESTION OF CHINA

Greece, 3, 6, 8, 10, 15, 67
Greenland, 48
Gregory X., 20
Grey, Sir George, 114, 276, 277
Griswold, 63-65
Gros, Baron, 73, 74
Grusenberg. *See* Borodin
Gutenberg, 27

HAARLEM, 27
Hailar, 224, 225
Hailsham, Lord, 197
Hanchengchen, 189
Hangchow, 18, 20, 166, 236
Hankow, 62, 96, 122, 127, 150, 153, 154, 156, 157, 160, 161, 163, 165-168, 174, 177, 189, 199, 218, 239, 240, 305, 307
—— Agreement, 164
Han R., 156, 160, 188
Hans, 12
Hanyang, 160, 161
Han-yeh-ping Iron Company, 136
Hanzawa, Gyokujo, 305, 307
Harbin, 103, 225
Harris, Townshend, 88, 89, 257, 258, 298
Hart, Sir Robert, 61, 81, 82, 108, 114, 116
Harvard, 159
Hawaii, 86, 97, 99, 138, 152
Hayashi, Baron, 172
Helena, 51
Henderson, Rt. Hon. Arthur, 198, 203, 204, 206
Herat, 19
Hewart, Lord, 278
Hideyoshi, 36, 38-43, 45, 49
Hinduism, 13
Hindustan, 19, 24
Hirado, 43, 44, 47
Hiung-nu, 11
Hizen, 89
Hōjō, 35
Holcombe, Professor, 143
Holland, 44, 47, 139
Honan, 141, 154, 171, 186, 187, 189, 240
Hong, 54, 55, 57, 58
Hongkong, 58, 71, 73, 87, 98, 99, 143, 150, 152, 164, 263, 283-285
—— and Shanghai Banking Corporation, 207

Hongkong University, 209, 215, 216, 269
Honolulu, 152, 170
Honshiu, 36
Hoover, President, 152
——, Professor, 291
Hornbeck, Professor, 198, 237
Houghton, Ambassador, 89, 257
Ho Yao-tsu, 167, 171
Hsien Feng, Emperor, 82
Huang Chen-wu, 206
Hudson R., 62
Hughes, Mr., 136
Hu Han-min, 169, 187, 188, 240
Hulatao, 229
Hunan, 154, 156, 160, 186, 189, 191
Hung Sui-tsuen, 67
Huns, 12
Hupeh, 154, 188, 189
Hu Shih, Dr., 13
Hu Yao-tsu, 171
Hwang Ch'ang-ku, 146
Hwangmotachen, 189

IEMOCHI, 89
Ignatieff, General, 73
Imperial Conference, 136
India, vi, 7, 8, 13, 15, 21, 29, 30, 34, 48, 54, 57, 58, 65, 119, 137, 138, 164, 168, 198, 220, 251, 261, 262, 274-276, 278, 279, 288, 291, 292, 294
Indian Empire, 37, 58
—— Mutiny, 71
Indus R., 19
Innocent X., 51, 52
Inouye, Y., 294
Institute of Pacific Relations, 152, 170, 190, 197, 224, 235, 236
International Relations of the Chinese Empire, The, viii
Ireland, 198
——, North, 212, 213, 215
Irene, Empress, 83
Irish Treaty of 1921, 137
Irwin, Lord, 281
Isabella of Spain, 29
Ishii, Viscount, 131
Islam, 19, 20, 148
Italy, 102, 116, 131, 139, 175, 196, 254
Ito, 92
Ivanov, 222

INDEX

Iwakura, 92
Iyeyasu, 36, 43-46, 49, 89, 90

JALAI NOR, 224
Java, 85
Jaxartes, 19
Jehol, 82
Jelal ed-Din, 19
Jerusalem, 112
Jesuits, 9, 37-39, 42-44, 52, 60
Joffe, M., 144
Johannesburg, 253, 277
John, King of England, 18
—— III., King of Portugal, 37
Johnson, Nelson T., 174-179
Johnston, Sir Reginald, 73, 272
Jordan, Sir John, 61, 260
Jukao, 189
Junglu, 82, 100-102

KAGOSHIMA, 37
Kalee Hotel, 176
Kalgan, 156
Kanagawa, Treaty of, 88
Kanbalu. *See* Khan-baligh (now Peiping)
Kanchow, 188
Kang Hsi, Emperor, 52
Kang-yi-wei, 99, 100
Kan R., 156
Kansu, 141, 188, 190, 192
Karakhan, 144
Kellogg Pact, 223, 227, 235
Ketteler, Baron von, 101
Khan-baligh, 20, 21 (now Peiping)
Khartoum, 75
Khingan Mountains, 225
Kiakhta, 72
Kiangsi, 154, 165, 188, 189, 191
Kiangsu, 75, 154, 166, 189
Kiaochow, 127, 278
—— Bay, 95
Kimberley, 253
Kins, 18, 19
Kiuhwashen, 189
Kiukiang, 165, 167
Kiushiu, 37, 38, 43, 46
Kolchak, 150
Komei, Emperor, 89
Koo, Wellington, 132
Korea, 28, 39-41, 49, 83, 92, 119, 120, 124, 152, 218, 231, 289
Kowloon, 73, 283
Kuang Hsü, Emperor, 99, 100

Kublai Khan, 19-21, 24, 25, 35, 51, 83, 111
Kung, Dr. H. H., 159
Kung-fu-tse. *See* Confucius
Kuo Min, 183
Kuomintang, 98, 125, 126, 141, 146, 148, 155, 158, 160, 161, 163, 166-169, 172-174, 180, 181, 184, 185, 187, 188, 197, 199, 202, 233, 284
Kwammu Tenno, Mikado, 34-36
Kwangsi, 129, 141, 142, 144, 180, 185, 186
Kwangtung, 67, 98, 129, 141, 154, 188
Kwan-yin Shan, 146
Kweichow, 129
Kyasthas, 24
Kyoto, 34, 35, 37, 42, 89-91, 197, 224, 251

Lady Hughes, 55
Lafayette, 143
Lampson, Mr. (afterwards Sir Miles), 161, 180, 204, 212, 216
Landecho, 42
Langham Place, 99
Lansing, Robert, 131
Laôtze, 8, 45, 109
Lazarists, 60
League of Nations, vi, 133, 134, 195, 223, 227, 235, 241, 247, 254, 273, 303, 304, 308, 311, 312
Leland Stanford University. *See* Dr. Wilbur
Lenin, 149, 150, 158
Leningrad, 251
Lexington, Battle of, 86
Liang Chung-chia, 224
Liaotung Peninsula, 92, 93, 95, 120, 127, 218, 221
Liefde, 43
Lienchieng, 189
Li Hung-Chang, 75, 82, 92, 94-96, 100, 103, 104, 124, 221
Linchwang, 189
Lincoln, President, 155, 296
Lin Tse-hsü, 57
Lisbon, 29, 30, 38, 43
Litvinov, 225
Liuchiu Islands, 92
Liverpool, 70, 87
Locarno Treaties, 267

London, 53, 63, 65, 70, 87, 99, 113, 126, 143, 161, 162, 170, 180, 198, 205, 209-211, 213-216, 232, 248, 256, 257
Louis Philippe, 59
—— of France. *See* St. Louis
Lou Tseng-tsiang, 132
Loyang, 240
Loyola, 37, 38
Luh, 64
Luther, 31, 37
Lytton Commission, 237

MACAO, 31, 51, 53, 56, 99
Macartney, Lord, 56, 58, 70
Macaulay, Lord, 292
Macdonald, Sir Claude, 278
Machiavelli, 298
Macmillan, Harold, 211, 271
MacNair, Professor, viii
Madras, 53
Madrid, 38, 44, 48, 180
Magalhães, 31
Magellan, 31
Mahan, Admiral, 142
Maintz, 27
Malabar, 30
Malacca, 19, 30, 31, 35, 37
Malay Peninsula, 17, 30, 219
Manchester Guardian, 204, 263, 279
Manchouli, 224
Manchuria, 12, 17, 74, 94, 102, 103, 111, 119, 120, 122, 127, 141, 153, 154, 172, 173, 217-220, 223, 224, 226, 227, 229-237, 239-241, 247, 252, 271, 289, 298
Manchuria Year Book, The, 219
Manchurian Railways, South, 127, 218, 228, 229, 231, 234
Manchus, 14, 52, 55, 66-68, 73, 75, 82, 98, 99, 101, 102, 108, 110-112, 114, 121, 122, 124, 155, 156, 240, 248
Manila, 32, 38, 97
Manji, 28
Manoel, King of Portugal, 29, 31
Maria, 51
Marquesas, 85
Martel, Charles, 35
Mecca, 30, 112
Mediterranean, 6, 15, 131
Meighen, Mr., 136

Meiji, Emperor, 89
Merovings, 35
Merv, 19
Mesopotamia, 30
Mexico, 32, 48, 145, 255, 256, 293
Michelborne, 48
Middle Ages, 8, 18, 27, 70, 91, 135
Mikado, 34-36, 40, 45
Milner, Sir Alfred (afterwards Lord), 114, 253, 277, 281
Mings, 25, 51, 68, 111, 112, 156
Mississippi, R., 62
Mogul, 24
Mohammed Shah, 19
Moluccas, 32, 48, 49
Moneypenny, 277
Mongol, 3, 4, 11, 14, 18-20
Mongolia, 127, 252
Monte-Corvino, John of, 26, 27
More, 191
Morocco, 27
Morrison, 280
Morrow, Dwight, 89, 255-257, 293, 294, 297
Morse, H. B., viii, 79, 115, 117
Moscow, 39, 113, 149, 167, 168, 223, 224, 226, 251
Mukden, 172, 173, 224, 225, 232, 234
Municipal Council, 77, 79, 80, 151, 170, 197, 198, 200, 201, 205, 265, 266
Mussolini, 183
Mustapha Kemal, 145

NAGASAKI, 37, 39, 43, 47
Nakamura, Captain, 234
Nanking, 18, 25, 57, 68, 75, 111, 114, 122-124, 157, 159, 166-178, 180-183, 185-189, 196-201, 203-206, 208, 210-212, 217, 222-225, 233, 238-240, 249-254, 279, 283, 293-296, 305, 311
——, Treaty of, 58, 59, 61, 66, 67, 70, 87, 112, 259, 283
Nanning, 152
Napier, Lord, 56, 57
Napoleon Bonaparte, 36, 39, 40
Nara, 251
Netherlands, 196, 197
New Caledonia, 86
Newchwang, 96, 103

INDEX

New England, 87
—— Guinea, 49
—— Hampshire, 120
—— Hebrides, 86
—— York, 62, 88, 159
New York Times, 231
New Zealand, 49, 85, 137, 152, 236
Nicholas, Czar, 94, 95
Nile, R., 276
Ningpo, 58
Nobunaga, 36-38, 45
Norfolk Island, 86
North, Lord, 258
North China Daily Herald, 175
North China Daily News, 174, 175, 178, 179, 305
North China Star, 178
North China Sunday News, 183
Norway, 44, 175, 177, 196

OBATA, MR., 174
Odes, Book of, 12
Odessa, 94
O-Kichi, 88
Okubo, 92
O'Malley, Mr., 161, 163, 174
Onon, R., 18
Ontario, 276
Orange River Colony, 253
Oregon, State of, 86
Ormuz, 30, 31

PACIFIC, 19, 32, 35, 43, 49, 65, 85, 86, 135, 136, 152, 217, 255
—— Conference. *See* Institute of Pacific Relations
Page, Walter Hines, 89, 257, 293
Pakhoi, 152
Palmerston, Lord, 58
Pamirs, 19
Pao-ting-fu, 125
Paris, 126, 132-134, 138, 139, 141, 240
——, Conference of, 142
——, Treaty of, 97
Parkes, Sir Harry, 61, 73, 90, 260
Pechihli, Gulf of, 96, 117
Peh Tai Ho, 117
Pehtang, 72
Pei-ho, R., 19
Peiping, 173-178, 186, 200, 205, 211, 235, 251-254, 259, 260, 284

Peixotto, Antonio, 34
Peking, viii, 18, 21, 25, 26, 31, 50-52, 54-58, 69, 71-75, 78, 79, 82-84, 89, 92, 95, 101-103, 107-115, 118, 121-123, 125-128, 130-133, 140-145, 149, 151, 153-157, 161, 163, 167, 171-173, 175, 176, 178-183, 196, 207, 222, 260, 278, 283, 292. (*See also* Peiping)
Penang, 284
Pepys, 53
Perry, Commodore (afterwards Admiral), 87, 257
Persia, 19, 119
Persian Gulf, 29, 30
Peru, 32
Pescadores Islands, 93
Philip II. of Spain, 38, 42, 43
Philippines, 31, 32, 38, 39, 49, 51, 138, 152, 236
Pines, Isle of, 86
Pingsiang, 156
Pioneer Fringe, The, 217
Pippin, 35
Pires, Thomé, 31
Pizarro, 32
Plunkett, Sir Horace, 148
Polo, Maffeo, 20, 21
——, Marco, 20, 21, 24, 26-29, 31
——, Nicolo, 20, 21
Port Arthur, 92, 93, 95, 102, 103, 120, 127, 217, 218, 221, 278
Portsmouth, Treaty of, 120, 218, 221
Portugal, 29, 31, 43, 44, 139, 196
Portuguese, 7, 28-32, 34, 36-38, 43, 46, 53, 56, 60, 145
Powhatan, 88
Pretoria, 253
Pugachev, 291
Pukow, 166, 171, 186
Pu Yi, Emperor, 121, 240

QUEBEC, 275
Quinsan, 206

RAZIN, STENKA, 291
Records, Book of, 12
Red Sea, 29, 30
Reuters, 181
Revue des Deux Mondes, 59
Rhodes, Cecil, 232
Ricci, 51

Roberts, Rev. Issachar J., 67
Rodjesventsky, 120
Roman Emperors, 3
—— Empire, 5, 12, 14, 52
Rome, 3, 6, 10, 20, 37, 38, 44, 52, 60, 112, 183
Roosevelt, President, 107, 120
Root, Elihu, 106
Ros, Com. Uff. Giuseppe, 183
Roxby, Professor P. M., 272
Roy, Mr., 168
Royal Institute of International Affairs, v, vii, viii, 170
Russia, v, 19, 71, 74, 92-96, 99, 102, 103, 105, 106, 119, 120, 122, 127, 128, 131, 132, 145, 207, 218, 220, 221, 228, 289. (*See also* Soviet Russia)
——, Soviet, 143-145, 149, 150, 159, 160, 217, 222-224, 227, 234, 239, 254, 288, 291, 292, 298

St. Augustine, Order of, 32, 38
St. Dominic, Order of, 32, 38, 51, 52, 60
St. Francis, Order of, 26, 32, 38, 39, 42, 43, 48, 51, 52, 60
St. Germain, Treaty of, 133
St. John's Island, 37
—— University, Shanghai, viii, 159
St. Lawrence, R., 62
St. Louis of France, 18
St. Petersburg, 72, 94, 126
Saburi, Mr., 174
Salisbury, Lord, 99
Samarkand, 19, 27
Samuel, Arthur, 210
Samurai, 47, 50
Sandwich Islands, 86
San Felipe, 42
San Francisco, 255
Sang Chiao-yen, 125
San Min Chu I, 146, 147
Saragossa, Treaty of, 32, 38
Sarajevo, 126
Saris, 43
Satsuma, 34, 89
Schaal, 51
Seoul, 40, 124
Seville, 48
Seymour, Sir Michael, 71
Shameen, 152, 163, 279

Shanghai, viii, 58, 62, 63, 65, 76-81, 96, 113, 117, 125, 139, 141, 142, 144, 150-152, 154, 159, 161, 163-165, 167-170, 173-179, 182, 183, 197, 198, 200-202, 204-206, 236, 238-241, 252, 253, 266, 284, 298, 305-307, 309, 310
——, Greater, 166, 167, 240
Shangti, 12, 52, 68
Shansi, 141, 154, 171, 186, 187
Shantung, 95, 101, 122, 127, 131-134, 136, 166, 171, 186, 219, 230
Sheng Hsüan-hwai, 121, 122
Shensi, 102, 141, 161, 188, 190, 192
Shidehara, Baron, 171, 173, 234
Shigemitsu, Mr., 175, 182
Shi Hwang-ti, Emperor, 11, 12, 125
Shimabara, 46
Shimonoseki, 92, 93
Shintos, 38
Shirō, Masuda, 47
Shoguns, 35
Siam, 17, 34, 219
Sianfu, 102, 161
Siang, R., 156
Siberia, 217
Silesia, 19
Simakow, 188
Simon, Sir John, 206, 279
Singapore, 48, 98, 284, 285
Siniticism, 13
Society Islands, 86
Socotra, 30
Soochow, 20, 205, 206
—— Creek, 63
Soong, Miss Mei-ling (afterwards Mrs. Chiang Kai-shek), 159
——, T. V., 159, 165, 168, 169, 185, 239, 240, 249
Soongs, 159, 160
Soshin, Nishi, 45
Sotelo, Father, 48
South Africa, 40, 114, 137, 198, 253, 276, 277, 284, 297
—— America, 29, 48, 59, 228
Spain, 29, 31, 32, 38, 44, 46-49, 96, 97, 196
Spaniards, 6, 32, 33, 37-39, 44, 46, 49, 60, 86
Spanish Armada, 35
Spice Islands, 31

INDEX

Stalin, 149
Stimson, Colonel Henry L., 175, 177
Straits Settlements, 284
Suez Canal, 276
Sui, 156
Sumatra, 30
Sun Chi-yuan, 186
—— Ch'uan-fang, 125, 154, 160, 165, 166
—— Fo, 168, 169, 188, 240
—— Wen. *See* Dr. Sun Yat Sen
—— Yat Sen, Dr., 98, 99, 110, 122-125, 141-145, 147-150, 155, 158, 159, 168, 172, 180, 197, 254, 280, 290, 293, 296, 301
—— —— ——, Madame, 159
Sungs, 18
Survey of International Affairs, viii, 190, 224, 279
Su Shun, 82
Suwang Fu, 117
Swatow, 152, 188
Sweden, 44, 78
Switzerland, 266, 292
Sze, Alfred, 132
Szechwan, 156, 157

TAHITI, 85
Taipings, 68
—— rebellion, 71, 78, 83, 101, 108, 192
Taiyüan, 186
Taku, 19, 73
Tanaka, Baron, 171, 173, 232
Tanegashima, 34
Tang Sheng-shih, 160
Tao Kuang, Emperor, 99
Taotai, 63, 76, 80
Tartars, 12, 18, 20, 21, 24-26, 51, 108, 112, 291
Tasmania, 86
Tawney, R. H., 113, 190, 245, 246
Templars, 35
Temuchin, 18
Thames, R., 63
Thorburn, 205, 206
Tibet, 12, 21
Tiehling, 102
Tien, 12, 13, 51, 52
Tientsin, 19, 62, 68, 72, 96, 101, 115, 141, 145, 165, 172, 252, 307
Tien-Wang, 67-69, 75

Tierra del Fuego, 86
Times, The, 180, 181, 204, 205, 231, 234, 250, 276, 277, 279
Timur, 51
Tokimune, 35
Tokugawas, 45, 47, 89-91
Tokyo, 90, 91, 126, 159, 175, 182, 231, 234, 238, 239, 251, 305
Tonga, 86
Tordesillas, Treaty of, 29
Tosa, 42, 89
Toynbee, Professor Arnold, viii, 224
Trans-Siberian Railway, 94, 103, 217
Transvaal, 253, 277, 285
Treaty Ports, 62, 70, 71, 78, 81, 96, 98, 108, 109, 112, 164, 174, 239, 247, 248, 259
Trotsky, 289
Ts'ai Lun, 7, 27
Ts'in, King of, 11
Tsinan, 101, 167, 171, 186
Tsing Hua College, 107
Tsingtao, 95, 133, 150, 171, 307
Tsou Lu, 146
Tsung-li Yamen, 74, 101
Tuan Ch'i-yui, 153
—— Yua, Prince, 82
Turkestan, 19, 26
Turkey, 145, 175, 217

UCHIDA, COUNT, 231
United Kingdom, 210, 212-215
United Press, 176-179, 182, 183
United States of America, vi, 58-60, 65, 66, 71, 74, 79, 86, 92, 97-99, 102, 105-107, 110, 126, 128, 131, 132, 134, 136, 138, 139, 143, 145, 152, 164, 175-177, 179, 194, 196, 197, 221, 223, 226, 235, 236, 241, 245, 254-258, 266, 276, 290, 291, 297-300, 303, 308, 311
Universities' China Committee, 209, 215, 216, 269, 272
Upper Burma, 83

VALEGNANI, 38
Vare, Com. Daniele, 183
Venice, 20
Venus, 85
Verbiest, 51

Versailles, Treaty of, 133, 134, 136, 257
Victoria, 31
Vladivostok, 74, 94, 221

WADE, MR., 92
Waichow, 152
Waldersee, Marshal von, 102
Wales, 193
Wang Ching-wei, 168, 240
——, Dr. C. T., 132, 169, 177, 181, 182, 196, 198-201, 203-205, 207, 208, 211, 212, 239, 269
——, Prince, 74
Wanghia, Treaty of, 59, 60
Wan Li, Emperor, 51
Ward, 56, 72, 75
Washington, 87, 106, 126, 131, 136, 162, 174-177, 179, 198, 246-249, 256, 257, 260, 261, 274, 296, 297, 304
—— Conference, 139, 142, 153, 171, 173, 272
—— Treaties, 140, 153, 161, 248
Webster, Daniel, 59
Weddell, Captain John, 53
Wei, S. Y., 132
Weihaiwei, 96, 201
West Indies, 29
Whampoa, 145, 159
——, Treaty of, 59
Whangpoo, R., 62
Wilbur, Dr. Ray Lyman, 152, 170
Willingdon, Lord, 104, 207
Willoughby, Professor, 106
Wilson, President, 126, 131, 133, 134, 139
Witte, Count, 94, 95, 103, 120, 221
Wittenberg, 31
Witwatersrand, 253
Woosung, 240
Wu, C. C., 169, 240
Wuchang, 125, 156, 160
Wuchang-Canton Railway, 155
Wuhan, 156, 157, 161, 165, 185
Wuhu, 167, 186

Wu P'ei-fu, 125, 141, 142, 153, 154, 160, 161, 165, 166

XAVIER, FRANCIS, 34, 37, 38, 51

YAHCHANG, 189
Yajiro, 37
Yale, 159
Yamaguchi, 92
Yang-chou, 26
Yangtze, R., 18-20, 25, 57, 62, 68, 69, 72, 75, 76, 83, 84, 94, 98, 100, 111-114, 121, 122, 126, 130, 136, 150, 155-157, 159, 160, 162, 163, 165, 166, 174, 180, 187-190, 193, 194, 233, 239-241, 252, 253, 294, 295
Yang Yu Ting, 233
Yedo, 87-90
Yeh, Commissioner, 71
Yehonala, 82, 83, 95, 96, 99-103, 120, 121
Yellow R., 19, 171, 186, 193
Yen Hsi-shan, 141, 154, 171, 172, 176, 180, 185, 186, 201
Yi, Prince, 82
——, Admiral Sun-sin, 40-42
Yochow, 160
Yokohama, 257
Yoritomo, 35
Yoshimitsu, 35, 41
Yoshinobu, 89
Young, Marshal. *See* Chang Hsüeh-liang
——, Patrick, 303, 312
——, Walter, 261, 271
Yuan Shih-kai, 100, 101, 121-130, 140, 143, 154, 290
Yuen, R., 156
Yui, Dr. David, 170
Yung Cheng, 52
Yungloh, 25
Yunhang, 188
Yunnan, 129, 144

ZEIMOTTO, FRANCISCO, 34
Zipangu, 28

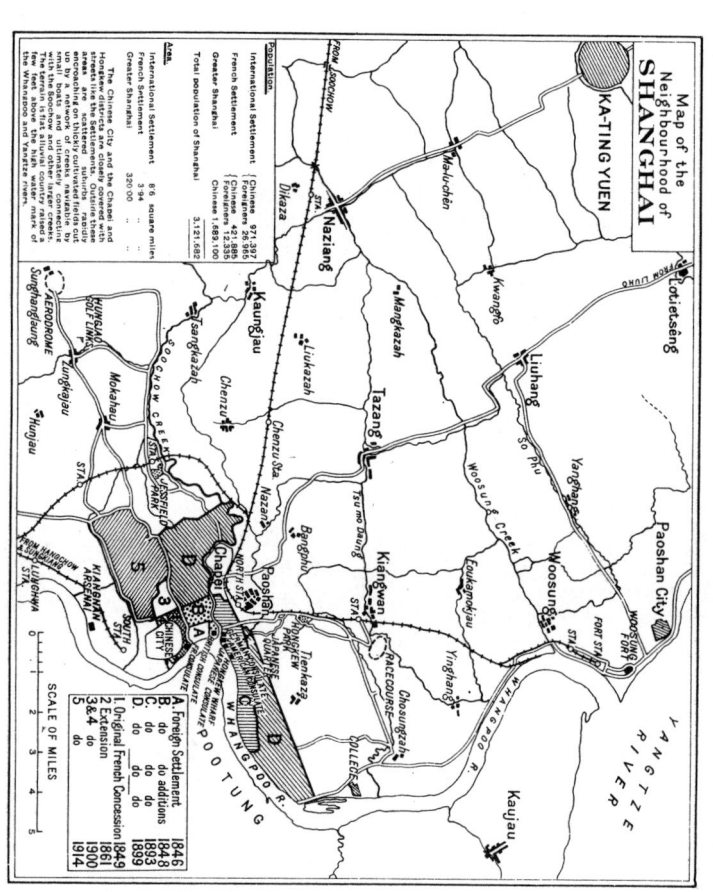

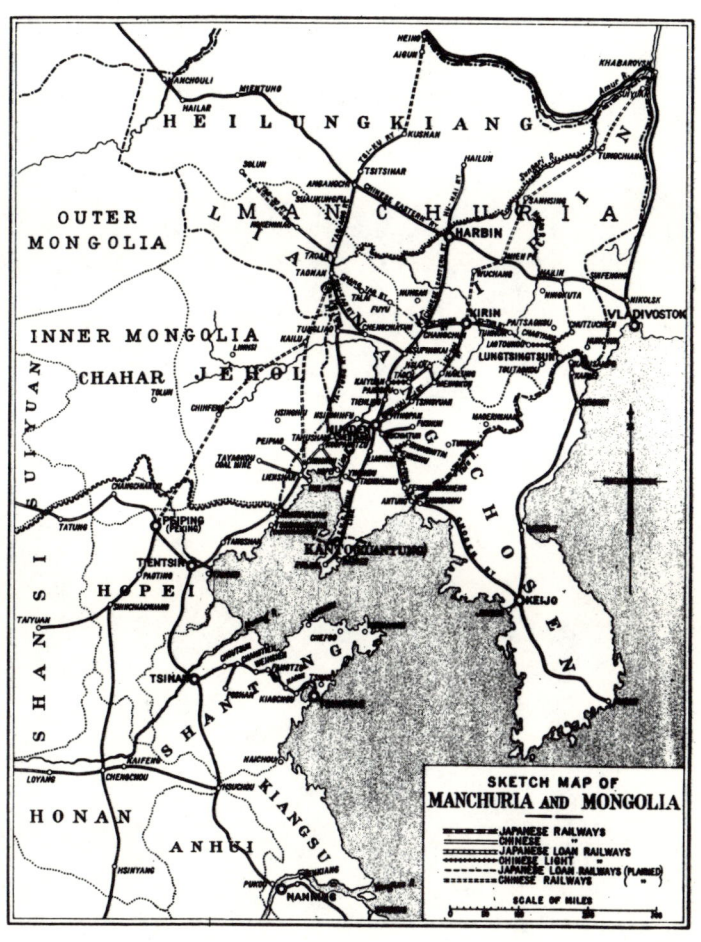

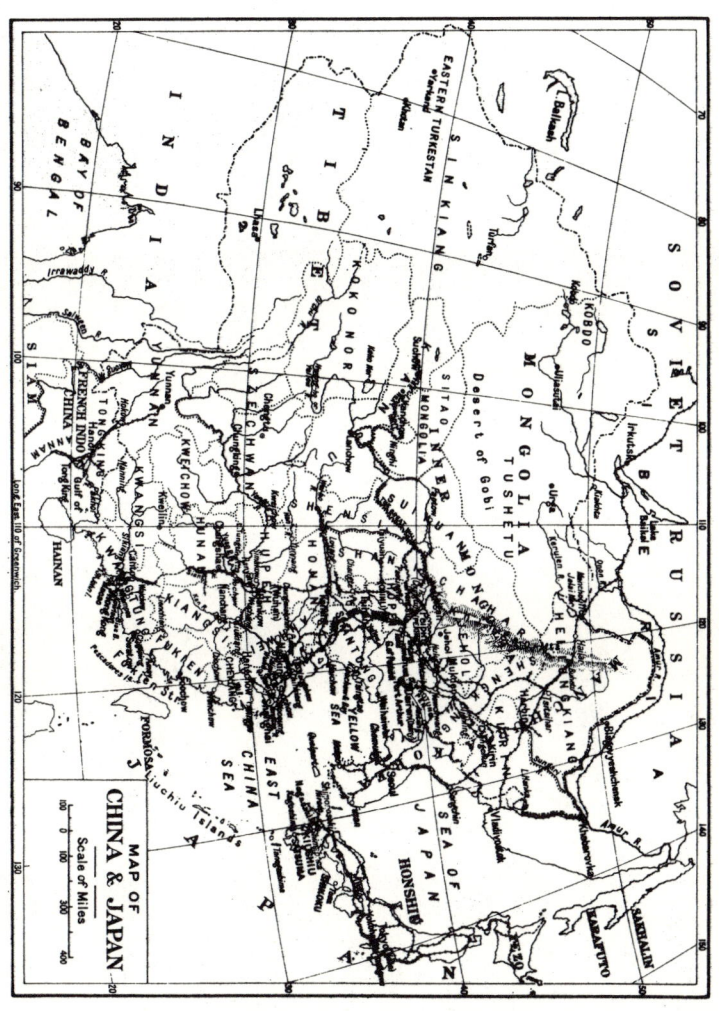